D0873905

SOCIETY FOR NEW TESTAMENT STUDIES
*MONOGRAPH SERIES*
General Editor: G. N. Stanton

58

JOSEPHUS' DESCRIPTION OF THE ESSENES
ILLUSTRATED BY THE DEAD SEA SCROLLS

# Josephus' Description of the Essenes Illustrated by the Dead Sea Scrolls

**TODD S. BEALL**

*Associate Professor of Old Testament*
*Capital Bible Seminary*

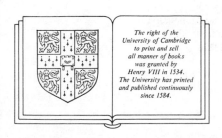

The right of the
University of Cambridge
to print and sell
all manner of books
was granted by
Henry VIII in 1534.
The University has printed
and published continuously
since 1584.

CAMBRIDGE UNIVERSITY PRESS

CAMBRIDGE
NEW YORK   NEW ROCHELLE
MELBOURNE   SYDNEY

Published by the Press Syndicate of the University of Cambridge
The Pitt Building, Trumpington Street, Cambridge CB2 1RP
32 East 57th Street, New York, NY 10022, USA
10 Stamford Road, Oakleigh, Melbourne 3166, Australia

First published 1988

Printed in Great Britain at
the University Press, Cambridge

*British Library cataloguing in publication data*
Beall, Todd S.
Josephus' description of the Essenes
illustrated by the Dead Sea Scrolls.
(Monograph series/Society for New
Testament studies; 58).
1. Josephus, Flavius
I. Title   II. Series
933'.0072024   DS115.9.J6

*Library of Congress cataloguing in publication data*
Beall, Todd S., 1952–
Josephus' description of the Essenes illustrated by
the Dead Sea scrolls.
(Monograph series / Society for New Testament
Studies ; 58)
Bibliography
Includes index.
1. Essenes – Historiography.   2. Josephus, Flavius –
Knowledge – Essenes.   3. Dead Sea scrolls – Criticism,
interpretation, etc.   I. Title.   II. Series: Monograph
series (Society for New Testament Studies); 58.
BM175.E8B38   1988   296.8'1   87-23828

ISBN 0 521 34524 3

WS

# CONTENTS

# PREFACE

This work is a revision of my dissertation completed while I was a New Testament Ph.D. candidate in the department of Biblical Studies at The Catholic University of America. It would not have been possible without the encouragement and support of many people. In particular, I would like to express my deep gratitude to Prof. Joseph A. Fitzmyer, who provided the inspiration for this study during a course on the Dead Sea Scrolls in 1979, and has closely guided the work from those incipient stages up to its present form. I greatly appreciate both his careful scholarship and his gracious encouragement during this endeavour.

I would like as well to express my thanks to my colleague at Capital Bible Seminary, Dr Richard A. Taylor, who read through the entire revised manuscript, and made numerous valuable suggestions. Special thanks also goes to Mr Keith Hogue, who graciously permitted me use of his computer in preparing this study.

Finally, I would like to express my deepest appreciation for the encouragement and friendship of Dr Homer Heater, former Academic Dean of Capital Bible Seminary. Without his support, I would not have been able to complete this project while at the same time carrying out my teaching responsibilities at the Seminary. His example of scholarly excellence, a warm love for people, and dedication to the Lord Jesus Christ remains a model for my own life and ministry as well.

# 1

## INTRODUCTION

### Ancient testimony to the Essenes

Prior to the discovery of the Dead Sea Scrolls in 1947, information concerning the pre-Christian Jewish sect of the Essenes was limited to the testimony of various Greek and Latin writers, only three of whom (Philo, Pliny, and Josephus) were contemporaneous with the group.[1] The earliest mention of the Essenes comes from Philo, an Alexandrian Jew, in two works written prior to A.D. 40: *Every Good Man is Free* (12–13 §75–91) and *Hypothetica* (11.1–18, preserved in Eusebius, *Praeparatio evangelica*). In addition, Philo devotes nearly an entire treatise (*On the Contemplative Life*) to the Therapeutae, a group in Egypt apparently similar to the Essenes who lived a more contemplative life than the Essenes.[2] A second contemporaneous writer who mentions the Essenes is Pliny the Elder. Pliny's description of the Essenes in his *Natural History* (5.15 §73), completed in A.D. 77, is brief but highly significant with regard to the identification of the Dead Sea Scroll community, as will be seen below.

### Josephus' account of the Essenes

But the most important contemporaneous description of the Essenes comes from the Jewish historian Flavius Josephus (*ca.* A.D. 37–100). In all, Josephus mentions the Essenes thirteen times in three works. Ten of the thirteen references to the Essenes are of comparatively minor importance for the present study, and are discussed briefly in the Appendix. But the other three passages form the basis for this study of Josephus' account of the Essenes. These are: (1) *Life* 1.2 §10–12, a brief passage in which Josephus states that he actually submitted himself to the Essene way of life for a time; (2) *J. W.* 2.8, 2–13 §119–61, the longest and most detailed description of the Essenes from any ancient writer; and (3) *Ant.* 18.1, 2, 5 §11, 18–22, a brief description of the Essenes that contains some important information not in the earlier account.

*1*

## Importance of Josephus' account

Josephus' description of the Essenes is uniquely important among the ancient testimonies concerning the Essenes for several reasons. First, Josephus is contemporaneous with the group (at least in one stage of its history). As mentioned above, only Philo and Pliny share this distinction with Josephus. While it is certainly possible that more precise information concerning the Essenes could have been preserved by later writers, it is more likely that, on the whole, the account closer to the actual existence of the group more accurately portrays the sect. Second, Josephus' account is not only contemporaneous but also detailed, and thus gives far more information about the group than, for example, Pliny. Third, Josephus was himself a Jew, and thus could be expected to have a somewhat better understanding of this Jewish sect than a non-Jewish writer. The only other Jew among the ancient witnesses to the Essenes was Philo. Fourth, Josephus was a Palestinian Jew, and thus almost certainly had better knowledge of a sect located (at least primarily) in Palestine than did Philo, an Alexandrian Jew. And finally, as indicated above, Josephus himself claimed to have spent time with the Essenes, indicating that (if his testimony is correct) he had close contact with the sect. This last point concerning Josephus' contact with the group is discussed more fully in connection with the commentary on *Life* 1.2 §10–12, below (p. 34).

## Problems in Josephus' account

Josephus' account of the Essenes, then, is the most important ancient secondary source of information regarding the group. Yet even Josephus' account is not without its difficulties. First, there are passages within Josephus' account that are obscure: in some cases, the obscurity stems from the Greek text itself (either syntax or vocabulary), while at other times it is caused by our inadequate knowledge of the customs and beliefs of the Essenes.

Second, it is widely recognized that Josephus was writing as an apologist as well as an historian. As G. A. Williamson observes, Josephus has several particular apologetic purposes in mind.[3] First, he gives an elaborate defense of the Romans, especially the two emperors Vespasian and Titus. In the *Jewish War*, as Thackeray points out, "the glamour of imperial Rome ... detracted from the historian's impartiality and on occasion raised serious doubts as to his veracity. The campaign is viewed through Roman spectacles."[4]

A second apologetic purpose evident in Josephus' writings, and one even more important than the first in terms of our present study, is to make a defense of the beliefs and customs of his own people, the Jews, to a Gentile world. As Williamson explains, Josephus desired "to rehabilitate his people in the eyes of their Roman conquerors, who ... were genuinely interested in their curious beliefs and customs, but through grievous misunderstanding were prone to despise them."[5] Thus, in both the *Jewish War* and *Antiquities* (and especially the latter work), Josephus is attempting to explain Judaism in the most favorable light to a Greek-speaking world, largely unacquainted with modes of Jewish life and its adherence to the Mosaic Law. This apologetic purpose results in a dual tendency towards idealization and accommodation to Greek thought in the writings of Josephus.[6]

A final apologetic purpose evident in Josephus is his defense of himself. His autobiography, *Life*, is a vigorous defense of his own conduct in the war against the charges of Justus of Tiberias, a rival historian. Similar self-justification appears in the *Jewish War* as well: as Thackeray notes, "the autobiographical notices of the historian in connexion with the outbreak of hostilities must be pronounced the least trustworthy portion of his writings."[7] Similarly, Williamson states that "although when Josephus has no axe to grind and is not indulging in patent exaggeration he is an informative and reliable historian, we must nevertheless use the greatest caution in accepting at its face value any statement that he makes about himself or about his personal enemies."[8]

Hence, although Josephus is generally regarded as a reliable historian, it is well to keep in mind these three apologetic purposes for his writing (especially the second one) as we examine his writings, since it remains uncertain to what degree these tendencies have colored his description of the Essenes.[9]

### Identification of the Qumran community with the Essenes

With the discovery of the Dead Sea Scrolls and the subsequent identification of the Qumran community with the Essenes by most scholars, a whole new treasure trove of possible first-hand information concerning the Essenes has been made available. This information may indeed shed valuable light upon the description of the Essenes by Josephus, if the Qumran group is Essene. Because the identification of the Qumran community with the Essenes is a "working hypothesis" in this book, the basic reasons for this identification will be briefly set forth below.

## Archaeological evidence

First, the archaeological and palaeographic data confirm that the Qumran community was in existence from the mid second century B.C. to A.D. 68, with a few of the manuscripts found in their possession dating back to the third century B.C. This is in complete agreement with the time frame mentioned by Josephus for the Essenes.[10] The archaeological data consist of stratigraphy, pottery, and coins. Based on these factors, de Vaux isolates five archaeological periods of occupation of the site of Khirbet Qumran: (1) a period dating from the eighth to the seventh century B.C.; (2) period 1a, from *ca*. 150–103 B.C., with a modest number of buildings; (3) period 1b, from 103–31 B.C., with much growth and expansion of the site, destroyed by the earthquake of 31 B.C. (Josephus, *Ant*. 15.5, 2 §121) and (probably) abandoned; (4) period 2, from 4 B.C.–A.D. 68, with only secondary modifications made to the buildings, ending with the destruction of Qumran by the Romans in A.D. 68; and (5) period 3, the period of Roman occupation.[11] In addition, all the pottery found in the caves belongs to the Hellenistic and (mainly) Roman periods, with none from other periods.[12] As de Vaux observes, "when we reflect that the manuscripts are numerous and the pottery plentiful, that the manuscripts constitute a homogeneous group, and that the pottery belongs to a single period, it is difficult to resist the conclusion that the manuscripts were deposited or abandoned in the caves at the same time as the pottery."[13] There are other similarities as well between the archaeological finds at Qumran and what our ancient sources say about the Essenes: among these are small cisterns probably meant for ritual baths, coins found in community buildings but not in living quarters (illustrating the practice of common sharing of money?), and an iron tool found in Cave 11 corresponding with Josephus' Essene hatchet.[14]

## Palaeographic and other evidence from the scrolls

The palaeographic evidence of the scrolls themselves confirms the results of the archaeological findings with regard to the date of the community and its writing. All the major palaeographic studies on the scrolls are in essential agreement about the date of their composition. Thus, for example, Birnbaum concludes that the Qumran manuscripts "must be assigned to some dates between roughly 300 B.C.E. and 68 C.E."[15] This conclusion is supported by the discoveries at Masada, whose ostraca and writings show the same script as at Qumran, yet must be earlier than A.D. 73 or 74, when the city fell to the Romans.[16] In addition, carbon-14 tests performed on the linen cloths in which the scrolls were wrapped indicate a date of 20 B.C., plus or minus 200 years.[17] Finally, a chemical analysis based on the temperature of shrinkage of fragments indicates that the Qumran fragments are younger than fifth-century B.C. documents, but are slightly older than those of Murabba'at (early second century A.D.).[18]

### Geographical evidence

While the archaeological and palaeographic data by no means necessitate the identification of the Qumran community with the Essenes, they at least point to the same chronological period for both. But it is the brief statement by Pliny in his *Natural History* (5.15 §73) concerning the Essenes that points to a geographical identity between Qumran and the Essenes as well. Having mentioned Jerusalem, "by far the most famous city of the East and not of Judea only," and Herodium, Pliny describes the Jordan River and the Dead Sea (*N.H.* 5.15 §70−2). Then he locates the Essenes on its western shore (*N.H.* 5.15 §73), Engedi "below them" ("infra hos Engada"), and then Masada ("inde Masada"). Though "infra hos" could mean an Essene settlement in the mountains overlooking Engedi, exploration of the area in the early 1960s has not revealed a trace of any ruins in the Roman period near Engedi.[19] Hence, the only other logical alternative is that by "infra hos" Pliny means "south of them" or "downstream." Thus, Pliny is in all probability describing Qumran, roughly eight miles south of Jericho; then Engedi, twenty miles south of Qumran; and finally, Masada, eleven miles south of Engedi, and somewhat inland. Furthermore, Pliny notes that the Essenes live among palm trees, which fits the area between Khirbet Qumran and Ain Feshkha, the spring just to the south of the Qumran community's farm area.[20] Thus, as de Vaux concludes, "if Pliny was not mistaken and if we are not mistaken, the Essenes of whom he speaks are the community of Qumran."[21]

### Internal evidence (compared with ancient testimony)

Finally, the identification of the Qumran community with the Essenes is supported by the numerous parallels between what is written in the scrolls and the ancient testimonies of Philo, Pliny, and Josephus regarding the Essenes. Many writers have appealed to details in

Josephus' description to illustrate passages in Qumran literature. But since one of the purposes of this study is to clarify the degree of agreement between the scrolls and Josephus' testimony concerning the Essenes, nothing further will be said at this juncture regarding the scrolls and ancient testimony to the Essenes.[22] It is helpful to cite merely one testimony from a reputable scholar who has gained his impressions from the preliminary survey. The following summary about the question of the identity of the Qumran sect is given by F.M. Cross:

> The scholar who would "exercise caution" in identifying the sect of Qumran with the Essenes places himself in an astonishing position: he must suggest seriously that two major parties formed communistic religious communities in the same district of the desert of the Dead Sea and lived together in effect for two centuries, holding similar bizarre views, performing similar or rather identical lustrations, ritual meals, and ceremonies. He must suppose that one, carefully described by classical authors, disappeared without leaving building remains or even potsherds behind; the other, systematically ignored by the classical sources, left extensive ruins, and indeed a great library. I prefer to be reckless and flatly identify the men of Qumran with their perennial house-guests, the Essenes. At all events, in the remainder of our paper, we shall assume the identification and draw freely upon both classical and Qumran texts.[23]

## Purpose of this study

With the identification of the Qumran community with the Essenes, scholars studying the Dead Sea Scrolls have quite naturally turned to Josephus' description of the Essenes to illumine various aspects of the Qumran material. For example, A. Dupont-Sommer, in his introductory book on the scrolls, refers to Josephus more than sixty times in the process of discussing the Qumran texts.[24] But no complete study has as yet been made that has sought to reverse the procedure: namely, to comment on Josephus' description of the Essenes by making reference to the relevant Dead Sea Scrolls material. J. Strugnell has recognized the need for such a study, as almost thirty years ago he suggested that "since now we have available Essene writings and, in addition, archeological remains of the Essene settlement, should we not use this new evidence as a help to the exact exegesis of the Greek and Latin authors?"[25] The purpose of this study, then, is to take up Strugnell's proposal, and provide a fresh translation of Josephus' description of the Essenes with a commentary in which the relevant passages from the Dead Sea Scrolls will be brought to bear on the text of Josephus. It is hoped that the study will result in the following contributions: most importantly, a better understanding of Josephus' description of the Essenes, as difficult passages in Josephus are illumined by the Qumran material; second, a better understanding of the Essenes themselves, as relevant data concerning them is systematized under the various topics described by Josephus; and finally, a delimitation of those areas in which problems still exist in the understanding of Josephus' description and its relation to the Qumran material.

### Primary source materials

#### Josephus

As mentioned above (p.1), the passages in Josephus that are treated in this book come from three different works: *The Jewish War*, *The Antiquities of the Jews*, and *Life*. The Jewish War was written first in Aramaic (*ca*. A.D. 73), with a new edition in Greek (A.D. 75–79). It consists of seven books, containing primarily an account of the war of the Jews against the Romans, but also containing a brief survey of Jewish history from the time of the Maccabean revolt. It is in the second book of this work that the longest and most famous account of the Essenes appears (2.8, 2–13 §119–61), though there are five other references to the Essenes in this work as well.[26] Josephus' second work, *The Antiquities of the Jews*, was completed in A.D. 93/94. Its twenty books depict the history of the Jews from creation to A.D. 66. Josephus mentions the Essenes seven times in this work, the last of which (18.1, 5 §18–22) gives important additional information concerning the Essenes.[27] The final reference to the Essenes in Josephus is in *Life* (1.2 §10–12), his autobiography, written shortly before his death.

The Greek text used for all three works of Josephus cited in this study is that of H. St J. Thackeray, R. Marcus, A. Wikgren, and L. H. Feldman, *Josephus* (LCL, 9 vols., Cambridge, Mass.: Harvard University Press, 1926–65). This text is based upon B. Niese's *editio maior*, but contains a number of changes suggested by scholars since Niese's day.[28] I have adopted a reading different from the Loeb edition on only one occasion, which is noted in the text.

### Dead Sea Scrolls

The primary Qumran material utilized in this study is the sectarian literature, especially the *Manual of Discipline* and the *Damascus Document*, but also the *War Scroll*, the *Hodayot*, the *Pesharim*, and the *Temple Scroll*. Each of these documents will be briefly described below. Full bibliographic data is available in the Primary Sources section of the Bibliography (pp. 167–9).

*Manual of Discipline*. The *Manual of Discipline* or *Serek hayyahad* (1QS) from Cave 1[29] is one of the two main community "rule books" found at Qumran. Its eleven columns were copied in the period 100–75 B.C. according to palaeographic analysis.[30] The date of composition is less certain, especially since it is quite possible that the document took shape over a period of time, reflecting changes in the community's situation.[31] In any event, it may have been composed as early as the first half of the second century B.C., with additions being made through at least the second half of the second century B.C.[32]

There are two important appendices to the *Manual of Discipline*, both of which are utilized in this study: *The Rule of the Congregation (for the End-Time)* (1QSa), which gives various rules for the group in an eschatological context, including a messianic assembly and banquet; and a *Collection of Benedictions* (1QSb), a poorly preserved text that contains blessings for various groups of people.

*Damascus Document*. A second community "rule book" of great importance to this study is the *Damascus Document* (CD). Originally called "Fragments of a Zadokite Work" (because the sect seemed to call itself "sons of Zadok"), two manuscripts of the *Damascus Document* were first discovered in the genizah of the Synagogue of Ezra in Old Cairo in 1896 by Solomon Schechter. MS A, a tenth-century copy, contains sixteen columns, while MS B, a twelfth-century copy, contains two columns (numbered 19 and 20) that roughly parallel cols. 7–8 of MS A. Numerous fragments of the *Damascus Document* have now been found at Qumran in Caves 4 (4QD[a-g]), 5 (5QD = 5Q*12*), and 6 (6QD = 6Q*15*).[33] While most of the Cave 4 CD MSS remain unpublished, Milik has stated that the original order of the sixteen columns of the document must be changed somewhat, as material from Qumran is integrated with MS A of CD. Thus, the order of the work is as follows: initial columns (preserved only in 4Q); CD 1–8 (with MS B 19–20 paralleling, but representing a different recension of, MS A 7–8); missing portion (partially preserved in 4Q); CD 15–16, 9–14; and final columns (preserved only in 4Q).[34]

Like the *Manual of Discipline*, the *Damascus Document* seems to contain references to various stages of the community's development, and thus is difficult to date precisely, since additions were undoubtedly made to the original core of material.[35] Its final form was probably written after the *Manual of Discipline*; for example, Dupont-Sommer dates the *Manual of Discipline* prior to 63 B.C. and the *Damascus Document* between 63 and 48 B.C.[36] However, P.R. Davies concludes that "the document as a whole is basically older than the Qumran community and that our available manuscripts ... represent a Qumranic recension."[37] If Davies' conclusion is correct, one must be careful in applying portions of the *Damascus Document* directly to the Qumran community.

*War Scroll.* The *War Scroll* (1QM) is also of importance to this study. The copy of the *War Scroll* found in Cave 1 consists of nineteen columns, of which several lines are missing from the bottom of each column. Fragments of six copies of the *War Scroll* have been found in Cave 4 as well (4QM[a-f]). According to Yadin, the *War Scroll* was composed during the second half of the first century B.C., since both the organization of the army and the armor used point to a dependence upon what was used in the Roman army of that time.[38] The scroll is essentially a book of instructions for the eschatological war between the sons of light (the sect itself) and the sons of darkness (the "Kittim," probably the Romans[39]). It consists of an introduction (col. 1); general regulations for battle, including prayers by the priests and Levites (cols. 2–14); and a final description of the battle (cols. 15–19), possibly written by another hand.[40]

*Hodayot.* The *Hodayot* (1QH), or *Thanksgiving Hymns*, consist of eighteen columns and sixty-six fragments[41] from Cave 1 which resemble the biblical Psalms in their prayers to God. Because of the poor condition of the scrolls, the precise order of the columns and even the number of hymns is not certain, with estimates ranging from twenty-five to forty separate hymns.[42] There are also apparently five unpublished fragments of the *Hodayot* from Cave 4, as well as four or five fragments that resemble the *Hodayot*, but whose text does not correspond to any known part of 1QH.[43] The *Hodayot* are valuable for this study, not so much for the information they shed upon sectarian daily life and customs (which is minimal), but rather for their theological assertions.

*Pesharim.* There are at least fifteen *Pesharim* that have been found at Qumran. These are: from Cave 1 — 1QpHab, 1QpMic, 1QpZeph, 1QpPs; and from Cave 4 — 4QpIsa[a-e], 4QpHos[a,b], 4QpNah, 4QpZeph, and 4QpPs[a,b]. In addition, as M. Horgan notes, three other texts are possibly *Pesharim*, namely, 3QpIsa, 4QpMic, and 4QpUnid.[44] The *Pesharim* are interpretations of individual biblical books (prophets or psalms), in which the text is applied or "actualized" to the current situation. Thus, as Dupont-Sommer observes, the *Pesharim* are "entirely dominated by sectarian outlook and concerns, and as a result they are a mine of valuable information concerning the sect's doctrine and history."[45] It is for this reason that the *Pesharim* are of value for the present study.

*Temple Scroll*. The *Temple Scroll* (11QTemple[a]) of Cave 11 is both the largest Qumran scroll known (over twenty-eight feet long, with sixty-six columns of text) and the most recent to be published (1977). According to Yadin, it was probably composed during the second half of the second century B.C.[46] The scroll consists of the following parts: an introduction (cols. 1–2); regulations concerning the Temple and the celebration of its feasts (cols. 3–47); and *halakot* on various subjects, including ritual cleanliness, judicial regulations, and regulations on the king and his army (cols. 48–66). Much of the *Temple Scroll* parallels the laws of the Torah, especially Deuteronomy 18–23, but an unusual feature is that it changes the scriptural quotation to the first person and makes God the speaker. This may indicate that the *Temple Scroll* was viewed by the sect as on the same level as the Hebrew Scriptures.[47] As A. Caquot remarks, the *Temple Scroll* seems to be written, not simply for an order or a sect, but rather for the whole nation of Israel, much as the biblical laws.[48] It is uncertain whether the *Temple Scroll* was actually composed by the Essenes or simply used by them. Yet, as Yadin and Caquot note, there are a number of items in the *Temple Scroll* that point specifically to the Essenes.[49] These passages will be treated at the appropriate point in this study. Hence, this document will form a part of the comparative analysis of Josephus and Qumran literature.

*Other Qumran literature*. Other Qumran literature used in this study are primarily smaller fragments from Cave 4, including 4QOrd[a] (4Q*159*), 4QFlor (4Q*174*), 4QTestim (4Q*175*), 4QAgesCreat (4Q*180–1*), 4QWiles (4Q*184*), 4QPrNab, 4QSirSabb, and 4QPBless. In addition, the Aramaic fragments of eleven MSS of *Enoch* found at Qumran (4QEn[a–g], 4QEnastr[a–d]), with nine copies of a possibly related Book of Giants (1QEnGiants, 2QEnGiants, 4QEnGiants[a–f], 6QEnGiants), have been utilized in this study. The Ethiopic form of *Enoch* has been used, with the exception of the Book of Parables, which was not found at Qumran (and which Milik regards as a Christian composition).[50]

## Approach and limitations of this study

The approach of this study will consist of a fresh translation of each of the major Essene passages in Josephus and a commentary upon each in the light of the Qumran literature discussed above. Sometimes there will be direct specific parallels from Qumran that illuminate the Josephus text; at other times, we may be able only to hint at possible correlations or suggest a general agreement (or disagreement) between Josephus and Qumran literature. While mention will be made of sections in Philo that correspond to each passage in Josephus, a detailed comparison between Philo and Josephus or Philo and Qumran literature is beyond the scope of this study.

There are some inherent difficulties in comparing Josephus' description of the Essenes with the Qumran literature. Not only do we have the problem of Josephus' objectivity and accuracy as a historian, mentioned above, as queried by some modern scholars, but there is also the even more difficult area of sorting out the various phases of the Qumran community itself. We cannot assume that Essene thought remained constant from the beginning of the sect's existence until the destruction of Jerusalem – a period of about 200 years. As Murphy-O'Connor contends, documents such as the *Manual of Discipline* and the *Damascus Document* probably had a long compositional history, and thus may not even be consistent within themselves, let alone with other Qumran literature.[51] This fact makes comparison of Josephus' account with these documents a much more complex matter, since we are not necessarily dealing with a homogeneous body of literature at Qumran. The approach of this work, then, will be to collect relevant passages from the Qumran literature for each section in Josephus, and then comment on their possible significance for the Josephus passage, at the same time recognizing the difficulties inherent in such a comparison.

## Abbreviations and transliteration

The abbreviations and Hebrew transliteration scheme used in this work are those of the *JBL/CBQ* Instructions for Contributors, except that *RQ* is used for *Revue de Qumran* rather than *RevQ*. In addition, unless otherwise indicated, all translations of Josephus or Qumran literature are my own.

# 2

## TEXT AND TRANSLATION OF JOSEPHUS' ESSENE PASSAGES

### A. Text of major passages

#### 1. Life 1.2 §10–12

(§10) Περὶ ἑκκαίδεκα δὲ ἔτη γενόμενος ἐβουλήθην τῶν παρ' ἡμῖν αἱρέσεων ἐμπειρίαν λαβεῖν· τρεῖς δ' εἰσὶν αὗται, φαρισαίων μὲν ἡ πρώτη καὶ Σαδδουκαίων ἡ δευτέρα, τρίτη δ' Ἐσσηνῶν, καθὼς πολλάκις εἴπομεν· οὕτως γὰρ ᾠόμην αἱρήσεσθαι τὴν ἀρίστην, εἰ πάσας καταμάθοιμι. (§11) σκληραγωγήσας οὖν ἐμαυτὸν καὶ πολλὰ πονηθεὶς τὰς τρεῖς διῆλθον· καὶ μηδὲ τὴν ἐντεῦθεν ἐμπειρίαν ἱκανὴν ἐμαυτῷ νομίσας εἶναι, πυθόμενός τινα Βαννοῦν ὄνομα κατὰ τὴν ἐρημίαν διατρίβειν, ἐσθῆτι μὲν ἀπὸ δένδρων χρώμενον, τροφὴν δὲ τὴν αὐτομάτως φυομένην προσφερόμενον, ψυχρῷ δὲ ὕδατι τὴν ἡμέραν καὶ τὴν νύκτα πολλάκις λουόμενον πρὸς ἁγνείαν, ζηλωτὴς ἐγενόμην αὐτοῦ. (§12) καὶ διατρίψας παρ' αὐτῷ ἐνιαυτοὺς τρεῖς καὶ τὴν ἐπιθυμίαν τελειώσας εἰς τὴν πόλιν ὑπέστρεφον. ἐννεακαιδέκατον δ'ἔτος ἔχων ἠρξάμην τε πολιτεύεσθαι τῇ Φαρισαίων αἱρέσει κατακολουθῶν, ἣ παραπλήσιός ἐστι τῇ παρ' Ἕλλησι Στωικῇ λεγομένῃ.

#### 2. J.W. 2.8, 2–13 §119–61

(§119) Τρία γὰρ παρὰ Ἰουδαίοις εἴδη φιλοσοφεῖται, καὶ τοῦ μὲν αἱρετισταὶ Φαρισαῖοι, τοῦ δὲ Σαδδουκαῖοι, τρίτον δέ, ὃ δὴ καὶ δοκεῖ σεμνότητα ἀσκεῖν, Ἐσσηνοὶ καλοῦνται, Ἰουδαῖοι μὲν γένος ὄντες, φιλάλληλοι δὲ καὶ τῶν ἄλλων πλέον.

## A. Translation of major passages

### 1. Life 1.2 §10–12

(§10) When I was about sixteen years old, I decided to get experience of the sects that existed among us. These are three, as we have said many times: the first, that of the Pharisees; the second, that of the Sadducees; and the third, that of the Essenes. For I thought that in this way I would choose the best, if I carefully examined them all. (§11) Therefore, submitting myself to strict training and many strenuous labors, I passed through the three groups. Having considered the experience thus gained to be insufficient for myself, and on learning of a certain man named Bannus, who lived in the desert, wore clothing supplied from trees, took as food only that which grew by itself, and washed many times in cold water both day and night for purification, I became his devotee. (§12) When I had lived with him for three years and had accomplished my purpose, I returned to the city. Being now nineteen years old, I began to conduct myself according to the rules of the sect of the Pharisees, which nearly resembles that called Stoic among the Greeks.

### 2. J.W. 2.8, 2–13 §119–61

(§119) For there are three philosophical classes among the Jews: the first are the sectarians called the Pharisees; the second, the Sadducees; and the third, who are reputed to cultivate solemnity, the Essenes. The last are Jews by birth, and have more mutual affection than do the others.

(§120) οὗτοι τὰς μὲν ἡδονὰς ὡς κακίαν ἀποστρέφονται, τὴν δὲ ἐγκράτειαν καὶ τὸ μὴ τοῖς πάθεσιν ὑποπίπτειν ἀρετὴν ὑπολαμβάνουσιν. καὶ γάμου μὲν παρ' αὐτοῖς ὑπεροψία, τοὺς δ' ἀλλοτρίους παῖδας ἐκλαμβάνοντες ἁπαλοὺς ἔτι πρὸς τὰ μαθήματα συγγενεῖς ἡγοῦνται καὶ τοῖς ἤθεσιν αὐτῶν ἐντυποῦσι, (§121) τὸν μὲν γάμον καὶ τὴν ἐξ αὐτοῦ διαδοχὴν οὐκ ἀναιροῦντες, τὰς δὲ τῶν γυναικῶν ἀσελγείας φυλαττόμενοι καὶ μηδεμίαν τηρεῖν πεπεισμένοι τὴν πρὸς ἕνα πίστιν.

(§122) Καταφρονηταὶ δὲ πλούτου, καὶ θαυμάσιον παρ' αὐτοῖς τὸ κοινωνικόν, οὐδὲ ἔστιν εὑρεῖν κτήσει τινὰ παρ' αὐτοῖς ὑπερέχοντα· νόμος γὰρ τοὺς εἰς τὴν αἵρεσιν εἰσιόντας δημεύειν τῷ τάγματι τὴν οὐσίαν, ὥστε ἐν ἅπασιν μήτε πενίας ταπεινότητα φαίνεσθαι μήθ' ὑπεροχὴν πλούτου, τῶν δ' ἑκάστου κτημάτων ἀναμεμιγμένων μίαν ὥσπερ ἀδελφοῖς ἅπασιν οὐσίαν εἶναι. (§123) κηλῖδα δ' ὑπολαμβάνουσι τοὔλαιον, κἂν ἀλειφθῇ τις ἄκων, σμήχεται τὸ σῶμα· τὸ γὰρ αὐχμεῖν ἐν καλῷ τίθενται, λευχειμονεῖν τε διαπαντός. χειροτονητοὶ δ' οἱ τῶν κοινῶν ἐπιμεληταὶ καὶ ἀδιαίρετοι πρὸς ἁπάντων εἰς τὰς χρείας ἕκαστοι.

(§124) Μία δ' οὐκ ἔστιν αὐτῶν πόλις, ἀλλ' ἐν ἑκάστῃ μετοικοῦσιν πολλοί. καὶ τοῖς ἑτέρωθεν ἥκουσιν αἱρετισταῖς πάντ' ἀναπέπταται τὰ παρ' αὐτοῖς ὁμοίως ὥσπερ ἴδια, καὶ πρὸς οὓς οὐ πρότερον εἶδον εἰσίασιν ὡς συνηθεστάτους· (§125) διὸ καὶ ποιοῦνται τὰς ἀποδημίας οὐδὲν μὲν ὅλως ἐπικομιζόμενοι, διὰ δὲ τοὺς λῃστὰς ἔνοπλοι. κηδεμὼν δ' ἐν ἑκάστῃ πόλει τοῦ τάγματος ἐξαιρέτως τῶν ξένων ἀποδείκνυται, ταμιεύων ἐσθῆτα καὶ τὰ ἐπιτήδεια. (§126) καταστολὴ δὲ καὶ σχῆμα σώματος ὅμοιον τοῖς μετὰ φόβου παιδαγωγουμένοις παισίν. οὔτε δὲ ἐσθῆτας οὔτε ὑποδήματα ἀμείβουσι πρὶν διαρραγῆναι τὸ πρότερον παντάπασιν ἢ δαπανηθῆναι τῷ χρόνῳ. (§127) οὐδὲν δ' ἐν ἀλλήλοις οὔτ' ἀγοράζουσιν οὔτε πωλοῦσιν, ἀλλὰ τῷ χρῄζοντι διδοὺς ἕκαστος τὰ παρ' αὐτῷ τὸ παρ' ἐκείνου χρήσιμον ἀντικομίζεται· καὶ χωρὶς δὲ τῆς ἀντιδόσεως ἀκώλυτος ἡ μετάληψις αὐτοῖς παρ' ὧν ἂν θέλωσιν.

(§128) Πρός γε μὴν τὸ θεῖον εὐσεβεῖς ἰδίως· πρὶν γὰρ ἀνασχεῖν τὸν ἥλιον οὐδὲν φθέγγονται τῶν βεβήλων, πατρίους δέ τινας εἰς αὐτὸν εὐχάς, ὥσπερ ἱκετεύοντες ἀνατεῖλαι.

(§120) They turn aside from pleasures as an evil, and regard self-control and not succumbing to the passions as a virtue. Marriage they regard with contempt, but in adopting other persons' children who are still pliable for learning, they consider them as their own kin and mold them according to their customs. (§121) They do not reject marriage and the propagation that comes from it, but they guard themselves against the licentious allurements of women and are persuaded that not one of them keeps her pledge to one man.

(§122) They despise riches, and their sharing of goods is admirable; there is not found among them any one who has greater wealth than another. For it is a law that those entering the sect transfer their property to the order; consequently, among them all there appears neither abject poverty nor superabundance of wealth, but the possessions of each are mingled together, and there is, as among brothers, one property common to all. (§123) They regard oil as a defilement; and if anyone is smeared (with it) accidentally, his body is purged clean of it. For to be dry of skin is held as a good thing, as well as always being dressed in white. They have elected overseers who take care of common matters, and without exception each one is (responsible) for the needs of all of them.

(§124) They have no one city, but many settle in each city; and when any of the sectarians come from elsewhere, all things they have lie available to them, just as if they were their own, and they take up lodging with those whom they have not seen before, as if they were their most intimate friends. (§125) Consequently when they journey, they carry nothing at all with them, except that they are armed on account of robbers. In every city, there is one of the order particularly appointed to take care of guests, providing clothing and other necessary things. (§126) In dress and bodily demeanor they are like children in fear of their tutors. They replace neither clothing nor sandals until they are altogether torn to shreds or worn out with age. (§127) Among one another they neither buy nor sell anything, but each one gives what he has to one in need and receives in turn what is useful for himself. Moreover, they may take freely from whomever they please without giving back something in return.

(§128) They are pious towards the Deity in a particular way: before the rising of the sun they do not talk about profane matters, but direct certain ancestral prayers towards it, as if entreating it to rise.

(§129) καὶ μετὰ ταῦτα πρὸς ἃς ἕκαστοι τέχνας ἴσασιν ὑπὸ τῶν ἐπιμελητῶν διαφίενται, καὶ μέχρι πέμπτης ὥρας ἐργασάμενοι συντόνως πάλιν εἰς ἓν συναθροίζονται χωρίον, ζωσάμενοί τε σκεπάσμασιν λινοῖς οὕτως ἀπολούονται τὸ σῶμα ψυχροῖς ὕδασιν, καὶ μετὰ ταύτην τὴν ἁγνείαν εἰς ἴδιον οἴκημα συνίασιν, ἔνθα μηδενὶ τῶν ἑτεροδόξων ἐπιτέτραπται παρελθεῖν, αὐτοί τε καθαροὶ καθάπερ εἰς ἅγιόν τι τέμενος παραγίνονται τὸ δειπνητήριον. (§130) καὶ καθισάντων μεθ᾽ ἡσυχίας ὁ μὲν σιτοποιὸς ἐν τάξει παρατίθησι τοὺς ἄρτους, ὁ δὲ μάγειρος ἓν ἀγγεῖον ἐξ ἑνὸς ἐδέσματος ἑκάστῳ παρατίθησιν. (§131) προκατεύχεται δ᾽ ὁ ἱερεὺς τῆς τροφῆς, καὶ γεύσασθαί τινα πρὶν τῆς εὐχῆς ἀθέμιτον· ἀριστοποιησαμένοις δ᾽ ἐπεύχεται πάλιν· ἀρχόμενοί τε καὶ παυόμενοι γεραίρουσι θεὸν ὡς χορηγὸν τῆς ζωῆς. ἔπειθ᾽ ὡς ἱερὰς καταθέμενοι τὰς ἐσθῆτας πάλιν ἐπ᾽ ἔργα μέχρι δείλης τρέπονται. (§132) δειπνοῦσι δ᾽ ὁμοίως ὑποστρέψαντες συγκαθεζομένων τῶν ξένων, εἰ τύχοιεν αὐτοῖς παρόντες. οὔτε δὲ κραυγή ποτε τὸν οἶκον οὔτε θόρυβος μιαίνει, τὰς δὲ λαλιὰς ἐν τάξει παραχωροῦσιν ἀλλήλοις. (§133) καὶ τοῖς ἔξωθεν ὡς μυστήριόν τι φρικτὸν ἡ τῶν ἔνδον σιωπὴ καταφαίνεται, τούτου δ᾽ αἴτιον ἡ διηνεκὴς νῆψις καὶ τὸ μετρεῖσθαι παρ᾽ αὐτοῖς τροφὴν καὶ ποτὸν μέχρι κόρου.

(§134) Τῶν μὲν οὖν ἄλλων οὐκ ἔστιν ὅ τι μὴ τῶν ἐπιμελητῶν προσταξάντων ἐνεργοῦσι, δύο δὲ ταῦτα παρ᾽ αὐτοῖς αὐτεξούσια, ἐπικουρία καὶ ἔλεος· βοηθεῖν τε γὰρ τοῖς ἀξίοις, ὁπόταν δέωνται, καὶ καθ᾽ ἑαυτοὺς ἐφίεται καὶ τροφὰς ἀπορουμένοις ὀρέγειν. τὰς δὲ εἰς τοὺς συγγενεῖς μεταδόσεις οὐκ ἔξεστι ποιεῖσθαι δίχα τῶν ἐπιτρόπων. (§135) ὀργῆς ταμίαι δίκαιοι, θυμοῦ καθεκτικοί, πίστεως προστάται, εἰρήνης ὑπουργοί. καὶ πᾶν μὲν τὸ ῥηθὲν ὑπ᾽ αὐτῶν ἰσχυρότερον ὅρκου, τὸ δὲ ὀμνύειν αὐτοῖς περιίστανται χεῖρον τῆς ἐπιορκίας ὑπολαμβάνοντες· ἤδη γὰρ κατεγνῶσθαί φασιν τὸν ἀπιστούμενον δίχα θεοῦ. (§136) σπουδάζουσι δ᾽ ἐκτόπως περὶ τὰ τῶν παλαιῶν συντάγματα, μάλιστα τὰ πρὸς ὠφέλειαν ψυχῆς καὶ σώματος ἐκλέγοντες· ἔνθεν αὐτοῖς πρὸς θεραπείαν παθῶν ῥίζαι τε ἀλεξητήριοι καὶ λίθων ἰδιότητες ἀνερευνῶνται.

(§137) Τοῖς δὲ ζηλοῦσιν τὴν αἵρεσιν αὐτῶν οὐκ εὐθὺς ἡ πάροδος, ἀλλ᾽ ἐπὶ ἐνιαυτὸν ἔξω μένοντι τὴν αὐτὴν ὑποτίθενται δίαιταν, ἀξινάριόν τε καὶ τὸ προειρημένον περίζωμα καὶ λευκὴν ἐσθῆτα δόντες.

(§129) After this they are each sent away by their overseers to the crafts in which each is proficient, and they labor earnestly until the fifth hour, when they come together again in one place. Girding themselves with linen wraps, they bathe their bodies in cold water. After this purification, they gather together in a private dwelling place, into which none of the uninitiated is permitted to enter; themselves now pure, they go into the dining-room, even as into some holy shrine. (§130) When they have sat down quietly, the baker serves the loaves in order, while the cook serves a plate of one kind of food to each one. (§131) The priest prays before the meal, and it is not allowed that anyone partake of the food before the prayer. When they have breakfasted, he prays again; both when they begin and when they end, they honor God as the supplier of life. Then, laying down their garments as holy things, they turn again to work until evening. (§132) When they return, they dine in like manner; and any guests who have happened to come to them sit down with them. Neither shouting nor uproar ever defiles their dwelling, but they yield to one another to speak in turn. (§133) To those outside, the silence of those within appears like some awful mystery; the reason for this is their uninterrupted sobriety and the measure of food and drink among them limited to what satisfies.

(§134) Now in other matters, they do nothing except by the order of their overseers, but these two things are left to their own discretion: succor and mercy. For they are themselves permitted both to help the deserving, when they ask, and to supply food to those who are destitute. But it is not permitted to give gifts to relatives without the consent of the stewards. (§135) They are upright managers of anger, masters of their temper, guardians of faithfulness, ministers of peace. Everything spoken by them is stronger than an oath, yet they avoid swearing, considering it worse than perjury. For they think that the one who is not believed apart from (swearing by) God has been condemned already. (§136) They are extraordinarily zealous in the writings of the ancients, choosing especially those that profit soul and body. With the help of these, they search out medicinal roots and the properties of stones for the healing of diseases.

(§137) Now for those who are eager to join their sect, entrance is not immediate; but while he remains outside for a year, they place him under their way of life: they give him a small hatchet, the above-mentioned loin cloth, and a white garment.

(§138) ἐπειδὰν δὲ τούτῳ τῷ χρόνῳ πεῖραν ἐγκρατείας δῷ, πρόσεισιν μὲν ἔγγιον τῇ διαίτῃ καὶ καθαρωτέρων τῶν πρὸς ἁγνείαν ὑδάτων μεταλαμβάνει, παραλαμβάνεται δὲ εἰς τὰς συμβιώσεις οὐδέπω. μετὰ γὰρ τὴν τῆς καρτερίας ἐπίδειξιν δυσὶν ἄλλοις ἔτεσιν τὸ ἦθος δοκιμάζεται καὶ φανεὶς ἄξιος οὕτως εἰς τὸν ὅμιλον ἐγκρίνεται. (§139) πρὶν δὲ τῆς κοινῆς ἅψασθαι τροφῆς ὅρκους αὐτοῖς ὄμνυσι φρικώδεις, πρῶτον μὲν εὐσεβήσειν τὸ θεῖον, ἔπειτα τὰ πρὸς ἀνθρώπους δίκαια φυλάξειν καὶ μήτε κατὰ γνώμην βλάψειν τινὰ μήτε ἐξ ἐπιτάγματος, μισήσειν δ᾽ ἀεὶ τοὺς ἀδίκους καὶ συναγωνιεῖσθαι τοῖς δικαίοις· (§140) τὸ πιστὸν ἀεὶ πᾶσιν παρέξειν, μάλιστα δὲ τοῖς κρατοῦσιν· οὐ γὰρ δίχα θεοῦ περιγενέσθαι τινὶ τὸ ἄρχειν· κἂν αὐτὸς ἄρχῃ, μηδέποτε ἐξυβρίσειν εἰς τὴν ἐξουσίαν, μηδ᾽ ἐσθῆτι ἤ τινι πλείονι κόσμῳ τοὺς ὑποτεταγμένους ὑπερλαμπρυνεῖσθαι· (§141) τὴν ἀλήθειαν ἀγαπᾶν ἀεὶ καὶ τοὺς ψευδομένους προβάλλεσθαι· χεῖρας κλοπῆς καὶ ψυχὴν ἀνοσίου κέρδους καθαρὰν φυλάξειν, καὶ μήτε κρύψειν τι τοὺς αἱρετιστὰς μήθ᾽ ἑτέροις αὐτῶν τι μηνύσειν, κἂν μέχρι θανάτου τις βιάζηται. (§142) πρὸς τούτοις ὄμνυσιν μηδενὶ μὲν μεταδοῦναι τῶν δογμάτων ἑτέρως ἢ ὡς αὐτὸς μετέλαβεν, ἀφέξεσθαι δὲ λῃστείας καὶ συντηρήσειν ὁμοίως τά τε τῆς αἱρέσεως αὐτῶν βιβλία καὶ τὰ τῶν ἀγγέλων ὀνόματα. τοιούτοις μὲν ὅρκοις τοὺς προσιόντας ἐξασφαλίζονται.

(§143) Τοὺς δ᾽ ἐπ᾽ ἀξιοχρέοις ἁμαρτήμασιν ἁλόντας ἐκβάλλουσι τοῦ τάγματος. ὁ δ᾽ ἐκκριθεὶς οἰκτίστῳ πολλάκις μόρῳ διαφθείρεται· τοῖς γὰρ ὅρκοις καὶ τοῖς ἔθεσιν ἐνδεδεμένος οὐδὲ τῆς παρὰ τοῖς ἄλλοις τροφῆς δύναται μεταλαμβάνειν, ποηφαγῶν δὲ καὶ λιμῷ τὸ σῶμα τηκόμενος διαφθείρεται. (§144) διὸ δὴ πολλοὺς ἐλεήσαντες ἐν ταῖς ἐσχάταις ἀναπνοαῖς ἀνέλαβον, ἱκανὴν ἐπὶ τοῖς ἁμαρτήμασιν αὐτῶν τὴν μέχρι θανάτου βάσανον ἡγούμενοι.

(§145) Περὶ δὲ τὰς κρίσεις ἀκριβέστατοι καὶ δίκαιοι, καὶ δικάζουσι μὲν οὐκ ἐλάττους τῶν ἑκατὸν συνελθόντες, τὸ δ᾽ ὁρισθὲν ὑπ᾽ αὐτῶν ἀκίνητον. σέβας δὲ μέγα παρ᾽ αὐτοῖς μετὰ τὸν θεὸν τοὔνομα τοῦ νομοθέτου, κἂν βλασφημήσῃ τις εἰς τοῦτον, κολάζεται θανάτῳ. (§146) τοῖς δὲ πρεσβυτέροις ὑπακούειν καὶ τοῖς πλείοσιν ἐν καλῷ τίθενται· δέκα γοῦν συγκαθεζομένων οὐκ ἂν λαλήσειέν τις ἀκόντων τῶν ἐννέα.

(§138) After he has given proof of his self-control in this time, they bring him closer to their way of life: he participates in the purer waters for purification, but he is not yet received into the common ways of living. For after this demonstration of perseverance, his character is tested for two more years; and if he appears deserving, then he is admitted into the community. (§139) But before he may touch the common meal, he must take awesome oaths: first, that he will practice piety towards the Deity; next, that he will cherish justice towards human beings and will wrong no one, either by his own decision or by (another's) order; that he will hate forever the unjust and fight together with the just; (§140) that he will forever show himself trustworthy to all, but especially to those in authority, for no one achieves his ruling authority apart from God; and that if he himself rules, he will never use his power arrogantly, or, either in his attire or any greater finery, outshine his subjects; (§141) that he will forever love the truth and expose liars; that he will keep his hands pure of stealing and his soul pure of unholy gain; and that he will neither hide anything from the members of his sect nor disclose anything about them to others, even if he be tortured to death. (§142) In addition, he swears that he will transmit their teachings to no one in a way other than as he received them; that he will refrain from brigandage; and that he will preserve in like manner both the books of their sect and the names of the angels. With such oaths as these they secure the allegiance of those who enter (their community).

(§143) But those who are caught in serious offenses they expel from the order. The one who is expelled is often brought to a most miserable fate. For since he is bound by their oaths and customs he is not able to partake of the food of others, but he feeds himself on wild herbs and his body wastes away from hunger until he dies. (§144) For this reason, they compassionately receive many back when they are close to breathing their last, considering the torture that has brought them to the verge of death to be sufficient for their offenses.

(§145) In their judgments they are most scrupulous and just, and they administer justice with not less than a hundred members assembled, but the decision reached by them is immutable. They have the greatest reverence, after God, for the name of the lawgiver, and if anyone blasphemes this one, he is punished by death. (§146) They also regard it as a good thing to obey the elders and the majority. For instance, if ten are sitting together, one would not speak against the will of the nine.

(§147) καὶ τὸ πτύσαι δὲ εἰς μέσους ἢ τὸ δεξιὸν μέρος φυλάσσονται, καὶ ταῖς ἑβδομάσιν ἔργων ἐφάπτεσθαι διαφορώτατα 'Ιουδαίων ἁπάντων· οὐ μόνον γὰρ τροφὰς ἑαυτοῖς πρὸ μιᾶς ἡμέρας παρασκευάζουσιν, ὡς μὴ πῦρ ἐναύοιεν ἐκείνην τὴν ἡμέραν, ἀλλ' οὐδὲ σκεῦός τι μετακινῆσαι θαρροῦσιν οὐδὲ ἀποπατεῖν. (§148) ταῖς δ' ἄλλαις ἡμέραις βόθρον ὀρύσσοντες βάθος ποδιαῖον τῇ σκαλίδι, τοιοῦτον γάρ ἐστιν τὸ διδόμενον ὑπ' αὐτῶν ἀξινίδιον τοῖς νεοσυστάτοις, καὶ περικαλύψαντες θοιμάτιον, ὡς μὴ τὰς αὐγὰς ὑβρίζοιεν τοῦ θεοῦ, θακεύουσιν εἰς αὐτόν. (§149) ἔπειτα τὴν ἀνορυχθεῖσαν γῆν ἐφέλκουσιν εἰς τὸν βόθρον· καὶ τοῦτο ποιοῦσι τοὺς ἐρημοτέρους τόπους ἐκλεγόμενοι. καίπερ δὲ φυσικῆς οὔσης τῆς τῶν λυμάτων ἐκκρίσεως ἀπολούεσθαι μετ' αὐτὴν καθάπερ μεμιασμένοις ἔθιμον.

(§150) Διῄρηνται δὲ κατὰ χρόνον τῆς ἀσκήσεως εἰς μοίρας τέσσαρας, καὶ τοσοῦτον οἱ μεταγενέστεροι τῶν προγενεστέρων ἐλαττοῦνται ὥστ', εἰ ψαύσειαν αὐτῶν, ἐκείνους ἀπολούεσθαι καθάπερ ἀλλοφύλῳ συμφυρέντας. (§151) καὶ μακρόβιοι μέν, ὡς τοὺς πολλοὺς ὑπὲρ ἑκατὸν παρατείνειν ἔτη, διὰ τὴν ἁπλότητα τῆς διαίτης, ἔμοιγε δοκεῖν, καὶ τὴν εὐταξίαν, καταφρονηταὶ δὲ τῶν δεινῶν, καὶ τὰς μὲν ἀλγηδόνας νικῶντες τοῖς φρονήμασιν, τὸν δὲ θάνατον, εἰ μετ' εὐκλείας προσίοι, νομίζοντες ἀθανασίας ἀμείνονα. (§152) διήλεγξεν δὲ αὐτῶν ἐν ἅπασιν τὰς ψυχὰς ὁ πρὸς 'Ρωμαίους πόλεμος, ἐν ᾧ στρεβλούμενοί τε καὶ λυγιζόμενοι, καιόμενοί τε καὶ κλώμενοι καὶ διὰ πάντων ὁδεύοντες τῶν βασανιστηρίων ὀργάνων, ἵν' ἢ βλασφημήσωσιν τὸν νομοθέτην ἢ φάγωσίν τι τῶν ἀσυνήθων, οὐδέτερον ὑπέμειναν παθεῖν, ἀλλ' οὐδὲ κολακεῦσαί ποτε τοὺς αἰκιζομένους ἢ δακρῦσαι. (§153) μειδιῶντες δὲ ἐν ταῖς ἀλγηδόσιν καὶ κατειρωνευόμενοι τῶν τὰς βασάνους προσφερόντων εὔθυμοι τὰς ψυχὰς ἠφίεσαν ὡς πάλιν κομιούμενοι.

(§154) Καὶ γὰρ ἔρρωται παρ' αὐτοῖς ἥδε ἡ δόξα, φθαρτὰ μὲν εἶναι τὰ σώματα καὶ τὴν ὕλην οὐ μόνιμον αὐτῶν, τὰς δὲ ψυχὰς ἀθανάτους ἀεὶ διαμένειν, καὶ συμπλέκεσθαι μὲν ἐκ τοῦ λεπτοτάτου φοιτώσας αἰθέρος ὥσπερ εἱρκταῖς τοῖς σώμασιν ἴυγγί τινι φυσικῇ κατασπωμένας, (§155) ἐπειδὰν δὲ ἀνεθῶσι τῶν κατὰ σάρκα δεσμῶν, οἷα δὴ μακρᾶς δουλείας ἀπηλλαγμένας, τότε χαίρειν καὶ μετεώρους φέρεσθαι. καὶ ταῖς μὲν ἀγαθαῖς, ὁμοδοξοῦντες παισὶν Ἑλλήνων, ἀποφαίνονται τὴν ὑπὲρ ὠκεανὸν δίαιταν ἀποκεῖσθαι καὶ χῶρον οὔτε ὄμβροις οὔτε νιφετοῖς οὔτε καύμασι βαρυνόμενον, ἀλλ' ὃν ἐξ ὠκεανοῦ πραῢς ἀεὶ ζέφυρος ἐπιπνέων ἀναψύχει· ταῖς δὲ φαύλαις ζοφώδη καὶ χειμέριον ἀφορίζονται μυχόν, γέμοντα τιμωριῶν ἀδιαλείπτων.

(§147) They avoid spitting in the midst of the group or on the right side. They are stricter than all Jews in not undertaking work on the seventh day, for not only do they prepare their meals on the day before, so as not to kindle a fire on that day, but they do not dare to move a vessel or even to relieve themselves. (§148) On the other days they dig a pit one foot deep with a hoe (for such is the purpose of the small hatchet that is given by them to the newly initiated) and, covering themselves completely with their outer garment so as not to insult the rays of the Deity, they relieve themselves into the pit. (§149) Then they push the soil that was dug out back into the pit. To do this they choose the more isolated places. Although this discharge of excrement is a natural process, yet it is a custom to wash after it as if they were unclean.

(§150) Now they are divided, according to the duration of their training, into four groups; the junior members are so inferior to the seniors that if seniors touch them, they must wash as if they had been in contact with a stranger. (§151) They are long-lived, as most of them remain alive over a hundred years on account of, I imagine, the simplicity and discipline of their way of life. They are fearless of danger and prevail over pain by their wills, whereas death, if it comes with glory, they consider better than immortality. (§152) The war with the Romans tested their souls in every way. In it, though racked, twisted, burned, mangled, and made to pass through every instrument of torture to force them to blaspheme the lawgiver or eat something forbidden, they did not submit to either, never once groveling before their torturers or shedding a tear. (§153) Rather, smiling in their pains and ridiculing those who inflicted the torments upon them, they gave up their souls cheerfully, confident that they would get them back again.

(§154) For this teaching is strong among them that bodies are corruptible and their matter is not lasting, but that souls are immortal and continue forever. Emanating from the finest ether, they are entangled with their bodies, as it were in prisons, into which they are dragged down by some natural sorcery. (§155) But when they are liberated from the bonds of the flesh, then, as though released from a long bondage, they rejoice and are carried aloft. Sharing the opinion of the Greeks, they declare that for the good (souls) there is in store a dwelling beyond the ocean, even a place unoppressed by rain or snow or blazing heat, but cooled by the mild west wind ever blowing from the ocean; whereas they assign evil (souls) to a gloomy and tempestuous recess filled with incessant punishments.

(§156) δοκοῦσι δέ μοι κατὰ τὴν αὐτὴν ἔννοιαν Ἕλληνες τοῖς τε ἀνδρείοις αὐτῶν, οὓς ἥρωας καὶ ἡμιθέους καλοῦσιν, τὰς μακάρων νήσους ἀνατεθεικέναι, ταῖς δὲ τῶν πονηρῶν ψυχαῖς καθ᾽ ᾅδου τὸν ἀσεβῶν χῶρον, ἔνθα καὶ κολαζομένους τινὰς μυθολογοῦσιν, Σισύφους καὶ Ταντάλους Ἰξίονάς τε καὶ Τιτυούς, πρῶτον μὲν ἀιδίους ὑφιστάμενοι τὰς ψυχάς, ἔπειτα εἰς προτροπὴν ἀρετῆς καὶ κακίας ἀποτροπήν. (§157) τούς τε γὰρ ἀγαθοὺς γίνεσθαι κατὰ τὸν βίον ἀμείνους ἐλπίδι τιμῆς καὶ μετὰ τὴν τελευτήν, τῶν τε κακῶν ἐμποδίζεσθαι τὰς ὁρμὰς δέει προσδοκώντων, εἰ καὶ λάθοιεν ἐν τῷ ζῆν, μετὰ τὴν διάλυσιν ἀθάνατον τιμωρίαν ὑφέξειν. (§158) ταῦτα μὲν οὖν Ἐσσηνοὶ περὶ ψυχῆς θεολογοῦσιν, ἄφυκτον δέλεαρ τοῖς ἅπαξ γευσαμένοις τῆς σοφίας αὐτῶν καθιέντες.

(§159) Εἰσὶν δ᾽ ἐν αὐτοῖς οἳ καὶ τὰ μέλλοντα προγινώσκειν ὑπισχνοῦνται, βίβλοις ἱεραῖς καὶ διαφόροις ἁγνείαις καὶ προφητῶν ἀποφθέγμασιν ἐμπαιδοτριβούμενοι· σπάνιον δ᾽ εἴ ποτε ἐν ταῖς προαγορεύσεσιν ἀστοχοῦσιν.

(§160) Ἔστιν δὲ καὶ ἕτερον Ἐσσηνῶν τάγμα, δίαιταν μὲν καὶ ἔθη καὶ νόμιμα τοῖς ἄλλοις ὁμοφρονοῦν, διεστὼς δὲ τῇ κατὰ γάμον δόξῃ· μέγιστον γὰρ ἀποκόπτειν οἴονται τοῦ βίου μέρος, τὴν διαδοχήν, τοὺς μὴ γαμοῦντας, μᾶλλον δέ, εἰ πάντες τὸ αὐτὸ φρονήσειαν, ἐκλιπεῖν ἂν τὸ γένος τάχιστα. (§161) δοκιμάζοντες μέντοι τριετίᾳ τὰς γαμετάς, ἐπειδὰν τρὶς καθαρθῶσιν εἰς πεῖραν τοῦ δύνασθαι τίκτειν, οὕτως ἄγονται. ταῖς δ᾽ ἐγκύμοσιν οὐχ ὁμιλοῦσιν, ἐνδεικνύμενοι τὸ μὴ δι᾽ ἡδονὴν ἀλλὰ τέκνων χρείαν γαμεῖν. λουτρὰ δὲ ταῖς γυναιξὶν ἀμπεχομέναις ἐνδύματα, καθάπερ τοῖς ἀνδράσιν ἐν περιζώματι. τοιαῦτα μὲν ἔθη τοῦδε τοῦ τάγματος.

## 3. Ant. 18.1, 2, 5 (§11, 18−22)

(§11) Ἰουδαίοις φιλοσοφίαι τρεῖς ἦσαν ἐκ τοῦ πάνυ ἀρχαίου τῶν πατρίων, ἥ τε τῶν Ἐσσηνῶν καὶ ἡ τῶν Σαδδουκαίων, τρίτην δὲ ἐφιλοσόφουν οἱ Φαρισαῖοι λεγόμενοι. καὶ τυγχάνει μέντοι περὶ αὐτῶν ἡμῖν εἰρημένα ἐν τῇ δευτέρᾳ βίβλῳ τοῦ Ἰουδαϊκοῦ πολέμου, μνησθήσομαι δ᾽ ὅμως καὶ νῦν αὐτῶν ἐπ᾽ ὀλίγον.

(§18) Ἐσσηνοῖς δὲ ἐπὶ μὲν θεῷ καταλείπειν φιλεῖ τὰ πάντα ὁ λόγος, ἀθανατίζουσιν δὲ τὰς ψυχὰς περιμάχητον ἡγούμενοι τοῦ δικαίου τὴν πρόσοδον.

(§156) The Greeks seem to me to have the same concept when they assign to their brave men, whom they call heroes and demi-gods, the islands of the blessed, whereas to the souls of the wicked the place of the ungodly down in Hades, where, as legend has it, people such as Sisyphus, Tantalus, Ixion, and Tityus are being tormented. Thus they were first maintaining that souls are everlasting, and then were encouraging virtue and discouraging evil. (§157) For the good are made better in their lifetime with the hope of a reward even after death, whereas the impulses of the wicked are hindered by fear, since they expect that even if they escape notice in life, they will undergo unending punishment after death. (§158) These, then, are the theological teachings of the Essenes concerning the soul, by which they set an inescapable bait for those who have once tasted of their wisdom.

(§159) Now there are some among them who profess to foreknow the future, being educated in holy books and various rites of purification and sayings of prophets; and rarely, if ever, do they err in their predictions.

(§160) Now there is another order of Essenes, who have the same views as the rest in their way of life, customs, and laws, but are at variance in their opinion of marriage. For they think that those who do not marry cut off the most important part of life, namely, genealogical succession; and further, if all were to hold the same opinion, the whole race would die out very quickly. (§161) They put their wives to the test, however, for a three-year period, and marry those who, having three periods of purification give proof that they are able to bear children. They do not have intercourse with them during pregnancy, demonstrating that they marry not for self-gratification but for the necessity of children. In the baths the women are covered with a garment, whereas the men wear a loin cloth. Such are the customs of this order.

### 3. Ant. 18.1, 2, 5 (§11, 18–22)

(§11) There were three philosophies among the Jews inherited from the most ancient times: that of the Essenes, that of the Sadducees, and the third the ones called the Pharisees. Indeed, I happen to have spoken already about them in the second book of *The Jewish War*, but I shall still give an account of them briefly here.

(§18) The doctrine of the Essenes is that they like to leave all things to God. They regard souls as immortal and believe that the path of righteousness is worth striving for.

(§19) εἰς δὲ τὸ ἱερὸν ἀναθήματα στέλλοντες θυσίας ἐπιτελοῦσιν διαφορότητι ἁγνειῶν, ἃς νομίζοιεν, καὶ δι' αὐτὸ εἰργόμενοι τοῦ κοινοῦ τεμενίσματος ἐφ' αὑτῶν τὰς θυσίας ἐπιτελοῦσιν. βέλτιστοι δὲ ἄλλως ἄνδρες τὸν τρόπον καὶ τὸ πᾶν πονεῖν ἐπὶ γεωργίᾳ τετραμμένοι.

(§20) ἄξιον δ' αὐτῶν θαυμάσαι παρὰ πάντας τοὺς ἀρετῆς μεταποιουμένους τόδε διὰ τὸ μηδαμῶς ὑπάρξαν Ἑλλήνων ἢ βαρβάρων τισίν, ἀλλὰ μηδ' εἰς ὀλίγον, ἐκείνοις ἐκ παλαιοῦ συνελθὸν ἐν τῷ ἐπιτηδεύεσθαι μὴ κεκωλῦσθαι· τὰ χρήματά τε κοινά ἐστιν αὐτοῖς, ἀπολαύει δὲ οὐδὲν ὁ πλούσιος τῶν οἰκείων μειζόνως ἢ ὁ μηδ' ὁτιοῦν κεκτημένος· καὶ τάδε πράσσουσιν ἄνδρες ὑπὲρ τετρακισχίλιοι τὸν ἀριθμὸν ὄντες. (§21) καὶ οὔτε γαμετὰς εἰσάγονται οὔτε δούλων ἐπιτηδεύουσιν κτῆσιν, τὸ μὲν εἰς ἀδικίαν φέρειν ὑπειληφότες, τὸ δὲ στάσεως ἐνδιδόναι ποίησιν, αὐτοὶ δ' ἐφ' ἑαυτῶν ζῶντες διακονίᾳ τῇ ἐπ' ἀλλήλοις ἐπιχρῶνται. (§22) ἀποδέκτας δὲ τῶν προσόδων χειροτονοῦντες καὶ ὁπόσα ἡ γῆ φέροι ἄνδρας ἀγαθούς, ἱερεῖς δὲ ἐπὶ ποιήσει σίτου τε καὶ βρωμάτων. ζῶσι δὲ οὐδὲν παρηλλαγμένως, ἀλλ' ὅτι μάλιστα ἐμφέροντες Δακῶν τοῖς Κτίσταις λεγομένοις.

## B. Text of minor passages (discussed in the Appendix)

### 1. J.W. 1.3, 5 (§78–80)

Θαυμάσαι δ' ἄν τις ἐν τούτῳ καὶ Ἰούδαν, Ἐσσαῖος ἦν γένος οὐκ ἔστιν ὅτε πταίσας ἢ ψευσθεὶς ἐν τοῖς προαπαγγέλμασιν, ὃς ἐπειδὴ καὶ τότε τὸν Ἀντίγονον ἐθεάσατο παριόντα διὰ τοῦ ἱεροῦ, πρὸς τοὺς γνωρίμους ἀνέκραγεν, ἦσαν δ' οὐκ ὀλίγοι παρεδρεύοντες αὐτῷ τῶν μανθανόντων, "παπαί, νῦν ἐμοὶ καλόν," ἔφη, "τὸ θανεῖν, ὅτε μου προτέθνηκεν ἡ ἀλήθεια καὶ τι τῶν ὑπ' ἐμοῦ προρρηθέντων διέψευσται· ζῇ γὰρ Ἀντίγονος οὑτοσὶ σήμερον ὀφείλων ἀνῃρῆσθαι. χωρίον δὲ αὐτῷ πρὸς σφαγὴν Στράτωνος πύργος εἵμαρτο· καὶ τοῦτο μὲν ἀπὸ ἑξακοσίων ἐντεῦθεν σταδίων ἐστίν, ὧραι δὲ τῆς ἡμέρας ἤδη τέσσαρες. ὁ δὴ χρόνος ἐκκρούει τὸ μάντευμα." ταῦτ' εἰπὼν σκυθρωπὸς ἐπὶ συννοίας ὁ γέρων διεκαρτέρει, καὶ μετ' ὀλίγον ἀνῃρημένος Ἀντίγονος ἠγγέλλετο κατὰ τὸ ὑπόγαιον χωρίον, ὃ δὴ καὶ αὐτὸ Στράτωνος ἐκαλεῖτο πύργος, ὁμωνυμοῦν τῇ παραλίῳ Καισαρείᾳ. τοῦτο γοῦν τὸν μάντιν διετάραξεν.

(§19) Sending votive offerings to the temple, they offer sacrifices [E and Lat. both have the negative here — they do *not* offer sacrifices] with a difference in the rites of purification that they employ; on account of this they are excluded from the common court and offer their sacrifices by themselves. Otherwise they are the noblest men in their way of life and have dedicated themselves to work entirely in agriculture. (§20) They are worthy of admiration above all those who lay claim to virtue, because such (qualities) did not exist among any Greeks or barbarians, not even to a small degree; but they have been with (the Essenes) for a long time and they have not been hindered in their pursuit of them. In addition, they hold their possessions in common, and the wealthy person does not benefit any more from his household possessions than the man who owns nothing at all. The men who live in this way are over four thousand in number. (§21) They neither bring wives into (the community) nor do they seek to acquire slaves, since they consider that the latter leads to injustice and the former inclines towards causing factions. Rather, they live by themselves and practice service for one another. (§22) They elect good men as treasurers of their revenue and what the land yields, and priests for the preparation of their bread and their food. They live no differently from, but most similarly to those who among the Dacians are called Ctistae.

### B. Translation of minor passages (discussed in the Appendix)

#### 1. J.W. 1.3, 5 (§78–80)

Now any one would be astonished at Judas on this occasion. He was an Essene by background, and there was never an occasion when he erred or spoke falsely in his predictions. At that time, when he saw Antigonus passing through the temple precincts, he cried out to his acquaintances (for not a few of his disciples were attending upon him), "Alas! It would be better for me to die, since the truth has already died before me and one of my predictions has proven false. For Antigonus lives, this one who ought to have been killed today; the place fated for his murder was Strato's Tower, and that is six hundred stades from here, and it is already the fourth hour of the day. So time knocks out prediction." Having said this, the old man remained downcast in his meditation. A little later it was announced that Antigonus had been killed in an underground place that was also called Strato's Tower, by the same name as the Caesarea Maritima. This, then, had thrown the seer into confusion.

## 2. J.W. 2.7, 3 (§111–13)

Παραλαβὼν δὲ τὴν ἐθναρχίαν Ἀρχέλαος καὶ κατὰ μνήμην τῶν πάλαι διαφορῶν οὐ μόνον Ἰουδαίοις ἀλλὰ καὶ Σαμαρεῦσι χρησάμενος ὠμῶς, πρεσβευσαμένων ἑκατέρων κατ᾽ αὐτοῦ πρὸς Καίσαρα ἔτει τῆς ἀρχῆς ἐνάτῳ φυγαδεύεται μὲν αὐτὸς εἰς Βίενναν πόλιν τῆς Γαλλίας. ἡ οὐσία δ᾽ αὐτοῦ τοῖς Καίσαρος θησαυροῖς ἐγκατατάσσεται. πρὶν κληθῆναι δ᾽ αὐτὸν ὑπὸ τοῦ Καίσαρος ὄναρ ἰδεῖν φασιν τοιόνδε· ἔδοξεν ὁρᾶν στάχυς ἐννέα πλήρεις καὶ μεγάλους ὑπὸ βοῶν καταβιβρωσκομένους. μεταπεμψάμενος δὲ τοὺς μάντεις καὶ τῶν Χαλδαίων τινὰς ἐπυνθάνετο, τί σημαίνειν δοκοῖεν. ἄλλων δ᾽ ἄλλως ἐξηγουμένων Σίμων τις Ἐσσαῖος τὸ γένος ἔφη τοὺς μὲν στάχυς ἐνιαυτοὺς νομίζειν, βόας δὲ μεταβολὴν πραγμάτων διὰ τὸ τὴν χώραν ἀροτριῶντας ἀλλάσσειν, ὥστε βασιλεύσειν μὲν αὐτὸν τὸν τῶν σταχύων ἀριθμόν, ἐν ποικίλαις δὲ πραγμάτων μεταβολαῖς γενόμενον τελευτήσειν. ταῦτα ἀκούσας Ἀρχέλαος μετὰ πέντε ἡμέρας ἐπὶ τὴν δίκην μετεκλήθη.

## 3. J.W. 2.20, 4 (§566–8)

Εἰς δὲ τὴν Ἰδουμαίαν ἑτέρους ἐπελέξαντο στρατηγοὺς Ἰησοῦν υἱὸν Σαπφᾶ τῶν ἀρχιερέων ἕνα καὶ Ἐλεάζαρον ἀρχιερέως υἱὸν Νέου· τῷ δ᾽ ἄρχοντι τότε τῆς Ἰδουμαίας Νίγερι, γένος δ᾽ ἦν ἐκ τῆς ὑπὲρ Ἰορδάνην Περαίας, διὸ καὶ Περαΐτης ἐκαλεῖτο, προσέταξαν ὑποτάσσεσθαι τοῖς στρατηγοῖς. ἠμέλουν δὲ οὐδὲ τῆς ἄλλης χώρας, ἀλλ᾽ εἰς μὲν Ἱεριχοῦν Ἰώσηπος ὁ Σίμωνος, εἰς δὲ τὴν Περαίαν Μανασσῆς, Θαμνᾶ δὲ τοπαρχίας Ἰωάννης ὁ Ἐσσαῖος στρατηγήσων ἐπέμφθη· προσκεκλήρωτο δ᾽ αὐτῷ Λύδδα καὶ Ἰόππη καὶ Ἀμμαοῦς. τῆς δὲ Γοφνιτικῆς καὶ Ἀκραβεττηνῆς ὁ Ἀνανίου Ἰωάννης ἡγεμὼν ἀποδείκνυται καὶ τῆς Γαλιλαίας ἑκατέρας Ἰώσηπος Ματθίου· προσώριστο δὲ τῇ τούτου στρατηγίᾳ καὶ Γάμαλα τῶν ταύτῃ πόλεων ὀχυρωτάτη.

## 2. J.W. 2.7, 3 (§111–13)

Now Archelaus, when he had taken possession of his ethnarchy, according to his remembrance of old quarrels, treated savagely not only Jews, but also Samaritans. Both of them sent envoys against him to Caesar, and in the ninth year of his reign he was banished to Vienne, a city of Gaul, and his possessions were assigned to Caesar's treasury. Before he was summoned by Caesar, it is said that he saw a dream such as this: he seemed to see nine full and large ears of grain being devoured by oxen. Having summoned the soothsayers and some of the Chaldaeans, he asked them what they thought it signified. When one after the other gave their interpretations, Simon, an Essene by background, said that he thought the ears of grain were years and the oxen a revolution, since in plowing they alter the land; so that he would reign the same number of years as the ears of grain and would die after various revolutions. Five days after he heard these things, Archelaus was summoned to his trial.

## 3. J.W. 2.20, 4 (§566–8)

Other generals were chosen for Idumaea: Jesus, son of Sapphas, one of the chief priests, and Eleazar, son of the high priest Neus; and they ordered Niger, then governor of Idumaea, who was of a family from Peraea beyond (the) Jordan (hence he was called the Peraean), to submit to these generals. Nor did they neglect the other regions: Joseph, son of Simon, was sent to be in command at Jericho; Manasseh was sent to Peraea; John the Essene was sent to the toparchy of Thamna – Lydda, Joppa, and Emmaus were also allotted to him; John, son of Ananias, was designated commander of Gophna and Acrabetta; and Josephus, son of Matthias, of the two Galilees. Gamala, the strongest city in that area, was also added to his command.

## 4. J.W. 3.2, 1 (§9–12)

'Ιουδαῖοι δὲ μετὰ τὴν Κεστίου πληγὴν ἐπηρμένοι ταῖς ἀδοκήτοις εὐπραγίαις ἀκρατεῖς ἦσαν ὁρμῆς καὶ ὥσπερ ἐκριπιζόμενοι τῇ τύχῃ προσωτέρω τὸν πόλεμον ἐξῆγον· πᾶν γοῦν εὐθέως ὅσον ἦν μαχιμώτατον αὐτοῖς ἀθροισθέντες ὥρμησαν ἐπ' 'Ασκάλωνα. πόλις ἐστὶν ἀρχαία τῶν 'Ιεροσολύμων εἴκοσι πρὸς τοῖς πεντακοσίοις ἀπέχουσα σταδίους, ἀεὶ διὰ μίσους 'Ιουδαίοις γεγενημένη, διὸ καὶ τότε ταῖς πρώταις ὁρμαῖς ἐγγίων ἔδοξεν. ἐξηγοῦντο δὲ τῆς καταδρομῆς τρεῖς ἄνδρες ἀλκήν τε κορυφαῖοι καὶ συνέσει, Νίγερ τε ὁ Περαΐτης καὶ ὁ Βαβυλώνιος Σίλας, πρὸς οἷς 'Ιωάννης ὁ 'Εσσαῖος. ἡ δὲ 'Ασκάλων ἐτετείχιστο μὲν καρτερῶς, βοηθείας δὲ ἦν σχεδὸν ἔρημος· ἐφρουρεῖτο γὰρ ὑπό τε σπείρας πεζῶν καὶ ὑπὸ μιᾶς ἴλης ἱππέων, ἧς ἐπῆρχεν 'Αντώνιος.

## 5. J.W. 5.4, 2 (§142–5)

Τῶν δὲ τριῶν τειχῶν τὸ μὲν ἀρχαῖον διά τε τὰς φάραγγας καὶ τὸν ὑπὲρ τούτων λόφον, ἐφ' οὗ κατεσκεύαστο, δυσάλωτον ἦν· πρὸς δὲ τῷ πλεονεκτήματι τοῦ τόπου καὶ καρτερῶς ἐδεδόμητο, Δαυΐδου τε καὶ Σολομῶνος, ἔτι δὲ τῶν μεταξὺ τούτων βασιλέων φιλοτιμηθέντων περὶ τὸ ἔργον. ἀρχόμενον δὲ κατὰ βορρᾶν ἀπὸ τοῦ 'Ιππικοῦ καλουμένου πύργου καὶ διατεῖνον ἐπὶ τὸν ξυστόν, ἔπειτα τῇ βουλῇ συνάπτον ἐπὶ τὴν ἑσπέριον τοῦ ἱεροῦ στοὰν ἀπηρτίζετο. κατὰ θάτερα δὲ πρὸς δύσιν, ἀπὸ ταὐτοῦ μὲν ἀρχόμενον, διὰ δὲ τοῦ Βηθσὼ καλουμένου χώρου κατατεῖνον ἐπὶ τὴν 'Εσσηνῶν πύλην, κἄπειτα πρὸς νότον ὑπὲρ τὴν Σιλωὰν ἐπιστρέφον πηγήν, ἔνθεν τε πάλιν ἐκκλῖνον πρὸς ἀνατολὴν ἐπὶ τὴν Σολομῶνος κολυμβήθραν καὶ διῆκον μέχρι χώρου τινός, ὃν καλοῦσιν 'Οφλᾶν, τῇ πρὸς ἀνατολὴν στοᾷ τοῦ ἱεροῦ συνῆπτε.

## 6. Ant. 13.5, 9 (§171–2)

Κατὰ δὲ τὸν χρόνον τοῦτον τρεῖς αἱρέσεις τῶν 'Ιουδαίων ἦσαν, αἳ περὶ τῶν ἀνθρωπίνων πραγμάτων διαφόρως ὑπελάμβανον, ὧν ἡ μὲν Φαρισαίων ἐλέγετο, ἡ δὲ Σαδδουκαίων, ἡ τρίτη δὲ 'Εσσηνῶν. οἱ μὲν οὖν Φαρισαῖοι τινὰ καὶ οὐ πάντα τῆς εἱμαρμένης ἔργον εἶναι λέγουσι, τινὰ δ' ἐφ' ἑαυτοῖς ὑπάρχειν συμβαίνειν τε καὶ μὴ γίνεσθαι. τὸ δὲ τῶν 'Εσσηνῶν γένος πάντων τὴν εἱμαρμένην κυρίαν ἀποφαίνεται, καὶ μηδὲν ὃ μὴ κατ' ἐκείνης ψῆφον ἀνθρώποις ἀπαντᾷ.

## 4. J.W. 3.2, 1 (§9−12)

Now the Jews, after the defeat of Cestius, uplifted by their unexpected military successes, were unrestrained in fervor, and as though stirred up by good fortune, extended the war further. Immediately, then, all their best warriors were mustered and pressed forward against Ascalon. This is an ancient city, about 520 stades from Jerusalem, which had always been odious to the Jews; because of this at that time it seemed nearer for the first attacks. This raid was led by three men outstanding in both courage and intelligence, namely, Niger the Peraean, and Silas the Babylonian, and besides them was John the Essene. Now Ascalon was strongly fortified with walls, but was nearly destitute of assistance, for it was garrisoned by one cohort of foot-soldiers and by one troop of horsemen, which Antonius commanded.

## 5. J.W. 5.4, 2 (§142−5)

Now of the three walls (of Jerusalem), the most ancient, on account of both the ravines and the hill above them, upon which it was built, was almost impregnable. But in addition to the advantage of its position it was also strongly built, since David and Solomon and the kings who followed them prided themselves on the work. Beginning on the north at the tower called Hippicus, it extended to the Xystus; then joining the council chamber, it terminated at the western colonnade of the temple. Beginning at the same place in the other direction, it reached down westward through the place called Bethso, to the gate of the Essenes; and then it turned to the south above the fountain of Siloam, from which also it again inclined to the east towards Solomon's pool, and passing through to a certain place they called Ophlas, joined the east colonnade of the temple.

## 6. Ant. 13.5, 9 (§171−2)

Now at this time there were three sects of the Jews, which held different opinions concerning human actions: the first was that of the Pharisees, the second the Sadducees, and the third the Essenes. Now the Pharisees say that some·things, but not all, are the work of fate; some are going to happen or not, depending on ourselves. But the sect of the Essenes maintains that fate is ruler of all things, and that nothing happens to people except it be according to its decree.

7. Ant. 13.10, 6 (§298)

... ἀλλὰ περὶ μὲν τούτων τῶν δύο καὶ τῶν Ἐσσηνῶν ἐν τῇ δευτέρᾳ μου τῶν Ἰουδαϊκῶν ἀκριβῶς δεδήλωται.

8. Ant. 13.11, 2 (§311–13)

Μάλιστα δ' ἄν τις θαυμάσειε καὶ Ἰούδαν τινά, Ἐσσηνὸν μὲν τὸ γένος, οὐδέποτε δ' ἐν οἷς προεῖπεν διαψευσάμενον τἀληθές· οὗτος γὰρ ἰδὼν τὸν Ἀντίγονον παριόντα τὸ ἱερὸν ἀνεβόησεν ἐν τοῖς ἑταίροις αὐτοῦ καὶ γνωρίμοις, οἳ διδασκαλίας ἕνεκα τοῦ προλέγειν τὰ μέλλοντα παρέμενον, ὡς ἀποθανεῖν αὐτῷ καλὸν διεψευσμένῳ ζῶντος Ἀντιγόνου, ὃν σήμερον τεθνήξεσθαι προειπὼν ἐν τῷ καλουμένῳ Στράτωνος πύργῳ περιόντα ὁρᾷ, καὶ τοῦ μὲν χωρίου περὶ σταδίους ἀπέχοντος νῦν ἑξακοσίους, ὅπου φονευθήσεσθαι προεῖπεν αὐτόν, τῆς δ' ἡμέρας ἤδη τὸ πλεῖστον ἠνυσμένον, ὥστ' αὐτῷ κινδυνεύειν τὸ μάντευμα ψεῦδος εἶναι. ταῦτ' οὖν λέγοντος αὐτοῦ καὶ κατηφοῦντος ἀγγέλλεται τεθνεὼς Ἀντίγονος ἐν τῷ ὑπογείῳ, ὃ καὶ αὐτὸ Στράτωνος ἐκαλεῖτο πύργος ὁμώνυμον τῇ παραλίῳ Καισαρείᾳ. τὸν μὲν οὖν μάντιν τοῦτο διετάραξεν.

9. Ant. 15.10, 4–5 (§371–9)

Ἀφείθησαν δὲ ταύτης τῆς ἀνάγκης καὶ οἱ παρ' ἡμῖν Ἐσσαῖοι καλούμενοι· γένος δὲ τοῦτ' ἔστιν διαίτῃ χρώμενον τῇ παρ' Ἕλλησιν ὑπὸ Πυθαγόρου καταδεδειγμένῃ· περὶ τούτων μὲν οὖν ἐν ἄλλοις σαφέστερον διέξειμι. τοὺς δὲ Ἐσσηνοὺς ἀφ' οἵας αἰτίας ἐτίμα, μεῖζόν τι φρονῶν ἐπ' αὐτοῖς ἢ κατὰ τὴν θνητὴν φύσιν, εἰπεῖν ἄξιον· οὐ γὰρ ἀπρεπὴς ὁ λόγος φανεῖται τῷ τῆς ἱστορίας γένει, παραδηλῶν καὶ τὴν ὑπὲρ τούτων ὑπόληψιν.

Ἦν τις τῶν Ἐσσηνῶν Μανάημος ὄνομα καὶ τἄλλα κατὰ τὴν προαίρεσιν τοῦ βίου καλοκαγαθίᾳ μαρτυρούμενος καὶ πρόγνωσιν ἐκ θεοῦ τῶν μελλόντων ἔχων. οὗτος ἔτι παῖδα τὸν Ἡρώδην εἰς διδασκάλου φοιτῶντα κατιδὼν βασιλέα Ἰουδαίων προσηγόρευσεν.

### 7. Ant. 13.10, 6 (§298)

... But concerning these two sects [i.e., the Pharisees and Sadducees], and that of the Essenes, it has been accurately reported in the second book of my *Judaica* (i.e., *Jewish War*).

### 8. Ant. 13.11, 2 (§311–13)

And especially one might marvel at a certain Judas, an Essene by background, who had never been faulted in the truth in his predictions. For when he saw Antigonus passing through the temple precincts, he cried out to his friends and acquaintances, who were with him for the sake of instruction in foretelling things to come, that it would be better for him to die, since he had spoken falsely about Antigonus who was (still) alive. He had predicted that he would die today at the place called Strato's Tower, and (now) he was seeing him going about alive. For the place where he had foretold that Antigonus would be killed was six hundred stades away from where he was then, and the greater part of the day was already over, so that his prophecy was likely to be false. Now as he was saying these things and was dejected, it was reported that Antigonus had been killed in the underground place that was also called Strato's Tower, by the same name as the Caesarea Maritima. It was this, then, which had thrown the seer into confusion.

### 9. Ant. 15.10, 4–5 (§371–9)

And those who are called Essenes by us were also pardoned from this necessity [viz., taking an oath of loyalty to Herod]. This is a sect that practices a way of life introduced to the Greeks by Pythagoras. Now I shall explain about these people more clearly elsewhere. But it is proper to state here the reasons why (Herod) held the Essenes in honor and why he thought more highly of them than their mortal nature would require. For the matter does not appear to be improper for this genre of history, since it will set forth the prevailing opinion about these men.

One of these Essenes was named Menahem, whose entire course of life testified to his virtue, and who had foreknowledge from God of the future. This man, upon seeing Herod (while he was still a child) going to his teacher, greeted him as "king of the Jews."

ὁ δ᾽ ἀγνοεῖν ἢ κατειρωνεύεσθαι νομίζων αὐτὸν ἀνεμίμνησκεν ἰδιώτης ὤν. Μανάημος δὲ μειδιάσας ἠρέμα καὶ τύπτων τῇ χειρὶ κατὰ τῶν γλουτῶν, "ἀλλά τοι καὶ βασιλεύσεις," ἔφη, "καὶ τὴν ἀρχὴν εὐδαιμόνως ἐπάρξεις· ἠξίωσαι γὰρ ἐκ θεοῦ. καὶ μέμνησο τῶν Μαναήμου πληγῶν, ὥστε σοι καὶ τοῦτο σύμβολον εἶναι τῶν κατὰ τὴν τύχην μεταπτώσεων. ἄριστος γὰρ ὁ τοιοῦτος λογισμός, εἰ καὶ δικαιοσύνην ἀγαπήσειας καὶ πρὸς τὸν θεὸν εὐσέβειαν, ἐπιείκειαν δὲ πρὸς τοὺς πολίτας· ἀλλ᾽ οὐ γὰρ οἶδά σε τοιοῦτον ἔσεσθαι, τὸ πᾶν ἐπιστάμενος. εὐτυχίᾳ μὲν γὰρ ὅσον οὐκ ἄλλος διοίσεις, καὶ τεύξῃ δόξης αἰωνίου, λήθην δ᾽ εὐσεβείας ἕξεις καὶ τοῦ δικαίου. ταῦτα δ᾽ οὐκ ἂν λάθοι τὸν θεόν, ἐπὶ τῇ καταστροφῇ τοῦ βίου τῆς ἀντ᾽ αὐτῶν ὀργῆς ἀπομνημονευομένης." τούτοις αὐτίκα μὲν ἥκιστα τὸν νοῦν προσεῖχεν ἐλπίδι λειπόμενος αὐτῶν Ἡρώδης, κατὰ μικρὸν δὲ ἀρθεὶς ἕως καὶ τοῦ βασιλεύειν καὶ εὐτυχεῖν, ἐν τῷ μεγέθει τῆς ἀρχῆς μεταπέμπεται τὸν Μανάημον καὶ περὶ τοῦ χρόνου πόσον ἄρξει διεπυνθάνετο. Μανάημος δὲ τὸ μὲν σύμπαν οὐκ εἶπεν· ὡς δὲ σιωπῶντος αὐτοῦ, μόνον εἰ δέκα γενήσονται βασιλείας ἐνιαυτοὶ προσεπύθετο, καὶ εἴκοσι καὶ τριάκοντα εἰπὼν ὅρον οὐκ ἐπέθηκε τῷ τέλει τῆς προθεσμίας, Ἡρώδης δὲ καὶ τούτοις ἀρκεσθεὶς τόν τε Μανάημον ἀφῆκεν δεξιωσάμενος, καὶ πάντας ἀπ᾽ ἐκείνου τοὺς Ἐσσηνοὺς τιμῶν διετέλει. ταῦτα μὲν οὖν εἰ καὶ παράδοξα δηλῶσαι τοῖς ἐντυγχάνουσιν ἠξιώσαμεν καὶ περὶ τῶν παρ᾽ ἡμῖν ἐμφῆναι, διότι πολλοὶ τοιούτων ὑπὸ καλοκαγαθίας καὶ τῆς τῶν θείων ἐμπειρίας ἀξιοῦνται.

## 10. Ant. 17.13, 3 (§346−8)

Σκιδναμένων δὲ ἑτέρων ἐφ᾽ ἑτέροις, οὐ γὰρ εἰς ἓν ἀνέκειτο πᾶσιν ἀφήγησις, Σίμων ἀνὴρ γένος Ἐσσαῖος ἀσφάλειαν αἰτησάμενος, μεταβολὴν πραγμάτων ἔλεγεν Ἀρχελάῳ φέρειν τὴν ὄψιν οὐκ ἐπ᾽ ἀγαθοῖς πράγμασι. βόας μὲν γὰρ κακοπαθείας τε ἀποσαφεῖν διὰ τὸ ἔργοις ἐπιταλαιπωρεῖν τὸ ζῷον μεταβολάς τε αὖ πραγμάτων διὰ τὸ τὴν γῆν πόνῳ τῷ ἐκείνων ἀρουμένην ἐν ταὐτῷ μένειν οὐ δύνασθαι· τοὺς δὲ ἀστάχυας δέκα ὄντας τοσῶνδε ἀριθμὸν ἐνιαυτῶν ὁρίζειν, περιόδῳ γὰρ ἑνὸς παραγίνεσθαι θέρος, καὶ τὸν χρόνον ἐξήκειν Ἀρχελάῳ τῆς ἡγεμονίας. καὶ ὁ μὲν ταύτῃ ἐξηγήσατο τὸ ὄνειρον. πέμπτῃ δὲ ἡμέρᾳ μεθ᾽ ὃ τὸ πρῶτον αὐτοῦ ἡ ὄψις Ἀρχελάῳ συνῆλθεν, ὁ ἀνακαλούμενος Ἀρχέλαος πεμπτὸς εἰς Ἰουδαίαν ὑπὸ Καίσαρος ἀφίκετο.

But Herod, thinking that the man either did not know him or was bantering him, reminded him that he was an ordinary citizen. But Menahem, smiling gently and slapping him on the backside, said, "But you shall indeed be king, and you shall exercise the reign well, for you have been found worthy by God. And remember the blows given by Menahem, so that this too may be a symbol to you of the changes of fortune. For the best attitude would be if you love both justice and piety towards God, and equity towards the citizens. But I know that you will not be such a one, since I understand everything. You will spend your life in such good fortune as no other person, and you will gain lasting glory, but you will forget piety and what justice means. These things, however, will not escape the notice of God, when at the end of your life his wrath will call these things to mind." At that very time Herod paid little heed to these words, lacking any hope of their fulfillment; but after gradually being raised to both kingship and good fortune, at the height of his reign, he sent for Menahem and questioned him about the length of time he would reign. But Menahem did not tell him at all. In view of his silence, Herod asked him only whether he would reign for ten years; and he said, "For twenty or thirty years," but he did not set a limit for the end of the appointed time. Yet Herod was satisfied even with these words and dismissed Menahem with a friendly gesture. From that time on he continued to hold all the Essenes in esteem. Now we have thought it proper to explain these things, however astonishing they may be, to our readers, and to reveal what has happened among us, since many of these people [Essenes] have because of their virtue been thought worthy of this acquaintance with divine things.

## 10.  Ant. 17.13, 3 (§346–8)

But when they [interpreters of Archelaus' dream] differed with one another (for all their interpretations did not come to one conclusion), Simon, an Essene by background, sought for assurance and said that the vision signified a change in the affairs of Archelaus, and not for the better. For the oxen signify both misery, since this animal suffers in its labors, and change in his affairs, since the land plowed by their toil cannot remain in the same state. The ears of grain, of which there were ten, designate the same number of years, since in the course of each year there is a harvest, and thus the time of the reign of Archelaus has expired. In such a way did this man interpret the dream. On the fifth day after Archelaus first had this vision, the other one called Archelaus, who had been sent to Judaea by Caesar, arrived.

# 3

## COMMENTARY ON JOSEPHUS' MAJOR ESSENE PASSAGES

Josephus' three major Essene passages will be discussed in turn below.

### A. Life 1.2 §10–12

*About sixteen years old* (§10). Josephus states earlier (1.1 §5) that he had been born in the year Gaius Caesar (i.e., Caligula) became emperor, i.e., A.D. 37/38; hence, his sixteenth year would have been A.D. 53/54. Later in this passage, he mentions that after passing through the three groups and living for three years with Bannus, he is nineteen years old (in A.D. 56/57). Thus, if Josephus' reckoning is accurate, he could not have spent longer than a year submitting himself to the rigors of the Sadducees, Pharisees, and Essenes. His time with the Essenes, then, was probably no more than six months. Since according to Josephus' own testimony (*J. W.* 2 §137[1]) a candidate for admission into the Essene community had to submit himself to their way of life for one year before full admission into the community, it is evident that Josephus did not even pass through the first stage of admission into the Essene community. Because of this fact, M. Black regards Josephus' claim to have spent time with the Essenes as a "fabrication;"[2] but we cannot be sure that there is not some truth in what Josephus says, with perhaps a bit of exaggeration on his part as well. As T. Rajak states, "there is evidently some rhetorical exaggeration in Josephus' language when he talks of 'hard labour' and of having to toughen himself up ... But, equally, it is again clear that there had to be a basis in truth."[3]

*Pharisees ... Sadducees ... Essenes* (§10). See below, pp. 35–6.

*Bannus* (§11). Nothing further is known about this man. A. Adam conjectures that his name may be an Aramaized form of βαλανεύς, "bather," presumably because of the man's practice of washing many times each day for purification.[4] These purification rituals might link him with the Essenes (perhaps a disenchanted member?). See

*J.W.* 2 §129, where Josephus discusses the Essene purification rites.

*Stoic* (§12). Josephus' comparison of the Pharisees to the Stoics is an example of his tendency to explain Jewish customs and sects by way of analogy to Greek models. Other examples of this tendency in his description of the Essenes are: *J. W.* 2 §156–8 (comparison of the Essene view of the immortality of the soul with the Greek doctrine); *Ant.* 18 §22 (comparing the Essene way of life to the Ctistae); and *Ant.* 15.10, 4 §371 (Essene way of life was introduced to the Greeks by Pythagoras).

## B. J.W. 2.8, 2–13 §119–61

### 1. J.W. 2.8, 2 §119–21

*Pharisees ... Sadducees ... Essenes* (§119). Josephus introduces the sects of the Pharisees, the Sadducees, and the Essenes as three "philosophical classes" (τρία ... εἴδη φιλοσοφεῖται), presumably to appeal to the Greek mode of thought. He refers to the three groups again in *Ant.* 13.5, 9 §171–2, *Ant.* 18.1, 2 §11, and (see above) *Life* 1.2 §10.[5] In *Ant.* 13.5, 9 §171–3 and *Ant.* 18.1, 2 §11–22 Josephus describes each group briefly, but here in *J. W.* he first gives a long explanation of the Essenes (*J. W.* 2 §119–61), followed by a few cursory remarks on the other two groups (*J. W.* 2 §162–6). The Pharisees and Sadducees are well known from the NT. The Essenes, however, are not mentioned in the NT, nor is the name "Essene" found at Qumran. There have been many proposals for the etymology of the group's name,[6] only the more important of which will be mentioned here. To begin with some older explanations, Philo does not use 'Εσσηνοί, but rather 'Εσσαῖοι, which he associates with ὅσιοι, "holy ones" (*Every Good Man is Free* 12 §75; 13 §91; see also Eusebius, *Praeparatio evangelica* 8.11, 1).[7] Some scholars think that Josephus suggests a similar interpretation in the present passage (2 §119) by his phrase δοκεῖ σεμνότητα ἀσκεῖν, taking σεμνότητα as "sanctity."[8] But σεμνότητα should probably be translated as "solemnity" or "dignity," rather than "sanctity" or "holiness."[9] Furthermore, Josephus' explanation does not make use of the 'Εσσαῖοι–ὅσιοι connection, since in this passage he uses σεμνότητα in place of ὅσιοι and 'Εσσηνοί rather than 'Εσσαῖοι.[10] Schürer, Cross, and many others regard the name as derived from the Syriac word *ḥassayyâ*, "pious ones," related to Hebrew *ḥasîdîm* ('Ασιδαῖοι

in 1 Macc 2:42; 7:13; 2 Macc 14:6).[11] Milik finds evidence for this
etymology from the expression *mṣd ḥsdyn* ("fortress of the pious
ones"), found in Mur 45:6, which he equates with the Essene settlement at Qumran.[12] While this etymology would accord well with the
testimony from Philo and Josephus, it does not take into account the
fact that the root *ḥs'* does not mean "pious" in the Palestinian dialect.
Since the group is living in Palestine, why would it be given an Eastern
Aramaic (Syriac) name?

Several recent suggestions have been made for the etymology of
"Essene" in light of the Qumran material. Dupont-Sommer proposes
that the word is derived from the Hebrew word *'ēṣâ*, which often
means "council" or "party" in Qumran literature; thus, the Essenes
would be "Men of the Council."[13] While it is true that the word
*'ēṣâ* does occur frequently in Qumran literature, the linguistic
derivation proposed is problematic, and it is not clear why *'ēṣâ* would
be chosen over *yaḥad*, "community," as the group's name. Furthermore, as Vermes notes, this explanation is not in accord with the
ancient testimonies of Philo and Josephus.[14] S. Goranson suggests
that the name is derived from Hebrew *'asâ*, the common Hebrew verb
meaning "to do, bear, bring forth." But his reason for the name being
used by the group seems more than a bit strained: it was used to
indicate that the Essenes sought "to *do* the will of God in order to
*bring forth* His redemption."[15]

Finally, Vermes links an old explanation with both the testimony of
Philo and Josephus and the new Qumran material.[16] He asserts that
"Essene" is derived from the Aramaic *'āsayyā'*, "healers," corresponding to the Greek Θεραπευταί (a term that, according to Vermes,
in Philo corresponds both to "healers" and "worshippers," and also
designates a contemplative group of Essenes living in Egypt). This
popular designation of the Essenes as healers is indirectly supported by
Josephus' testimony that the Essenes sought out medicinal roots and
stones for healing diseases (*J. W.* 2 §136). In addition, the concepts
both of spiritual healing (1QS 4:6; CD 8:4−5; 1QH 2:8−9; 9:24−5)
and even physical healing (1QapGen 20:20 − Abraham heals
Pharaoh, whom the Egyptian *'sy'* were unable to cure) are evident
in the Qumran literature.[17] While this theory is intriguing, Cross
points out that the transcription *ess-* presupposes *ḥas-* rather than the
*'ās-* that *'āsayyā'* requires.[18] Furthermore, it is not certain that the
Therapeutae are to be equated with Essenes; they may have been only
a group similar to the Essenes. The etymology of "Essene" thus
remains unclear, despite the new evidence from Qumran.

*Jews by birth* (§119). Apparently the Essenes did not permit any non-Jew to become a member of the sect. This finds support in Qumran literature in the requirements for admission into the community, discussed in 1QS 6:13–14: "And anyone of Israel who devotes himself to join the council of the community ..." The same is implied in 1QS 1:21–3; 1QSa 1:1; and CD 4:2, 4.

*More mutual affection* (§119). Josephus notes that not only are all the Essenes of the same race (γένος), but they also have a love for one another that is greater than that of the other Jewish sects. This sense of community was apparently so characteristic of the Essenes that it is one of the first facts Josephus mentions about the group in his discussion. Mutual affection is likewise emphasized in Qumran literature. In 1QS 1:9, the sect members are to "love all the sons of light," i.e., the members of the community (see 1QS 2:16; 3:13, 25). And in 1QS 2:24–5, they are all to be "in the community of truth, of virtuous humility, of affectionate love (*'hbt ḥsd*), and of right-minded intention towards one another." The same emphasis is evident in another rule book, the *Damascus Document*. For example, in CD 6:20–1; 7:1, among the obligations of the members of the community are that they "love each man his brother as himself ... and ... seek each man the well-being of his brother." In addition, the penal code of the *Manual of Discipline*, 1 QS 7:1–25, contains many laws against acting unkindly towards a fellow sect member, including insulting him (1QS 7:4), deceiving him (1QS 7:5–6), bearing a grudge against him (1QS 7:8), interrupting him (1QS 7:9), and falsely reporting about him (1QS 7:15). Each of these actions was penalized severely. See further 1QS 8:1–2; 9:16, 19; CD 8:5–7; and CD 9:2–8 for additional examples of the importance of mutual affection at Qumran.

*Turn aside from pleasures as an evil* (§120). Though Josephus often uses the word ἡδονή ("pleasure") in a general sense, it is possible that he is using the term here to mean "sensuous pleasures," as also later in the passage (*J. W.* 2 §161 – "They do not have intercourse with them during pregnancy, demonstrating that they marry not for self-gratification [ἡδονήν] but for the necessity of children").[19] This connotation of ἡδονή would fit well with Josephus' subject matter in §120 and §121, namely, the Essene view of marriage and the infidelity of women. In any event, this first statement serves as a general introductory remark, with concrete examples to follow. Qumran literature contains numerous condemnations of sensual pleasures and lust. 1QS 4:9–11 states that "to the spirit of perversity belong abundant desire (*rḥwb npš*) ... quick temper, great vileness, burning insolence, and abominable deeds committed in the spirit of lust.'' In 1QH 10:29–31, the servant of God is one who is filled with the knowledge of his truth, and who detests gain and the "pride of pleasures" (*rwm 'dnym*). Both 1QS 1:6 and CD 2:16 warn against "lustful eyes" ('*yny znwt*), with CD 2:17–3:12 citing examples of those drawn by their own lusts and wills. In CD 4:17–5:11, the first of Belial's three nets is lust (*znwt*), an example of which is a man marrying two women in his lifetime (CD 4:21). Other condemnations of sensual pleasures are found in CD 7:1–2; 8:5–8; and 4Q*184*.

*Self-control* (§120). Self-control (ἐγκράτεια) and overcoming the passions (πάθη) are regarded as a virtue (ἀρετή) in the same way that sensual pleasures are considered to be evil. The two phrases are thus complementary. Those places in Qumran literature where sensual pleasures are condemned (see above) are applicable here as well, especially 1QS 4:9–11.

*Marriage they regard with contempt* (§120). Josephus indicates in this passage that the Essenes look down on marriage. He makes a similar statement in *Ant.* 18 §21: "They neither bring wives into (the community) nor do they seek to acquire slaves, since they consider that the latter leads to injustice and the former inclines towards causing factions." That Josephus means that the Essenes he describes here are celibate is made clear by *J.W.* 2 §160–1, in which he asserts that there is another order of Essenes who *do* marry. Thus, taking the passages together, Josephus presents the Essenes as primarily celibate, but with at least one group of them who marry.

Philo is even more resolute on the question of Essene marriage. He states quite plainly that "no Essene takes a wife" (*Hypothetica* 11.14–17), and asserts that this is because a wife is a threat to the communal life since she entices a man to please only herself, and not the entire community.[20]

Scholars have long debated the accuracy of Philo and Josephus concerning Essene celibacy. W. Bauer maintained that Philo and Josephus were simply ascribing to the Essenes what was then a widely held Hellenistic attitude towards marriage and women.[21] Likewise, R. Marcus indicates that Josephus has probably "misled us" in his presentation: "it is not too bold, I think, to suggest that the avoidance of marriage ascribed to most Essenes by Josephus is a hellenizing distortion."[22]

The data from Qumran do indeed contradict Philo's flat assertion that "no Essene takes a wife." The *Manual of Discipline* is silent on the subject, and taken by itself it might seem to support celibacy.

Yet, its appendix includes women and children among the new arrivals (1QSa 1:4), and in 1QSa 1:9–12 a young man is prohibited from sexual relations with a woman until he is twenty.[23] Furthermore, the *Damascus Document* contains numerous references to women and marriage: CD 4:19–5:2 speaks against "marrying two women" during the man's lifetime (thus against polygamy, not marriage[24]); CD 5:6–7 prohibits sexual relations with a menstruating woman; CD 7:6–7 speaks of those living in camps who take a wife and beget children; CD 12:1–2 prohibits sexual relations in the city of the Sanctuary; and CD 16:10–12 concerns annulling the oaths and vows of a wife (thus presuming marriage in the first place). In addition, the *Temple Scroll* contains a prohibition of polygamy and divorce: the king may not take another woman while his wife is still alive, since she alone is to be with him as long as she lives (11QTemple[a] 57:15–19). Again, it should be recognized that neither the *Damascus Document* nor the *Temple Scroll* may have been composed originally at Qumran, so that differences between these documents and the *Manual of Discipline* may reflect differing stages in the sect's existence. Nonetheless, it is evident that at least among the sectarians responsible for the *Rule of the Congregation*, the *Damascus Document*, and the *Temple Scroll*, marriage was certainly permitted, though a strict view of marriage was taken.[25]

Yet, the evidence from Qumran is not entirely in favor of a sexually mixed community. According to de Vaux, in the large main cemetery at Qumran "all the skeletons in that part of the cemetery which is carefully planned are male." Skeletons of women and children were found only in the surrounding area.[26] Milik deduces from this evidence that there existed an older celibate community that only later permitted women among its ranks,[27] though it is equally possible that the two groups (celibate and married) existed at the same time, as Josephus seems to imply. Hence, while it is safe to say that Philo's assertion of total Essene celibacy is in error, there does seem to be evidence at Qumran to support Josephus' contention of a group of celibate Essenes in addition to a group of married Essenes.[28] The relationship of these two groups of Essenes to one another, both in time (did one emerge from the other, or did both exist simultaneously?) and size (which group was larger, and was one more "normative" than the other?) cannot be answered with certainty from the evidence at Qumran.

*Adopting other persons' children* (§120). This celibate group of Essenes, Josephus continues, secures younger members by adopting other peoples' children at an "early" age (ἁπαλοὺς ἔτι πρὸς τὰ μαθήματα) and training them in the Essene way of life. Philo reports no such custom, indicating only that no Essene is a mere child, but that all are full grown and verging on old age (*Hypothetica* 11.3).

There is no clear support from Qumran for the custom of adoption as Josephus describes it, though voluntary joining of the community is frequently noted (*hndbym* or *hmtndbym*, "those who volunteer": 1QS 1:7, 11; 5:1, 6, 8, 10, 21–2; 6:13; 1QpMic 10:5). Children, in fact, are mentioned very infrequently in Qumran literature.[29] There is, however, one intriguing line in the *Hodayot* which should be noted here: "For my father did not know me and my mother abandoned me to you" (1QH 9:34–5). In the context, "you" is the Lord, who acts as a foster father (*'wmn*) to all his children of truth.[30] The statement that God is the psalmist's foster father is certainly metaphorical (see Ps 27:10; Isa 63:16);[31] but it may, in fact, be based upon a real situation in the community, as described by Josephus.

Josephus' statement regarding the education of these children "according to their customs (ἤθεσιν)" can now be illustrated by Qumran literature. That the Qumran community was interested in educating the people in the particular teachings and customs of the community is evident even from the existence of different collections of rules, namely, the *Manual of Discipline*, the *Damascus Document*,[32] and even the *War Scroll*. Specifically, in 1QSa 1:4–5 new arrivals, including women and children, are to be read "all the precepts of the covenant" and are to be instructed "in all their ordinances lest they stray." 1QSa further states that the young person "[shall be in]structed in the Book of Meditation and shall be taught the precepts of the covenant in accordance with his age, and [shall receive] his [edu]cation in their ordinances for ten years [from] the time of entry into the children's [class]" (1QSa 1:6–8). CD 15:5–6 does not indicate this period of education specifically, but simply mentions that the sons of every member of the community who have reached the age to pass before the census (presumably twenty years old, as in 1QSa 1:8–9) must pledge themselves by the oath of the covenant. Most likely "their sons" (*bnyhm*) refers to the parents' natural children, not adopted, especially since the *Damascus Document* contains several references to women and children (for example, CD 7:7: "[if they] take a wife and beget children, they shall walk in obedience to the Law"; see further pp. 38–9 above). Yet, this does not rule out the possibility that Josephus' statement regarding the adoption of children may not be essentially correct for the celibate group of Essenes he is describing. In any event, Josephus' remarks concerning the training of these children are entirely in keeping with Qumran thought.

*They do not reject marriage* (§121). As mentioned above, Josephus does not echo Philo in his statement of the Essenes' total rejection of marriage. Here, Josephus states that the Essenes recognize that marriage does have a place — namely, for propagation of the race — and thus should not be rejected completely. Elsewhere, Josephus notes that there is in fact a married group of Essenes (*J. W.* 2 §160). Yet in that passage as well as here, Josephus is quick to point out that the purpose of marriage for the Essenes is not for fulfillment of sensual pleasure, but rather for the totally utilitarian goal of perpetuating the race.

While there is no specific statement regarding the purpose of marriage in Qumran literature that parallels Josephus' comment, this austere, non-pleasure-seeking view of marriage is certainly in harmony with Qumran thought. The *Manual of Discipline* does not even mention marriage,[33] while the references in 1QSa and the *Damascus Document* deal primarily with restrictions on sexual relations (see above, pp. 38–9). And the statement in CD 7:6–7 speaks of those who "live in camps according to the rule of the land, and take a wife and beget children," thus closely associating marriage with begetting children, much as Josephus does here.[34]

*Licentious allurements of women* (§121). Josephus next gives a reason for Essene celibacy. It is not that they are against marriage per se, but rather they desire to protect themselves from the licentiousness (ἀσέλγεια) and infidelity (lack of πίστις to one man) of women. Josephus gives two additional reasons for celibacy elsewhere (the evil of self-gratification [*J. W.* 2 §161], and the tendency of women to cause factions [*Ant.* 18 §21]). Though Josephus' explanation is certainly not flattering to women, it pales in comparison with Philo's misogynist diatribe in *Hypothetica* 11.14–17. Philo states that no Essene takes a wife because she is a selfish, jealous, beguiling, seducing, arrogant person who completely enslaves her husband.

Cross and others suspect that both Philo and Josephus are guilty of placing their own misogynist beliefs on the lips of the Essenes.[35] Yet, it seems more likely that the apparently independent testimonies of Philo and Josephus contain at least a grain of truth. Various alternative explanations for Essene celibacy have been suggested that exonerate the Essenes from misogyny. Buchanan observes that the regulations for ritual purity (in which menstrual periods, seminal discharges, and other emissions rendered a person unclean) could easily lead to the formation of a celibate order.[36] Others, such as Marx, regard Essene celibacy as a result of their combat, "holy war" ideology, which led them to forsake anything non-essential to the struggle against evil.[37] Coppens links Essene celibacy specifically with the sect's eschatological expectations, a notion also seen in the NT (Luke 20:34–6; 1 Cor 7:26–35).[38] Cross sees all these currents of thought (ritual purity, "holy war," and apocalypticism) as playing a role in Essene celibacy: "The Essene in his daily life thus girds himself to withstand the final trial, purifies himself to join the holy armies, anticipates the coming conditions in God's inbreaking kingdom. This is the situation which prompts counsels against marriage."[39]

While these attempts by scholars to explain Essene celibacy have much to commend them, one must not, therefore, *ipso facto* assume that Josephus' explanation is entirely incorrect. As Strugnell observes, "the association of women with trouble-making belongs quite naturally to the Wisdom literature of the OT."[40] The book of Proverbs is replete with warnings against associations with "loose" women (*'šh zrh*) and invectives against contentious women (*'št mdwnym*).[41] Sir 25:24 contains an even stronger statement: "From a woman sin had its beginning, and because of her we all die" (see also Sir 9:2–9; 19:2–3; 23:22–6; 25:13–26; 26:5–9; 42:9–14; and 47:19). Furthermore, this tradition seems to be represented at Qumran by 4Q*184*, which Allegro orginally called "The Wiles of the Wicked Woman."[42] In this piece, the author rails against the woman who is acting wantonly and seductively "to seek out a righteous man and lead him astray" (4Q*184* 1:13–14). The question is, precisely whom is the author condemning? Allegro sees the subject as being "the harlot," but suspects that the terminology is used figuratively, perhaps for Rome;[43] Dupont-Sommer contends that woman in general is the subject of the invective;[44] Carmignac supposes that the poem is a satirical allegory whose real subject is the rival sect;[45] while Strugnell thinks that the poem is a personification of "la Dame Folie," much as Wisdom is personified in Proverbs.[46] Regardless of the interpretation adopted, it is clear that 4Q*184* does provide an example in Qumran literature of the deprecation of at least a particular kind of woman, whether further symbolic meaning is intended or not; hence, one should perhaps reserve judgment whether or not Josephus' statements on women may in fact represent the Essene point of view after all.

## 2. J.W. 2.8, 3 §122–3

*They despise riches* (§122). Josephus' statement regarding riches is stronger than Philo's. The latter asserts that the Essenes love frugality and "shun expensive luxury as a disease of both body and soul" (*Hypothetica* 11.11); but Josephus states that the Essenes despise riches (πλοῦτος) in general.

Qumran literature is replete with references to riches.[47] In the *Manual of Discipline*, the man of understanding is exhorted to hate "all the men of the Pit because of their spirit of hoarding (*str*, 'hiding'),'' and to "surrender his property (*hwn*) to them [the men of the Pit]," since "beyond the will of God he shall desire nothing" (1QS 9:21–4). Furthermore, according to 1QS 10:18–19, he is not to covet the "riches of violence" (*hwn ḥms*). In 1QS 11:1–2 those who "acquire possessions" (*mqny hwn*) are linked with the "proud of spirit," and "those that brandish a stick, that point the finger and utter wounding words."

The *Damascus Document* likewise contains numerous condemnations of riches, especially CD 4:17, in which the second net by which Belial ensnares Israel consists of riches (*hwn*). Other passages in the *Damascus Document* condemn the "riches of iniquity" (CD 6:15 – *hwn hrš'h*; CD 8:5 – *hwn rš'h*)[48] or regard "riches and gain" (*hwn wbṣ'*) as of little importance (CD 8:7; 10:18; 11:15; 12:6–7). In the *Hodayot*, riches are seen as a source of pride for the ungodly (1QH 10:24–5 – *wytrwmmw [b]mqnh wqnyn*), and as something to be loathed by God's servant (1QH 10:29–30). No riches may compare with God's truth (1QH 14:20; 15:22–3).

Finally, the *Pesharim* present an equally bleak picture of riches. In 1QpHab 6:1, the Kittim are said to gather in their riches (*hwnm*), while in 1QpHab 8:10–13 the Wicked Priest's betrayal of God and his precepts is blamed on riches (*hwn*). And 1QpHab 9:4–5 states that the priests of Jerusalem have heaped up riches and gain (*hwn wbṣ'*) by plundering the people. Essentially the same statement is made in 4QpNah 3–4 i 11 as well.

An indication of the Qumran community's dislike for riches may also be found in the expression *'bywnym* ("poor ones"). This word, while apparently not a technical designation for the community (as, for example, *yḥd* and *'dh*), nonetheless does refer to the community on occasion. This seems to be the case in 1QM 11:9, 13; 13:12–14; 1QH 5:22 (*'bywny ḥsd*, "the poor of grace"); 1QpHab 12:3, 6, 10; and especially 4QpPs[a] 1–10 ii 10; 1–10 iii 10. The last two references are the only texts that contain the definite article (*'dt h'bywnym*, "the congregation of the poor ones").[49] Thus, this expression may well be a further indication of the despising of riches in the Qumran community.

*One property common to all* (§122). Josephus indicates in this section that those entering the community transfer (δημεύειν) their property to the order, and that their possessions are mingled together (ἀναμεμιγμένων) so that there is one property common to all. He makes a similar statement in *Ant.* 18 §20: "they hold their possessions in common." Philo's assertions are in agreement with Josephus: "None of them allows himself to have any private property ... but they put everything together into the public stock and enjoy the benefit of them all in common" (*Hypothetica* 10.4; see also *Every Good Man is Free* 12 §77).

This pooling of goods spoken of by Josephus and Philo is illustrated in Qumran literature. In the *Manual of Discipline*, there are several statements indicating a transference of property to the community upon entrance. 1QS 1:11−12 states that all the volunteers are to "bring all their understanding and powers and possessions (*hwnm*) into the Community of God." Furthermore, 1QS 5:1−2 specifies as the rule for the members of the community that they separate from perverse men and that they "become as community in doctrine and property (*yḥd btwrh wbhwn*)." The matter is more specifically spelled out in 1QS 6:17−22, where three stages are set forth for admission into the order. First, he must complete one full year of examination within the community. During this year he must not touch the purification or "mingle with the property of the Many" (*'l yt'rb bhwn hrbym*). Next, he must complete a second year within the community, still unable to partake of the common meal. His property and wages (*hwnw w't ml'ktw*), however, are to be handed over to the overseer of the funds of the Many (*mbqr 'l ml'kt hrbym*), but kept in a separate account for him, and not spent for the community as a whole. Finally, after the second year, he is permitted to become a full member of the community in matters of law, justice, purification, and the mingling[50] of his property (*wl'rb 't hwnw*) with that of the community.[51]

There is evidence, however, of some sort of personal property in the community as well. In 1QS 7:6−8, the person who is negligent to the detriment of the community's property is to reimburse it or, if unable, to be punished for sixty days. This implies that some did have personal property that had not been given to the community.[52]

Ownership of property is even more clearly brought out in the *Damascus Document*. According to CD 9:10–16, property could be lost or stolen from its owner. And in CD 14:12–13, the Many are to pay the overseers and judges the wage of at least two days a month, in order to provide for their needs.

Thus, it seems that at least for the community situation represented by the *Damascus Document*, not all possessions were held in common, contrary to our ancient sources. But we should beware of forcing a reconciliation between the *Damascus Document* and the *Manual of Discipline* on this subject, since the two documents may well represent different stages in the community's development.[53] That there was probably a time in the group's history when possessions were for the most part pooled is indicated not only by the *Manual of Discipline* but by the archaeology of Qumran as well. De Vaux reports that hundreds of coins were found in the main administration buildings, but not a single coin in the living quarters of the community.[54] Hence, the testimony of Josephus concerning common ownership of property seems to be consistent with the situation at Qumran, at least during one phase of the community's existence.

*They regard oil as a defilement* (§123). Josephus is alone among the ancient writers in mentioning the Essene avoidance of oil. Oil is regarded as a "defilement" (κηλίς, lit., "stain"), and any accidental contact with it is to be washed off the person's body.

Prior to the discovery of the Dead Sea Scrolls, it was thought by C. Ginsburg that oil was prohibited by the Essenes because it was an extravagance, "contrary to the simplicity of their manner of life."[55] But the *Damascus Document* supports the view that ritual purity was the cause of this prohibition. CD 12:15–17 states that "all wood, stones, and dust which are defiled by the uncleanness of man (*ygw'lw bṭm't h'dm*), by virtue of the stains of oil on them (*lg'wly šmn bhm*),[56] according to their uncleanness shall the one who touches them become unclean." J. Baumgarten argues cogently that oil touched by an unclean person is rendered impure, and that this impurity is transmitted to anyone who touches the oil (or an oil-stained material).[57] Thus, the oil that carries impurity is to be avoided, since any unclean person, i.e., a non-member of the community, and probably even an Essene of a lower order (see *J.W.* 2 §150: "the junior members are so inferior to the seniors that if seniors touch them, they must wash as if they had been in contact with a stranger"), may have contaminated it previously. Josephus' statement that the Essenes always desired to keep their skin dry and wipe off any oil accidentally spilled on them is entirely in harmony with this concept of ritual purity seen in the *Damascus Document*.

There is another reference to oil in the *Temple Scroll*. 11QTemple[a] 21:12–22:16 speaks of the feast of fresh oil, where oil is offered on the altar. According to the reconstruction of the text by Yadin at 22:16, this new oil, which is poured out once a year, expiates for all the fresh oil of the land: "after which they shall eat and they shall pour out the new oil and the olives, for in this day they will expiate for all the fresh oil of the land (*ykprw* [ʾ]*l* [*kw*]*l* [*yš*]*hr h'rṣ*) before the Lord one time in a year, and they will rejoice." If Yadin's reconstruction is correct, this may be a further indication that any oil not made clean by the yearly rite described in the *Temple Scroll* is, in fact, impure.[58]

*Always being dressed in white* (§123). Josephus mentions in *J. W.* 2 §137 that one of the three items given a candidate to the sect was a white garment. Presumably ritual purity was behind the Essene preference for white garments.[59] The priests in the OT wore white linen garments (Exod 28:39–42). And in *J. W.* 2 §131 the Essenes' linen (2 §129) garments are laid down after breakfast "as holy things" (ὡς ἱεράς).

One possible indication of a preference for white at Qumran may be seen in the description of the battle garments of the priests in 1QM 7:9–10: "seven priests of the sons of Aaron, clothed in garments of fine white linen (*bgdy šš lbn*): a linen tunic and linen trousers, and girded with a linen girdle." As Yadin observes, the addition of "linen" (either šš or *bd*)[60] to every item, including the girdle, plus the special emphasis on "white" (*lbn*), may well be an indication of the Essene fondness for white garments.[61]

*Elected overseers* (§123). Josephus explains that the management of the Essene community is carried out by the elected ἐπιμεληταί ("overseers," "administrators"). These officials are mentioned three times by name in *J. W.*: here (2 §123), where each[62] of the overseers is said to take care of the needs of the community as a whole; in *J. W.* 2 §129, where they are in charge of directing the work of each Essene; and in *J. W.* 2 §134, where it is said that virtually nothing is done apart from the order of these overseers (though one may help the needy without special permission). In addition, the same officials are probably meant in *Ant.* 18 §22, which states that the Essenes "elect good men as treasurers (ἀποδέκτας) of their revenue and what the land yields, and priests for the preparation of their bread and their food." Hence, if these treasurers (ἀποδέκτας) are to be identified with the ἐπιμεληταί of *J. W.*, it seems that the latter are primarily financial guardians of the community, responsible for the labor force as well as for the collection and disbursement of all community wealth.[63]

Many scholars have identified Josephus' ἐπιμελητής with the *mĕbaqqēr* found in the Dead Sea Scrolls.[64] In the *Manual of Discipline*, *mˇebaqqēr* is used to describe the presiding officer in the council of the community (he alone could speak without permission of the Many – 1QS 6:12) and the one in charge of "the revenues of the Many" (1QS 6:20). Whether two different officials are meant in 6:12 and 6:20 or only one with several functions, is not clear, though the use of the same term (*mĕbaqqēr*) in both passages seems to favor the latter interpretation. In any event, the *mĕbaqqēr* of 6:20 clearly parallels Josephus' ἐπιμελητής, as both are in charge of the funds of the community.

In the *Damascus Document*, the *mĕbaqqēr* is involved in a wide variety of activities. He bears evidence in criminal cases (CD 9:18–22); instructs the priest in the Law (CD 13:5); teaches the Many about God's works (CD 13:7–8); examines and teaches potential new members of the congregation (CD 13:11; 15:8–14); exercises control over the community's commercial dealings (CD 13:16); and, along with the judges, receives wages from the Many (equal to at least two days per month) to be disbursed to people in need (CD 14:13–16).[65] These last two duties of the *mĕbaqqēr* in the *Damascus Document* (control over commercial dealings and receipt/disbursement of wages) are most closely parallel to the tasks of Josephus' ἐπιμελητής, who takes care of the needs of all (*J. W.* 2 §123).

Mention should also be made of the *pāqîd*, another title for a Qumran official, which occurs in 1QS 6:14 and (as a verb) in CD 14:6 and elsewhere. It seems that in the *Manual of Discipline* the term *pāqîd* is essentially synonymous with *mĕbaqqēr*, since the *pāqîd* of 1QS 6:14 has the same task as the *mĕbaqqēr* in CD 13:11 and 15:8–14 (namely, examining potential new members).[66] Yet, in CD 14:6, the *pāqîd* is clearly distinguished from the *mĕbaqqēr* over all the camps in 14:8–12. Furthermore, the *pāqîd* of CD 14:6 is a priest, whereas the *mĕbaqqēr* is presumably a lay person, since in CD 13:5 he instructs the priest in the Law. Hence, at least in one stage of the community's existence, leadership appears to have been shared between the priestly *pāqîd* and the lay *mĕbaqqēr*.[67] J. Priest argues that the *pāqîd* was originally the real leader of the community, with the *mĕbaqqēr* initially only a minor official (overseer of the property, 1QS 6:20); only later was the *mĕbaqqēr* equal (1QS 6:12–24?) and finally superior to the *pāqîd* (most of CD).[68] If Priest is correct, then the early *mĕbaqqēr* would correspond almost exactly to Josephus' ἐπιμελητής.

### 3. J.W. 2.8, 4 §124–7

*Many settle in each city* (§124). In this section (§124–7) Josephus elaborates on the hospitality, frugality, and sharing of the Essenes. He first observes that the Essenes do not live in one particular city, but rather many of them settle (μετοικοῦσιν)[69] in each city. This statement is reflected by Philo as well: "They live in many cities (πόλεις) of Judaea, and in many villages (κώμας), and are grouped in great societies of many members" (*Hypothetica* 11.1). Elsewhere, however, Philo asserts that the Essenes "live in villages (κωμηδόν) and avoid the cities (πόλεις) because of the iniquities which have become inveterate among city dwellers" (*Every Good Man is Free* 12 §76). Thus, Philo seems to contradict himself about the Essene attitude towards the cities.[70] Both Philo (*Every Good Man is Free* 12 §75) and Josephus (*Ant.* 18 §20) agree that the total number of Essenes is over four thousand.

Evaluation of Josephus' statement concerning the dwelling places of the Essenes by means of the Qumran literature is not an easy task. Geographic references are sparse in these documents, and when they do appear, scholars disagree whether the references should be taken literally or figuratively (as, for example, the "land of Damascus" in the *Damascus Document*).[71] Numerous reconstructions of the history of the Qumran sect have been proposed based upon the archaeological data at Qumran and the (often unclear) geographical references in the scrolls, but a consensus has not yet been reached.[72] To take one reconstruction as an example, J. Murphy-O'Connor regards the Essenes as Jews from Babylon ("Damascus") who return to Palestine after the victory of the Maccabees, find Palestinian Judaism too liberal, exhort their fellow Jews to join with them (CD 2:14–6:1), and move to more remote villages (because of the reasons Philo suggests). Finally, those who follow the Teacher of Righteousness found Qumran, while those who follow the Man of Lies preserve Essenism outside of Qumran.[73] Murphy-O'Connor thinks that Philo and Josephus are describing this second, non-Qumran branch of Essenism, and not Qumran Essenism at all.[74] While Murphy-O'Connor's reconstruction is based upon his careful reading and evaluation of the Qumran material, nearly every text he uses is subject to a different interpretation by other scholars, such as F.M. Cross.[75] Thus, the geographic links he sees between Philo and Josephus and the Essenes are wedded to the accuracy of his reconstruction of Essene history.

Regardless of one's understanding of Essene history, however, there is evidence in the terminology used in the *Damascus Document* to support a multiplicity of dwelling places for the group. These settlements are apparently called "camps" (*mḥnwt*) in the *Damascus Document*.[76] The word *mḥnh* ("camp") occurs fifteen times in the *Damascus Document* (and not at all in the *Manual of Discipline*), six times in the plural. For example, CD 7:6–7 states "And if they live in camps according to the rule of the land and take a wife and beget children, they shall walk in obedience to the Law" (also CD 19:2). CD 12:23 and 13:20 speak of "the organization of the camps," while CD 14:3 refers to "the organization of all the camps," and CD 14:9 speaks of an overseer "in charge of all the camps" (in contrast to CD 13:7, which refers to the overseer of an individual camp). In CD 9:11 ("the camp from which it was stolen"), while the singular *mḥnh* is used, it is evident that this camp is only one among many (otherwise, the qualifying phrase would not be necessary). Hence the use of the term *mḥnh*, especially its plural use, indicates that the author is addressing a multiplicity of settlements – each with its own overseer and organization (CD 13:7), yet with one chief overseer over all the camps (CD 14:9).

Another interesting geographic term used in the *Damascus Document* but not in the *Manual of Discipline* is '*yr* ("town" or "city"). This word occurs six times in the *Damascus Document*, three times apparently in reference to Jerusalem (CD 12:1–2, the city of the Sanctuary; CD 20:22, the Holy City), but three times with reference to the sectarian dwelling place(s). CD 10:21 prescribes that on the Sabbath a man may not walk "farther than a thousand cubits outside his town (*ḥwṣ l'yrw*)"; similarly, CD 11:5–6 states that a man may not "go after the herd to pasture it outside his town (*ḥwṣ m'yrw*) except two thousand cubits" on the Sabbath. The significance in both these passages lies in the third-person pronoun added to '*yr* in order to define which town the author is indicating – hence, this implies that the sectarians lived in more than one town. Finally, CD 12:19 speaks of the "rule concerning the organization of the towns of Israel (*'ry yśr'l*)," thus indicating that there may have been a separate set of rules for the towns and for the camps (CD 12:22 has an identical expression with reference to the camps).[77] Unfortunately, if there was a separate set of rules, it has not survived in our copies of the *Damascus Document*, since the next section (CD 12:19b–22) does not seem to be directly related to the title in CD 12:19a.

The use of the terms *mḥnh* and '*yr* in the *Damascus Document*, then, does seem to point to groups of the sectarians living in areas outside of Qumran.[78] Whether or not (as Cross thinks) Josephus "distorts the situation" somewhat in stating that *many* settle in each city is difficult to ascertain given the present data.[79]

*When they journey* (§124–5). In this section, Josephus describes the hospitality of the Essenes toward visiting members of the sect. Such visiting Essenes need not take anything with them on their journey (except arms to guard against robbers), since in each city they are welcomed as close friends (συνηθεστάτους) by the Essenes living there, and are given everything they need. In fact, an appointed official is specifically entrusted with the task of taking care of the guests in that Essene community. Philo's description of Essene hospitality is similar: "No one's house is his own in the sense that it is not shared by all, for beside the fact that they dwell together in communities, the door is open to visitors from elsewhere who share their convictions (τῶν ὁμοζήλων, 'those of like zeal')" (*Every Good Man is Free* 9 §85).[80]

Specific confirmation of the kind of hospitality mentioned here by Josephus and Philo is lacking in Qumran literature, though the practice is entirely in harmony with Qumran teaching, since it is an outgrowth of the principle of brotherly love. As the characteristic has already been discussed previously (*J.W.* 2 §119 – see p. 37 above), further elaboration will not be necessary here. Several passages, however, should be mentioned in the context of hospitality. CD 6:20–7:1 states that the sectarians are "to love each man his brother as himself, and to support the hand of the needy, the poor, and the stranger (*gr*), and to seek each man the well-being (7:1) of his brother, and not to betray, each man him who is flesh of his flesh." Likewise, in the *Temple Scroll* a travelling Levite is to be accorded his rights, including a meal (11QTemple[a] 60:12–15 – see Deut 18:6–8).

Finally, in line with Josephus' statement that an official is appointed in each city for the care of such guests, CD 14:13–15 prescribes that the wage of at least two days per month be given to the overseer and the judges, to be used to meet the needs of the poor and needy, the homeless (*ynw'*), and other indigent people. While not specifically mentioning visiting Essenes, this passage does indicate that officials of the community were assigned the task of providing for the welfare of certain needy groups.[81]

*They replace neither clothing nor sandals* (§126). Josephus speaks of the discipline and frugality of the Essenes' dress and bodily demeanor (σχῆμα σώματος)[82] in the Hellenistic picture of children in fear of their tutors (παιδαγωγουμένοις). He then gives an example of this Essene frugality: they only replace clothing or sandals when they are torn to shreds or totally worn out. Philo also notes the frugality of the Essenes: he states that they show their love for God in various ways, including their frugality (ὀλιγοδείαν), simple living, and contentment (*Every Good Man is Free* 12 §84; see also 12 §77, where frugality and contentment are regarded by the Essenes as "an abundance of wealth").

Frugality and hatred of riches have already been seen as major tenets at Qumran (see *J. W.* 2 §122 above, pp. 43–4). In particular, scorn is indicated for the one who is interested only in heaping up possessions rather than using up what he has: the man of understanding, according to the *Manual of Discipline*, is told to hate "all the men of the Pit because of their spirit of hoarding," and is told to desire nothing apart from the will of God (1QS 9:21–4). Those who "acquire possessions" are viewed as enemies of the righteous (1QS 11:1–2). Hence, Josephus' statement fits well with the general attitude of the Qumran community towards possessions.

There is, in fact, one statement in the penal code of the *Manual of Discipline* that appears to refer more specifically to the Essenes' frugality of dress. 1QS 7:13–14 states that "whoever allows his 'hand' (*ydw*) to protrude from beneath his garment, if this garment is in rags (*whw'h pwḥ[ḥ]*) and reveals his nakedness he shall be punished for thirty days." As Brownlee and others suggest, *pwḥ* (from *pwḥ*, "to blow") should probably be emended to *pwḥḥ* (from *pḥḥ*, meaning "to have holes in one's garments, to be clad in rags, be exposed"),[83] as reflected in the preceding translation.[84] Whatever the meaning of this prohibition (i.e., whether *ydw* is to be taken literally or euphemistically[85]), if the suggested emendation is correct, then this text provides a good indication of the tendency of the sectarians to wear their clothes until they were so worn out as to be ineffective as a covering.

*Each one gives what he has to one in need* (§127). This free sharing of goods to meet the needs of another sectarian is also mentioned by Philo in connection with the absence of slavery among the Essenes: "Not a single slave is to be found among them, but all are free, exchanging kindnesses (ἀνθυπουργοῦντες) with one another" (*Every Good Man is Free*, 12 §79).

The evidence for such a pooled community of resources at Qumran has already been discussed above (*J. W.* 2 §122, pp. 44–5). In addition, concern for meeting the needs of the brethren provides the basis for the customs of hospitality mentioned previously by Josephus (*J. W.* 2 §124–5; see p. 50 above). Once again, CD 6:20–7:1 seems particularly applicable to this section of Josephus: the sectarian is to "love each man his brother as himself, and to support the hand of the needy, the poor, and the stranger, and to seek each man the well-being of his brother."

### 4. J.W. 2.8, 5 §128–33

*Before the rising of the sun they ... direct certain ancestral prayers towards it* (§128). Josephus next speaks about the various activities in a typical day of the Essenes, especially the ritual worship of the community (§128–33). He first remarks about the particular (ἰδίως) way the Essenes show their piety towards the Deity (τὸ θεῖον) – namely, the way in which they offer up their morning prayers. Josephus' words could be taken to mean that the Essenes prayed to the sun, i.e., that they were sun-worshippers. This is in fact the position of A. Dupont-Sommer, who cites this passage as evidence that there was an Essene sun cult, similar to that of the Pythagoreans.[86] This interpretation may also be supported by Josephus' statement later in *Jewish War* that the Essenes cover themselves during defecation "so as not to insult the rays of the Deity" (*J.W.* 2 §148). But it is highly unlikely that Josephus would report so approvingly of the piety of a Jewish sect that worshipped the sun.[87] A. Leaney understands this passage to indicate veneration of the sun, rather than worship; but it is difficult to see the distinction between worship and veneration.[88]

Others think that it is not a question of veneration, but rather of invocation: thus Vermes states that "from Talmudic times the recitation of the morning *Shema'* has been preceded by a benediction thanking God for the creation of light."[89] S. Talmon refers the pronoun αὐτόν in the phrase πατρίους δέ τινας εἰς αὐτὸν εὐχάς ("but direct certain prayers towards *it*") to God (τὸ θεῖον) rather than to the sun (τὸν ἥλιον).[90] But this is unlikely, since τὸ θεῖον would require the neuter pronoun αὐτό. In addition, τὸν ἥλιον is the nearest antecedent to αὐτόν, and the next clause uses ἀνατεῖλαι ("to rise"), the normal term to designate the rising of the sun. Finally, J. Daniélou, J. Strugnell, and F.M. Cross think that Josephus is simply speaking of the direction of the Essenes' prayers, namely, towards the east (rather than the normal Jewish orientation towards the Temple at Jerusalem), and that this is the aspect of Essene morning prayer that Josephus considers unusual.[91] Thus, according to Strugnell, εἰς αὐτόν would be translated "towards it," i.e., in the direction of the sun.[92] Moreover, the following clause, ὥσπερ ἱκετεύοντες ἀνατεῖλαι, is introduced by a comparative ὥσπερ and warns one against pressing the "entreaty" too literally. Daniélou observes that the early Christian orientation of prayer was also towards the east, perhaps patterned after that of the Essenes.[93]

At Qumran, not surprisingly, there is no evidence of sun-worship. In fact, in the *Temple Scroll*, there is a specific prohibition against worshipping the sun, nearly identical to Deut 17:2−5 (11QTemple[a] 55:15−21; see also Ezek 8:16−19). There are, however, numerous references to prayer in the scrolls, several of which specifically refer to prayer at dawn. In the *Manual of Discipline*, there is a much-debated section dealing with the times for worship (1QS 9:26−10:8).[94] The first portion of this section prescribes morning and evening prayer:

> He will bless Him [with the offering] of the lips at the times which He has ordained (*ḥqq'*) at the beginning of the dominion of light, during its circuit ('*m tqwptw*), and when it is gathered towards its appointed dwelling place; at the beginning of the watches of darkness, when he opens up their reservoir and sets them up on high, and at their circuit when they are gathered from before the light; when the heavenly lights appear from the realm of holiness, (and) when they are gathered to the dwelling place of glory.     (1QS 10:1−3)

The passage probably refers to two times of prayer, morning and evening (described in three ways: first, morning−evening, then evening−morning, then evening−morning again).[95] This interpretation is supported by a parallel statement several lines down: "When day comes and the night, I will enter the covenant of God; when night and morning depart, I will recite His precepts" (1QS 10:10; see also 1QS 10:13−14).[96] A similar indication of prayer at dawn and dusk is given in the *War Scroll*: "We shall exalt [Thy magnificence] because of Thy lofty deeds [during] the seasons and times appointed by the eternal testimonies, at the [com]ing of day and night and [when] evening and morning depart" (1QM 14:13−14).[97]

In the *Hodayot*, there are several intriguing references to prayer at dawn. 1QH 4:5−6 states: "I thank thee, O Lord, for Thou hast illumined my face by Thy covenant, and [...] I seek Thee, and sure as the dawn (*wkšḥr nkwn*) Thou hast appeared to me as [perfect Light] (*l'w[rtw]m*)." This passage perhaps comes the closest of any in Qumran literature to linking God with the sun in the same manner as Josephus. Dupont-Sommer, in fact, translates the phrase, "at daybreak Thou hast appeared to me" (reading *l'wrtym* as a pseudo-dual of *'wrh*), and considers that it is "doubtless connected with the prayer to the sun" described by Josephus.[98] But it should be recognized that the same terminology is used in Hos 6:3 ("His going forth is as sure as the dawn"; cf. Prov 4:18; Wis 16:28), and thus one should not ascribe sun-worship to the Essenes on the basis of the language of this passage.

Another section in the *Hodayot*, 1QH 12:4−7, is very similar to 1QS 10:1−3 (discussed above):

> [with blessings and th]anksgiving and prayers, bowing down and imploring always from one season to another: when the light comes from [its] dwe[lling place] at its appointed hour in the circuit of the day according to the laws of the great luminary; when evening approaches and light withdraws at the beginning of the dominion of darkness at the hours of night in its circuit; when the morning draws near and (darkness) vanishes before the light to return to its dwelling place, when the night withdraws and day breaks.

As in 1QS 10:1−3, prayer twice a day seems to be indicated, here described in terms of a morning−evening−morning cycle of prayer.

Finally, a further possible indication of the Qumran sectarians' regard for the sun may be seen in their calendar. Unlike the lunar calendar followed by official Judaism, the Qumran community apparently adopted a solar calendar of 364 days, similar to that used in *Jubilees* (*Jub.* 2:9; 6:32, 38) and part of *1 Enoch* (*1 Enoch* 72−82, the Astronomical Book, fragments of which have been found at Qumran [4QEnastr[a,b,c,d]][99]). Evidence of the use of a solar calendar at Qumran is clearly found in 11QPs[a] Dav Comp 27:6, which makes reference to "all the days of the year, 364." The solar calendar is also confirmed by fragments of the *Book of Priestly Courses* found in Cave 4.[100]

Hence, while neither Josephus nor the Qumran texts seem to indicate sun-worship, Josephus does hint (both in this passage and in *J. W.* 2 §148) that the Essenes had a high regard for the sun. And this regard for the sun also shows up at Qumran, as reflected in their description of God in terms of the sun's light (1QH 4:5−6) and in their retention of the solar calendar.[101]

*They labor earnestly until the fifth hour* (§129). Josephus relates that after their morning prayers, the Essenes are sent away by their overseers (ἐπιμελητῶν, as in *J. W.* 2 §123 and §134 − see pp. 46− 7 above) to their various crafts, in which they work zealously (συντόνως) until the fifth hour (i.e., about 11 a.m.).[102] Elsewhere Josephus states that the Essenes "have dedicated themselves to work entirely in agriculture" (*Ant.* 18 §19). Philo writes that some of the Essenes work on the land (sowing, planting, and taking care of cattle), while others work on crafts, though they make nothing that might be used for war (*Every Good Man is Free* 12 §76–8; *Hypothetica* 11.6–9).[103]

The Qumran scrolls are of little help regarding the kind of work done by the community. Other than the fact that manual work was done ("the work of his hands," 1QS 9:22), little else is said. However, archaeology of the Qumran area indicates that the inhabitants were occupied in both agriculture and craft work. At Qumran itself several workshops have been excavated: one is a well-preserved potter's workshop, another contains a large furnace and a water supply, and a third was used for grinding corn or barley. At Feshkha (two miles south of Khirbet Qumran), de Vaux excavated a farm containing a large building primarily for storage, a hangar probably used for drying dates, and an enclosure north of the large building designed for some sort of industrial use (a place either for curing hides or raising fish).[104] In addition, the reeds growing near Ain Feshkha were probably used for roofs and weaving; and it is likely that both salt and bitumen were manufactured as well (asphalt has been found both at Khirbet Qumran and at Feshkha).[105] Hence, de Vaux concludes that Feshkha was "an agricultural and industrial establishment used to benefit the community of Qumran," and that the Qumran sectarians "laboured in the workshops at Khirbet Qumran or on the farm at Feshkha."[106]

*Girding themselves with linen wraps, they bathe their bodies* (§129). After the Essenes finish their morning labors, Josephus reports that they come together in one place, don linen wraps, and bathe themselves in cold water[107] prior to the common meal. In the next phrase, he specifically calls this washing a "purification" (ἁγνείαν), which renders the Essenes "pure" (καθαροί). Participation in these daily washings was apparently permitted only after a one-year probationary period: only then did the novice participate in "the purer waters for purification" (*J.W.* 2 §137–8).[108] Josephus mentions two other occasions when the Essenes wash to rid themselves of impurity: after defecation, they wash "as if they were unclean" (*J.W.* 2 §149), and when senior Essenes are touched by juniors, "they must wash as if they had been in contact with a stranger" (*J.W.* 2 §150). Philo mentions only that the Essenes demonstrate their love of God by their continual "purity" (ἀγνείαν), but gives no specifics.

The evidence from the scrolls indicates that the Qumran community did practice purificatory washings. In the *Manual of Discipline*, 1QS 3:4—5 indicates that a man who scorns God's ordinances "shall not be absolved by expiation, or purified by lustral waters (*bmy ndh*), or sanctified by seas and rivers, or cleansed by all the waters of washing"; yet, the one who humbles himself towards God's precepts will "be cleansed when sprinkled with lustral water and sanctified in flowing water." In 1QS 4:20—1 lustral terminology is apparently used as a simile for spiritual truth: "Then God will purify by His truth all the works of every man, and will refine for Himself the (bodily) fabric of every man, to banish all spirit of perversity from his members, and purify him of all wicked deeds by the spirit of holiness; and He will cause the spirit of truth to gush forth upon him like lustral water."[109] But 1QS 5:13—14 seems to be a clear reference to a purifying bath: the one who is not obedient to God's precepts is not to "enter the water to touch the purity of the holy men (*lg't bṭhrt 'nšy hqwdš*), for they will not be cleansed unless they have turned from their wickedness." By "purity" (*ṭhrt*) is probably meant ritually pure articles, especially food.[110] This passage comes closest to Josephus' description of a purificatory washing followed by a communal meal, though there is no statement in the scrolls that this was a daily practice, as Josephus indicates.

In the *Damascus Document*, there are several references to washing. CD 10:10—11 states: "Let no man bathe in dirty water or in a quantity too little to cover a man completely." And in CD 11:21—2, the washing is definitely purificatory in nature: "Whoever enters the House of Prostration [i.e., the Temple?] let him not enter in a state of uncleanness; let him wash himself."[111] Again, as in the *Manual of Discipline*, there is no specific mention in these texts of daily purificatory washings.

Archaeological excavations also provide evidence of baths at Qumran. Some have pointed to seven large cisterns with steps found there as proof of the bathing practices of the community,[112] but similar cisterns with steps have been found elsewhere that were not used for bathing.[113] Two or three smaller basins have been found at Qumran, however, that were certainly used for bathing.[114] Whether or not "the baths taken in them had a ritual significance," de Vaux cautiously remarks, "archaeology is powerless to determine." But surely the evidence from the scrolls (especiallly 1QS 5:13—14) coupled with the archaeological findings indicates that the Qumran community did engage in purificatory washings, even if we cannot determine today the specific significance then attached to them by the Qumran Essenes.

Some scholars have seen a sacramental meaning in the purificatory washings of the Essenes. K. G. Kuhn, for example, states that the baths had, over and above a purificatory function, "the sacramental function of mediating in the divine forgiveness of sins ... The baths, and apparently also the communal meal, took on a new meaning, mediating salvation from God."[115] But neither Josephus nor Qumran provides evidence for the sacramental understanding of these washings.[116] Rather, both in Josephus and Qumran literature, the washings were performed for reasons of ritual purity.

*They go into the dining-room, even as into some holy shrine* (§129). Josephus reports that after the purificatory bath, the Essenes gather together in a private dwelling place, where the uninitiated (ἑτεροδόξων) are not permitted to enter. Then they proceed into the dining-room for their common meal.[117] Philo also mentions the common meals (συσσίτια) of the Essenes (*Every Good Man is Free* 12 §86, 91; *Hypothetica* 11.5, 11 [ὁμοτράπεζοι, "partakers of a common table," is the term used here]), but does not go into any further detail.[118]

Evidence from Qumran literature indicates clearly that the sectarians had a common meal. In the *Manual of Discipline*, 1QS 6:2–3 states that "they shall eat together (*wyḥd yw'klw*), and they shall bless together, and they shall deliberate together." 1QS 6:4–5 further describes the common meal (see below, pp. 58–61). And *The Rule of the Congregation (for the End-Time)* gives the rule for a meal at the "end of days" (1QSa 1:1) with the Messiah of Israel present (1QSa 2:17–22). That this meal is related to the daily meals of the Essenes seems evident from the last line of the text: "And they shall proceed according to this rite at every mea[l where] at least ten persons [are as]sembled" (1QSa 2:21–2; cf. 1QS 6:3–6).[119]

There is archaeological evidence for the common meal at Qumran as well. De Vaux has identified the largest room in the ruins of Qumran as a refectory. This identification is supported by the existence of a pantry for crockery adjoining the large room, containing more than one thousand vessels needed for eating: "jars to distribute the water, jugs and beakers from which to drink, dishes from which to serve the food, plates and bowls for eating."[120] Hence, both the scrolls and the archaeological evidence attest to the common meal at Qumran.

Josephus' statement that the Essene meal is only for the fully initiated member of the community ("none of the uninitiated is permitted to enter"; see also *J. W.* 2 §139) is also illustrated in Qumran literature. The *Manual of Discipline* stresses that the meal was only for community members in good standing, not for the outsider, the novice, or the erring member. According to 1QS 5:13, those who do not keep God's covenant (i.e., outsiders) may not "enter the water to touch the purity of the holy men," i.e., they may not take the purificatory bath preparatory to eating the meal.[121] In the rules for admission into the community, it is stated that the novice "shall not touch the purity of the Many until he has been examined concerning his spirit and his deeds upon his having completed one full year" (1QS 6:16–17). At that time, if he passes muster, he becomes a full member, participating in "law and justice and purity (*ṭhrt*) and the mingling of his property" (1QS 6:22). This passage appears to indicate that the novice may share in the common meal after a one-year probation, but must become a full member of the community (at least two years' probation) before partaking of the common drink.[122] Apparently the special precaution taken with regard to the common drink was necessary because liquids were especially powerful conveyors of uncleanness.[123] Hence, to protect the purity of the group, only full members were permitted to partake of the common drink. Finally, several passages in the *Manual of Discipline* deny the common meals to disobedient members: for lying (1QS 6:24–5), for speaking against a priest (1QS 7:2–3), and for slandering (1QS 7:15–16), the punishment was one year's separation from the "purity of the Many." The one who left the community and then returned apparently received a probation period similar to the initiate: "during the first year he shall not touch the purity of the Many, and during the second year he shall not touch the drink of the Many" (1QS 7:19–20). And in 1QS 8:16–18, the person who "turned aside from all that is laid down" is denied the "purity of the holy men ... until his deeds are purified of all perversity and he walks in perfection of way." Thus, the common meal at Qumran was limited to full community members in good standing.

*When they have sat down quietly* (§130). The quietness[124] of the Essenes is mentioned by Josephus both in their sitting down for the meal and during the meal itself (*J. W.* 2 §133). Quietness and order in speaking is emphasized in Qumran literature as well. See below, pp. 61–2.

*The baker serves the loaves in order* (§130). Josephus next mentions how thc meal is served. Loaves of bread are served by the baker in order (ἐν τάξει), i.e., according to rank, and a single dish is given to each by the cook. Josephus stresses the order, frugality (*one* plate of *one* kind of food given to each), and equality of treatment (each receiving the same portion) in the Essene community with respect to the meal.

As mentioned above, there are only two places in Qumran literature where the meal is specifically described (1QS 6:4–5 and 1QSa 2:17–22), and one of these (1QSa 2:17–22) describes a meal at the "end of days" with the Messiah of Israel present. Hence, there is not much basis for detailed comparison with Josephus' account of the meal. But is is noteworthy that the traits stressed by Josephus – order, frugality, and equality of treatment – are given prominence in the Qumran documents as well. The manifest concern for hierarchy within the community (discussed more fully below, pp. 99–100), is evident at their meetings and meals. In 1QS 6:4, 8–9, the community are enjoined to sit "each according to his rank" (*'yš ktkwnw*) when they assemble. Presumably this includes the common meal as well, since it is described in the middle of the same section (1QS 6:4–5). And in the eschatological assembly and meal described in 1QSa 2:11–22, part of the hierarchy is specifically given: the priest (Messiah of Aaron?),[125] then the Messiah of Israel, then the rest of the community, "each according to his rank" (*'yš lpy kbwdw*).[126] Hence, Josephus' ἐν τάξει may well reflect the ordering of the community described by the Qumran documents. In addition, the frugality and equality of treatment stressed by Josephus, while not specifically mentioned at Qumran in connection with the meal, are nonetheless important tenets of the sect (see the previous discussion on frugality, pp. 43–4 [*J. W.* 2 §122] and pp. 50–1 [*J. W.* 2 §126], and on equality of treatment, p. 37 [*J. W.* 2 §119] and pp. 44–5 [*J. W.* 2 §122].[127]

The kind of food served by the cook is not described by Josephus, nor is there any mention of the beverage that was drunk. Josephus mentions only the bread served by the baker. Philo states that the Essene-like Therapeutae ate common bread seasoned with salt and drank only spring water, even during their sacred banquets (*On the Contemplative Life* 4 §37; 9 §73–4). At Qumran, according to 1QS 6:4–5 (and 1QSa 2:17–21), the meal included "bread" (*lḥm*) and "wine" (*tyrwš*). As E. F. Sutcliffe points out, the word *lḥm* often has a wider meaning than simply "bread," and may simply refer to the food of the meal, whether bread or not.[128] With regard to the "wine," since *yyn* (the normal word for fermented wine) was not used, *tyrwš* probably refers either to new, sweet wine (i.e., lightly fermented wine)[129] or to unfermented grape juice.[130] Biblical usage favors the former alternative, while later rabbinic usage favors the latter (*y. Ned.* 7.40b). Complete abstention from even lightly fermented wine would perhaps be more in harmony with the ascetic lifestyle of the community, but it is impossible to be certain in this matter. If the *Temple Scroll* reflects the practices of the community, then *tyrwš* is probably to be equated with new wine, since in the feast of new wine it is used synonymously with *yyn ḥdš* ("new wine" – 11QTemple[a] 21:7, 8).[131] *Yyn* itself may have been regarded negatively by the community (CD 8:9, 10 [= CD 19:22, 23]),[132] so that their *tyrwš* was probably only lightly fermented if at all.

Neither the baker nor the cook described by Josephus is mentioned in Qumran literature, a not surprising fact in the light of the small amount of space given to the meal there. Elsewhere, Josephus states that priests are elected "for the preparation of their bread and their food" (*Ant.* 18 §22). This was apparently necessary to insure ritual purity (see also *J. W.* 2 §143). Thus it is possible that the baker and the cook were priests.[133] Or, perhaps the priests whom Josephus mentions (in *Ant.* 18 §22) simply supervised the work done by the (lay) baker and cook.[134]

*The priest prays before the meal* (§131). Josephus continues his description of the meal by recording that the priest prays both before anyone partakes of the food and after the meal is over, thus honoring God "as the supplier of life." The only other time Josephus mentions priests in connection with the Essenes is in *Ant.* 18 §22 (mentioned above), where he states that priests are elected to prepare their food.

Striking similarity is found between Josephus and Qumran literature on this point. The brief description of the meal in 1QS 6:4–5 emphasizes the role of the priest in blessing the food before anyone eats: "And then when they set the table to eat or (prepare) the wine to drink, the priest shall first stretch out his hand to pronounce a blessing on the first-fruits of bread and wine." Likewise, in the meal at the "end of days" described in 1QSa 2:17–21, the blessing of the food by the priest (and only subsequently by the Messiah of Israel) is stressed:

> And [when] they gather for the community table, [or to drink w]ine, and arrange the community table [and mix] the wine to drink, let no man [stretch out] his hand over the first-fruits

of bread and [wine] before the priest; for [it is he who] shall bless the first-fruits of bread and w[ine, and shall] first [stretch out] his hand over the bread. And after[wards], the Messiah of Israel shall [str]etch out his hands over the bread. [And afterwards,] all the congregation of the community shall [bl]ess, ea[ch according to] his rank.

1QS 10:14–15 also gives a blessing prior to eating, but does not say specifically who offers it. There is no mention in Qumran literature of a prayer at the end of the meal. Given the paucity of information about the meal in the scrolls (the two passages cited above comprise all that is said), this is not surprising. What is unusual is the prominence given to the priest's blessing both by Josephus and in the scrolls.

Josephus states that these prayers are made in order to honor God as the "supplier of life." The concept of God as the supplier of life is common in Qumran literature. In the *Manual of Discipline*, 1QS 3:15–18 says that "from the God of Knowledge comes all that is and shall be, and before (beings) were, He established all their design." Similarly, 1QS 11:11 says that "without Him nothing is made," while 1QS 11:18 asserts that "all that is brought into being exists by Thy will." The concept of God as creator is also seen in the *War Scroll* (1QM 10:8, 11–16) and, especially, the *Hodayot* (1QH 1:7–20; 10:9; 13:7–13; 15:22).

*When they return, they dine in like manner* (§132). After their meal, Josephus writes that the Essenes lay down their dining attire "as holy things" (ὡς ἱεράς) and return to work. Then, at evening, they share a meal similar to the first, at which any guests (ξένων) who have come are present as well. Presumably the "guests" are visiting Essenes (as in *J. W.* 2 §125), since otherwise it would be difficult to see how a non-sectarian could participate in the common meal (see above, p. 58 [*J. W.* 2 §129]). For the hospitality of the Essenes towards visiting members, see above, p. 50 (*J. W.* 2 §124–5). No further elaboration on the custom of a second daily meal is found in Qumran literature.

*The silence of those within appears like some awful mystery* (§132–3). Josephus returns to the subject of the quietness of the Essenes during their meal time,[135] a trait he had mentioned earlier (*J. W.* 2 §130) with respect to their seating. He states that the Essenes do not shout or create an uproar; rather, they speak in turn. This (relative) silence appears to those outside the sect as some "awful mystery" (μυστήριον φρικτόν), but it is really due to their continual sobriety and limitation of food and drink to what satisfies their needs. Philo similarly states that the Essene-like Therapeutae maintain an orderly silence during their festive meals, unlike the common rowdy Greek banquets (*On the Contemplative Life* 5–11 §40–89, esp. 10 §75, 81).

Quietness and especially order in speaking are characteristics of the Qumran sect as well. In the *Manual of Discipline*, the rules for speaking in the assembly are very strict: "Let no one interrupt the words of another before he has finished speaking. Also, let no one speak out of turn ... Whoever desires to put a question to the council of the community shall rise to his feet and say: I have something to say to the Many. If they order him to speak, he shall speak" (1QS 6:10–13). In the penal code, several laws are directed against speaking loudly or out of turn: "And whoever utters a foolish word from out of his mouth: three months. And for whoever interrupts the words of another: ten days ... And whoever laughs stupidly (and) loudly shall be punished for thirty days" (1QS 7:9–10, 14–15). Similarly, in the *Damascus Document*, the people are to be seated in a particular order, and are to speak according to this order (CD 14:6).

Josephus traces the cause of the Essene quietness and orderly behavior back to their sobriety (νῆψις, from νήφω, "to drink no wine"), especially with regard to their food and drink.[136] Earlier, Josephus mentioned the Essene disdain for pleasure and love of self-control (*J. W.* 2 §120), a characteristic found in Qumran literature as well (see above, pp. 37–8 [*J. W.* 2 §120]). CD 8:4–10, a section condemning those who have "defiled themselves in the ways of lust and in the riches of iniquity," cites Deut 32:33, which mentions wine in a pejorative way: "they kept not themselves from the people, but lived in license deliberately, walking in the way of the wicked, of whom God said, Their wine is the poison of serpents and the head of asps is cruel." Essene sobriety thus seems characteristic of the Qumran community as well.

Before leaving the Essene common meal, the question must be raised in what sense it is a sacred meal. At first glance, Josephus seems to present it as such. After the purificatory bath, they go into the dining-room "as into some holy shrine"; a priest is present, who prays before and after the meal to honor God; their garments are laid down "as holy things"; and the quietness surrounding the meal appears "like some awful mystery" to those outside the sect. But the last statement (about the quietness surrounding the meal) reveals Josephus' methodology throughout his discussion: he is describing the common meal as it would appear to an outsider. Thus, the dining-room is not actually a shrine, nor are their garments actually holy − they merely appear (ὡς)[137] that way to the outsider. And the same is true with respect to their quietness at meals: to the outsider, it appears like (ὡς) an "awful mystery," but it is simply an out-growth of Essene sobriety. Josephus, then, does not actually say that the meals of the Essenes are sacred, but rather, because of the Essenes' extreme concern for purity, quietness, and order, their sober meal times appear sacred in character to an outsider.[138]

Evidence for the sacred (or even, as some say, sacramental)[139] character of the meals at Qumran is also sparse. Aside from the fact that, as in Josephus, a priest says the blessing before the meal, there is nothing else "sacred" in the meal's description (either in 1QS 6:4−5 or in the end-time meal described in 1QSa 2:17−22).[140] Because of 1QSa 2:17−22, some have said that the common meal was an anticipation of the messianic banquet in the last days.[141] But this interpretation seems unlikely, since the instructions given in 1QSa 2:17−22 (esp. 2:21−2) hardly fit a one-time "banquet" but rather apply to the normal meal, only in the end-time when the Messiah of Israel is present. And the importance of the Messiah of Israel at the meal should not be over-emphasized, since the priest will still have first place at the gathering.

Other scholars regard the common meal as a substitute for the Temple sacrifices, which may not have been performed by the Essenes (see further below, pp. 115−19 [*Ant.* 18 §19]). Thus, the sacredness of the meal is seen as derived from its sacrificial role.[142] Possible support for this concept has been adduced in the discovery of animal bone deposits in various open spaces at Qumran. The bones were covered between sherds of pitchers or pots, or stored in capped jars hardly buried in the ground. De Vaux concludes that "the care with which the bones were set apart after the flesh had been cooked and eaten reveals a religious preoccupation. It is possible that these are the remnants of sacrifices."[143] But de Vaux himself notes that no altar has been found at Qumran, nor is there any evidence that sacrifices were practiced there. Other explanations for the bones have been given. E.F. Sutcliffe proposes that they are the bones of the red heifer used in purifying those in contact with dead bodies (since the cemetery was nearby) according to Numbers 19.[144] And J. van der Ploeg thinks that the animal bones may have been considered unclean by the sect (analogous to the uncleanness of human bones) and therefore buried.[145] Thus, it is not clear whether the animal deposits are remains of sacrifices or not.

Since the priest is prominent in both Josephus' and the Qumran description of the meal, it is certainly possible, as M. Burrows suggests, that the procedure and significance of the common meal may have been "determined by the pattern of the priest's meal after the temple sacrifice," regardless of whether the sectarians sacrificed at Qumran or not.[146] Possibly as well the purificatory baths taken before the meal are to be associated with the ritual cleansing of the priests accompanying temple sacrifice.[147] But even this hypothesis goes beyond the direct evidence provided by either Josephus or Qumran, where concern for ritual purity seems to be the pre-eminent emphasis in both the bath and the meal. Theories that go further and link the purificatory baths and the common meal at Qumran to the Christian sacraments of baptism and the Eucharist are on even more tenuous ground.[148] There is no evidence of connection between description of Qumran meals and NT texts about the institution of the Eucharist.

### 5. J.W. 2.8, 6 §134–6

*They do nothing except by the order of their overseers* (§134). Having described the daily activities of the Essenes (especially their ritual worship), Josephus presents further characteristics of the sect in *J. W.* 2 §134–6. He says that the Essenes only act on their own with respect to helping someone or showing mercy. In everything else, they follow the orders of their overseers (ἐπιμελητῶν – see above, pp. 46–7 [*J. W.* 2 §123]). Essene obedience to authority is also mentioned by Josephus later in the passage: "They also regard it as a good thing to obey the elders and the majority" (*J.W.* 2 §146).

Obedience to authority is an important tenet at Qumran as well. Many portions of the Qumran rule books deal with this issue. For example, in the *Manual of Discipline*, 1QS 5:2–3 states that those who join the community must "submit to the authority of the sons of Zadok, the priests who keep the covenant, and to the authority of the majority (*rwb*) of the men of the community who hold fast to the covenant. On their authority shall go forth the decisive edict on every matter of law, property, and precept" (see also 1QS 5:9). Several times, the one in lower rank is instructed to obey the higher: "They shall all obey one another, the lower (obeying) the higher (*hqtn lgdwl*)" (1QS 5:23); "And in regard to property and money, the lower shall obey the higher" (1QS 6:2). In 1QS 6:11–13, no one is permitted even to speak in the assembly "without the consent of the Many, unless he is the overseer of the Many." The penal code specifies a one-year punishment for one who rebels "against the word of his fellow member who is registered above/before him (*hktwb lpnyhw*)" (1QS 6:25–6), as well as a permanent expulsion for the one "who murmurs against the authority of the community" (1QS 7:17). Similarly, in the *Damascus Document*, no one may be introduced into the congregation apart from the consent of the overseer (CD 13:12–13), no partnership for trade may be made without his knowledge (CD 13:15–16), and everything that a man has to say regarding any litigation or judgment must be said to the overseer (CD 14:11–12). Thus, obedience to those in authority is a principle stressed in the rule books of Qumran.

*Succor and mercy* (§134). There are only two exceptions, Josephus states, to the overseer's authority in all matters. The sectarians may help the deserving (τοῖς ἀξίοις)[149] when asked and they may supply food to the destitute without securing permission. But they cannot give gifts to relatives without permission. Philo, too, emphasizes the charity of the Essenes, especially their thoughtful treatment of the sick and the elderly (*Every Good Man is Free* 12 §87; *Hypothetica* 11.13).

For Essene charity, see above (*J.W.* 2 §119, 122, 124, pp. 37, 44–5, and 50). Three passages are particularly noteworthy with regard to assistance for the needy. In the closing hymn of the *Manual of Discipline*, the writer promises to show "loving charity towards the disheartened and to strengthen the hands of the feeble" (1QS 10:26). In the *Damascus Document*, the sectarian is told "to love each man his brother as himself, and to support the hand of the needy, the poor, and the stranger" (CD 6:20–1). Finally, CD 14:12–16 sets forth a special fund for charity to be distributed by the overseer and judges: "The wage of at least two days a month, this is what they shall pay into the hands of the overseer and the judges. They shall set apart a portion of this sum for [orph]ans, and with the other they shall support the hand of the poor and the needy and the old man [dy]ing, and the man that is homeless and him that is taken captive into a foreign nation, and the virgin [with no] near kin and the you[ng woman wh]om no man seeks." This passage seems to indicate that (at least at the time the *Damascus Document* was written) the matter of providing for the needy was so important to the sectarians that a special fund was set aside to be used at the discretion of the overseer and judges. Josephus, on the other hand, depicts a more voluntary situation, with only those cases involving a relative going before the overseer. If Josephus' account is accurate,[150] he may be reflecting the Essene customs at a different time period from the *Damascus Document*, or perhaps he is simply speaking of voluntary acts of charity performed in addition to the organized effort.

*Masters of their temper* (§135). Josephus next lists four qualities of the Essenes in compact fashion. The first two qualities are nearly synonymous: they are upright managers of anger (ὀργῆς ταμίαι δίκαιοι)[151] and they are masters of their temper (θυμοῦ καθεκτικοί). These qualities are a specific outgrowth of their self-control, an attribute mentioned by Josephus at the beginning of the passage (*J. W.* 2 §120 – see p. 38 above).

There are many references to the control of one's temper at Qumran. According to the *Manual of Discipline*, to the spirit of truth belong "the spirit of humility and forbearance (*'wrk 'pym*)" (1QS 4:3), while to the spirit of perversity belongs "shortness of temper (*qṣwr 'pym*)" (1QS 4:10). In 1QS 5:25, the sectarian is instructed not to speak to his brother "with anger (*b'p*) or murmuring." In the penal code, 1QS 6:25–7 states that "whoever answers his fellow disrespectfully or speaks (to him) with shortness of temper (*bqṣwr 'pym*)" shall be punished, as will one who speaks in anger (*bḥmh*) against a priest (1QS 7:2). The hymn writer in 1QS 11:1–2 echoes a similar sentiment: rather than get angry, he will "respond with humility to those who are haughty in spirit, and with a broken spirit to those who brandish a stick, who point the finger and utter wounding words." In the *Damascus Document*, the sectarian is told "to bear no malice from one day to the next" (CD 7:2–3), while the one who brings an action against his fellow "in the heat of anger" (*bḥrwn 'pw*) is liable to punishment by death (CD 9:4–6). Similarly, in the *Hodayot*, the exhortation is to "be slow to anger" (*h'rykw 'pym* – 1QH 1:36–7). And in several places the reminder is given that God is "long-suffering" (*'rwk 'pym* – 1QH 1:6; 16:16; 17:17; see also CD 2:4). Thus, the concept of control of one's temper is firmly rooted in Qumran thought.

*Guardians of faithfulness* (§135). The next quality Josephus lists is that the Essenes are πίστεως προστάται, "guardians of faithfulness." The word πίστις has numerous shades of meaning, and with such a limited context it is difficult to determine the precise nuance Josephus has in mind. According to K. H. Rengstorf, in Josephus' writings πίστις may mean trust, belief, faith, faithfulness, loyalty,

trustworthiness, honesty, etc.[152] In *J. W.* 2 §121, as seen above
(p. 41), the word is used to describe a woman's "faithfulness" or
"pledge" to her husband. Accordingly, I have translated the word
as "faithfulness" in this passage as well, i.e., faithfulness with respect
to keeping the community teachings and perhaps faithfulness in
keeping one's own word as well (i.e., trustworthiness).

There are a number of references to faithfulness and
trustworthiness[153] at Qumran. The Hebrew words *'mn* and *'mwnh*,
similar in range of meaning to πίστις, are used frequently in Qumran
literature.[154] Two passages in the *Manual of Discipline* in particular
seem to echo Josephus' πίστεως προστάται ("guardians of
faithfulness"). 1QS 8:1−3 speaks of the appointment of twelve men
and three priests "to practice truth, righteousness, justice, loving
charity, and modesty one towards the other, to maintain faithfulness
(*lšmwr 'mwnh*) in the land with steadfast intent and a contrite spirit."
Similarly, the writer of the hymn at the end of the *Manual of
Discipline* states: "With wise intent, I will conceal knowledge and with
understanding prudence I will fence [it] in with a firm boundary, to
maintain faithfulness (*lšmwr 'mnym*) and the strong decree of God's
righteousness" (1QS 10:24−5). The use of *'mn* in the sense of
trustworthiness may be seen in the *Damascus Document*, where
witnesses must be trustworthy (*n'mnym*) for their testimony to be
accepted (CD 9:21, 23; 10:2). Also, in the *Temple Scroll*, the royal
guard for the king must consist of "trustworthy men" (*'nšy 'mt* −
11QTemple[a] 57:8).

*Ministers of peace* (§135). The final quality Josephus mentions in
cryptic fashion is that the Essenes are ministers of peace (εἰρήνης
ὑπουργοί). Philo goes so far as to say that the Essenes are pacifists:
"As for darts, javelins, daggers, or the helmet, breastplate, or shield,
you could not find a single manufacturer of them, nor, in general,
any person making weapons or engines or plying any industry
concerned with war" (*Every Good Man is Free* 12 §78). But Josephus
mentions earlier in this passage that the Essenes do carry arms to protect themselves from robbers when journeying (*J. W.* 2 §125), and in
*J. W.* 3.2, 1 §9−12 he depicts John the Essene as leading the battle
at Ascalon (see also *J. W.* 2 §152). Hence, unlike Philo, Josephus does
not present the Essenes as total pacifists.

That the Qumran commuity was also peace-loving is evident from
the scrolls. In the *Manual of Discipline*, those who walk in the spirit
of truth will be visited with "healing and abundance of peace (*wrwb
šlwm*), with length of days and fruitfulness" (1QS 4:6−7; see also

1QS 2:4, 9; 3:15). With regard to their treatment of one another, 1QS 5:24−6 states that "they shall reprove each other in truth and humility and loving charity one towards the other. Let no man speak to his neighbor with anger, or ill-temper, or disrespect, or impatience, or a spirit of wickedness." Thus, their dealings with one another were to be peaceful. The *Damascus Document* reflects a similar sentiment. Those who "stirred up civil strife" (*wysysw lryb 'm*) were punished by God (CD 1:21−2:1). According to CD 6:21−7:3, the sectarian is "to seek each man the peace of his brother," and "to bear no malice from one day to the next." The *Hodayot* contain eleven references to peace, with the fragmented 1QH 13:5 perhaps coming closest to Josephus' "ministers of peace": "and eternal grace to all the peace-[makers] (*lkwl* [ ] *lšlwm*)."[155]

Despite the basic peace-loving nature of the Qumran sectarians, the *War Scroll* reveals another, warlike side of the group. The entire document describes the preparation and execution of the eschatological war between the sons of light and the sons of darkness in great detail. As Y. Yadin states, "its purpose was to supply an urgent and immediate need, a guide for the problems of the long-predicted war, which according to the sect would take place in the near future."[156] Since it was probably composed at the end of the first century B.C., and the "Kittim" of the document probably refers to the Romans,[157] it is very possible, as Milik suggests, that the *War Scroll* was used as a propaganda piece for the later war with the Romans.[158] But even the *War Scroll* does not contradict the essential peace-loving nature of the group, since the document itself makes clear that the purpose of the war is to provide ultimate peace for the sons of light: "Then in the time of God His sublime greatness shall shine for all the times [of the ages] unto peace and blessing, glory and joy, and length of days for all the sons of light" (1QM 1:9; see also 1QM 3:5; 12:3; 17:7). And further, the apocalyptic character of the *War Scroll* indicates that the "war" may be a spiritual battle rather than a military one.[159] Qumran literature, then, supports Josephus' view of the group as peace-loving, yet not afraid of going to war; it does not support Philo's description of the group as complete pacifists.

*They avoid swearing* (§135). Josephus next elaborates on the trustworthiness[160] of the Essenes and their disdain for swearing. He observes that what they say is more binding than an oath, but they do not swear, since they think "that the one who is not believed apart from (swearing by) God has been condemned already." Especially strong is Josephus' statement that the Essenes consider swearing as worse than perjury.[161] Elsewhere (*Ant.* 15.10, 4 §371) Josephus notes that Herod did not require the Essenes to take an oath of loyalty to him. Philo also mentions that the Essenes demonstrate their love for God "by abstinence from oaths" (*Every Good Man is Free* 12 §84). Josephus himself, however, describes in great detail the "awesome oaths" (ὅρκους ... φρικώδεις) that the Essenes must take upon final admission into the sect (*J. W.* 2 §139). Hence, according to Josephus, not all types of oaths were banned by the Essenes.

Qumran literature indicates that oaths, though not banned by the community, were restricted in use. In the *Manual of Discipline*, the only oath mentioned is in 1QS 5:8, taken upon entrance into the community (see below, p. 76).[162] This accords well with Josephus' account. But the situation in the *Damascus Document* is more complex. In addition to "the oath of the covenant" taken by those who desire to join the community (CD 15:5–11; see below, pp. 76–7), other oaths are mentioned. CD 9:8–10 states that a person "who causes another to swear out in the field, and not in the presence of the judges or on their order, will have meted out justice by his own hand," which is unlawful. So oaths are here restricted to the presence of judges. In CD 9:10–12, the owner of a lost object is to swear "by an oath of malediction" (*bšbw't h'lh*), so that the one "who hears shall be guilty if he knows the thief and does not denounce him" (see also Judg 17:2; Lev 5:1). Yet, even the form of this "oath of malediction" was apparently restricted. According to the fragmented text of CD 15:1–5, it was forbidden to swear "by *Aleph* and *Lamed* or by *Aleph* and *Daleth*" or even by "the law of Moses." Rather, one must swear only "by the curses of the covenant" (*b'lwt hbryt*) in the presence of the judges. Presumably, then, CD 15:1–5 prohibited the oath of malediction (CD 9:10–12) from invoking God's name in any form (even abbreviations of El or Elohim ['*l*] or Adonai ['*d*] or invoking the Mosaic Law). In CD 16:6–7, every "binding oath which a man has undertaken" (*kl šbw't 'sr 'šr yqym 'yš 'l npšw*) must be fulfilled, "even at the price of death." This injunction may include the oath of admission (note the similarity in language to 1QS 5:8), but probably includes other oaths as well, since *kl* ("every") is used. In addition, the following passage (CD 16:8–12) forbids a husband from annulling the oath of his wife (as Num 30:7–16 permits) except if the oath violates the community covenant. Finally, the *Temple Scroll* contains a large section on oaths (11QTemple[a] 53:9–54:5), which is almost verbatim from Deut 23:21—4 and Num 30:2—17. Unlike the *Damascus Document*, the *Temple Scroll* passage follows Num 30:7—16 and permits a husband to annul his wife's oath.

Thus, while the *Manual of Discipline* seems to be in accord with Josephus, the *Damascus Document* permits other oaths in addition to the oath of entrance, though the use of these oaths is restricted in comparison with the *Temple Scroll* and OT law (as seen, for example, in the treatment of Num 30:7—16). Perhaps Josephus is simply exaggerating the Essene avoidance of oaths, or, more likely, perhaps the *Damascus Document* and the *Temple Scroll* (if the latter is of Essene origin) represent different stages in the community's development when a more tolerant attitude towards oaths was permitted than in the community described by the *Manual of Discipline* and Josephus.[163]

*Zealous in the writings of the ancients* (§136). Josephus writes that the Essenes are very interested in the writings of the ancients (τὰ τῶν παλαιῶν συντάγματα), especially with regard to what would profit soul and body. Later, Josephus mentions that the Essenes who profess to tell the future are "educated in holy books," thus giving another reason for their esteem of ancient writings (*J. W.* 2 §159). Philo also notes that the Essenes study "the laws of their fathers" very industriously, particularly setting aside the seventh day to hear the books read and expounded (*Every Good Man is Free* 12 §80—2).

What books does Josephus mean by "the writings of the ancients"? Certainly these would include the biblical books.[164] But the word "ancients" is sufficiently broad to encompass more than these books alone.[165] This interpretation is confirmed by Josephus' next statement, that the books are used to search out medicinal roots and properties of stones to heal diseases, since there is little in the biblical books that would be of help for that purpose. Books such as *Enoch* and *Jubilees*, however, do treat these subjects (see below), and are undoubtedly to be included in Josephus' "writings of the ancients" consulted by the Essenes.

Evidence at Qumran for the use of books is, of course, overwhelming. In terms of biblical material, portions of every canonical OT book have been found with the exception of Esther, and sections of three deuterocanonical books (Tobit, Sirach, and the Epistle of Jeremy) have been found as well. The pseudepigraphical works of *Jubilees* and *Enoch* appear in abundance at Qumran (see n. 99, p. 147), as well as the *Genesis Apocryphon*, *Testaments of the Twelve Patriarchs*, the Temple Scroll (which B. Z. Wacholder regards as the "sectarian Torah"[166]), the *Targumim*, the *Pesharim*, and many other similar works.[167]

The Qumran rule books also attest to the study of books. In the *Manual of Discipline*, 1QS 6:6−8 states that "in the place where the ten are, there shall not lack a man who studies the Law day and night continually ... and the Many shall keep vigil in common for a third of all the nights of the year, to read the book and to study its decree." Similarly, after quoting Isa 40:3, 1QS 8:15−16 declares that "this means the study of the Law which He commanded by the hand of Moses, that they may act according to all that is revealed, season by season, and according to that which the prophets have revealed by His Holy Spirit." In the *Damascus Document*, after the citation of Amos 5:26−7 and 9:11, CD 7:17 explains that "the faithfulness of the images is the books of the prophets whose words Israel has despised." And CD 16:1−5 mentions study of both the Law and the book of *Jubilees*:

> For this reason a man will undertake to return to the Law of Moses, for by it all things are carefully taught. And the exact detail <of the> times of the blindness of Israel with regard to all these, this is what is carefully taught in the Book of the Divisions of the Times into their Jubilees and their Weeks.[168] And on the day that a man undertakes to return to the Law of Moses, the angel Mastema[169] will depart from him if he fulfills his promises.

This passage is especially interesting in that the Law and the book of *Jubilees* are mentioned in the same context, both apparently viewed as equally authoritative by the community.

Finally, the *Damascus Document* mentions the *spr hhgy*, the "Book of Meditation": according to CD 10:6, the judges "must be learned in the Book of Meditation and in the constitutions of the covenant," and CD 13:2 states that "where there are ten of them, let there not lack a man who is a priest learned in the Book of Meditation" (see also CD 14:8). This book is also mentioned in *The Rule of the Congregation (for the End-Time)*: according to 1QSa 1:7, every native in Israel was to be instructed in the "Book of Meditation" and "taught the precepts of the covenant." Dupont-Sommer believes that *spr hhgy* refers to the *Manual of Discipline*; G. Molin thinks the *Hodayot* are meant; C. Rabin considers the term "an etymological substitute for *mishnah*"; and G. Vermes regards it as a reference to the Torah (citing Josh 1:8 and Ps 1:2, which speak of constant meditation in the Law).[170] If B.Z. Wacholder is correct in his understanding of 11QTemple[a] as the "sectarian Torah" (see p. 136 n. 47), this work might well be the *spr hhgy*. Though the identity of the *spr hhgy* remains uncertain, the use of the term is yet another indication of the sect's esteem for books.

*Healing of diseases* (§136). Josephus adds that the Essenes use these writings to search out "medicinal roots and the properties of stones" (ῥίζαι τε ἀλεξητηρίοι καὶ λίθων ἰδιότητες) to heal diseases. Direct confirmation of this practice is lacking at Qumran, but there are numerous indications of the group's interest in healing. In the *Manual of Discipline*, the ones walking in the spirit of truth are visited with "healing (*mrp'*) and abundance of peace, with length of days and fruitfulness" (1QS 4:6–7). Furthermore, in the *Damascus Document*, apostates "will be sick < without > any healing" because of their wickedness (CD 8:4). In the *Hodayot*, the writer (whom Dupont-Sommer identifies with the Teacher of Righteousness)[171] states: "I have been a snare for sinners, but healing for all that are converted from sin" (1QH 2:8–9), perhaps a metaphorical use of *mrp'* (see also CD 12:5; 1QH 9:24–5). An interesting reference to healing occurs in the *Genesis Apocryphon*. The Egyptian physicians (*'sy'* – 1QapGen 20:19, 20) could not heal the Pharaoh, but Abraham, speaking in the first person, states: "So I prayed for that [ ] ..., and I laid my hands upon his [he]ad. The plague was removed from him and the evil [spirit] was commanded (to depart) [from him], and he was cured." And in the *Prayer of Nabonidus* there is also a probable reference to a healer, though the text is not entirely clear. Nabonidus states that he has had a bad inflammation for seven years, and that he prayed, and "an exorcist remitted my sins for Him (*wḥṭ'y šbq lh gzr*): he was a Jew fr[om (among) the deportees]" (4QPrNab 1–3 i 4).[172] Dupont-Sommer identifies this exorcist who healed the king as Daniel.[173]

Further evidence that the Qumran community was interested in healing and books about healing may be seen in their interest in *Jubilees* and *Enoch*. As mentioned above, not only have numerous fragments from both books been found at Qumran, but *Jubilees* is specifically mentioned in CD 16:2–5. And in both books there is mention of healing. In *Jub.* 10:10–14, Noah is taught the use of herbs for healing, to protect his sons from the demons:

> And one of us (angels) He commanded that we should teach
> Noah all their medicines; for He knew that they would not
> walk in uprightness, or strive in righteousness ... And we

explained to Noah all the medicines of their diseases, together with their seductions, how he might heal them with herbs of the earth. And Noah wrote down all things in a book as we instructed him concerning every kind of medicine. Thus the evil spirits were precluded from (hurting) the sons of Noah. And he gave all that he had written to Shem, his eldest son.

In *Enoch*, the name of the angel who was to heal and teach healing to Noah and his sons is given as Raphael (from *rp'*, "to heal"): "The Lord said to Raphael ... heal the earth which the angels have corrupted, and proclaim the healing of the earth, that they may heal the plague, and that all the children of men may not perish" (*1 Enoch* 10:4−8).[174] Earlier, the wicked angels had taken wives, "and they taught them charms and enchantments, and the cutting of roots, and made them acquainted with plants" (*1 Enoch* 7:1; see also 8:3). So presumably Raphael was to undo this work with a counter work of healing. Again, in *1 Enoch* 25:1−6 a fragrant tree is mentioned, whose "fruit shall be food to the elect: it shall be transplanted to the holy place, to the temple of the Lord the Eternal King ... And its fragrance shall be in their bones, and they shall live a long life on earth, such as thy fathers lived: and in their days shall no sorrow or plague or torment or calamity touch them" (see also the trees and plants described in *1 Enoch* 28:1−32:6). Thus, healing (including the healing properties of plants) is mentioned in numerous places in the literature that the Qumran community possessed.[175]

Finally, it should be recalled in this regard that G. Vermes thinks that the very name "Essene" is derived from the Aramaic *'āsayyā'*, "healers," and thus was a popular characterization of the group (see discussion above, pp. 35−6 [*J.W.* 2 §119]).

## 6. J.W. 2.8, 7 §137−42

*Entrance is not immediate* (§137−8). In this section (2 §137−42) Josephus discusses the process for admission into the sect and the oaths that the novice must take. He describes a three-year initiation period. During the first year, while the novice remains outside (ἔξω), he is put under their way of life (and given a hatchet, a loin cloth, and a white garment). Then, having given proof of his self-control (ἐγκρατείας),[176] he is brought closer to their way of life (διαίτη): he may join in the "purer waters for purification" (καθαρωτέρων τῶν πρὸς ἁγνείαν ὑδάτων), i.e., the purificatory baths,[177] but is not received into the common ways of living (συμβιώσεις), including the common meal.[178] This second stage lasts for two years. Finally, after taking "awesome oaths" (ὅρκους ... φρικώδεις), the novice is admitted as a full member into the community and is permitted to eat (ἄψασθαι) the common meal.[179]

Strikingly similar to Josephus' description of the stages of entrance into the sect is the lengthy section in the *Manual of Discipline* on the same subject, 1QS 6:13–23. First, there is an unspecified period of time spent outside the sect in which the community's way of life is learned. Only then is the novice permitted to "draw near to the council of the community" (1QS 6:13–16). There follows a two-year period of probation within the community: during the first year, the novice may not touch the "purity (*ṭhrt*) of the Many," i.e., their food,[180] and he may not mingle his property with them; during the second, he may not touch the drink (*mšqh*) of the Many,[181] and his money may be collected by the overseer, but not spent with that of the Many (1QS 6:16–21). This two-year period is also mentioned in 1QS 8:10–11 ("When they have established themselves in the institution of the community, in perfection of way, for two years day for day ..."). After the completion of each phase, the novice is examined. Finally, upon passing the third phase, "he shall be regularly inscribed in his rank among his brethren in whatever concerns the Law and justice and purity and the mingling of his property; and he may give his opinion to the community together with his judgment" (1QS 6:22–3).

In comparing Josephus' discussion with the *Manual of Discipline*, we find many points of similarity. First, both accounts indicate that the joining of the community is a voluntary decision. Josephus speaks of novices who are "eager (ζηλοῦσιν) to join their sect," while the *Manual of Discipline* repeatedly emphasizes that those who join are "volunteers": 1QS 6:13 begins with the words, "whoever, born of Israel, volunteers (*hmtndb*) to join" (see also 1QS 1:7, 11; 5:1, 6, 8, 10, 21–2; 1QpMic 10:5). Second, in both there is a period of time spent outside the sect. Josephus specifies the length of time as one year, while in the *Manual of Discipline* the amount of time is unspecified. Third, as Michel and Bauernfeind note, the terminology used by Josephus to describe the novice's closer contact with the sect after the initial one-year period corresponds well with the language of 1QS: Josephus states that after the year, "they bring him closer to [their] way of life" (πρόσεισιν μὲν ἔγγιον τῇ διαίτῃ), while 1QS 6:16 mentions that after his examination the novice "shall either draw near" (*yqrb*) to the council of the community or depart.[182] Fourth, in both Josephus and 1QS, there is a two-year period of initiation within the community itself. In 1QS, a clear distinction is made between the first and second years (with an examination after each year), while Josephus simply describes the two-year period as a whole. Fifth, Josephus records that during this two-year period, the novice may participate in the purificatory baths. 1QS does not specifically mention this point, but it is certainly possible that drawing "near to the council of the community" (1QS 6:16) includes participation in the baths.[183] Sixth, Josephus mentions that the novice may not participate in the "common ways of living," i.e., the meal, during the two-year period. Again, 1QS is in general agreement, but provides further detail: the novice cannot touch the meal for one year, and the drink for two years. Josephus either does not know of this distinction, or chooses to simplify the procedure for his reader. Finally, according to both Josephus and 1QS, after a further examination (stated specifically in 1QS 6:21 ["they shall examine him"] and implied in Josephus ["his character is tested for two more years, and if he appears deserving, then he is admitted"]) he is admitted into the community with full rights and privileges. At some stage prior to full acceptance into the community, the novice must take an oath of obedience to the community − in 1QS, the oath probably comes at the beginning of the two-year initiation period within the community (1QS 5:8−10; CD 15:5−10), whereas Josephus seems to depict the oath at the end.[184] Thus, the description of the stages of entrance into the community given in 1QS 6:13−23 corresponds quite well for the most part with Josephus' account.[185]

Josephus mentions that the novice is given a small hatchet, a loin cloth, and a white garment at the time he begins the initiation process (while still outside the community). On the Essene hatchet, see below, pp. 97−8 (*J. W.* 2 §148). The loin cloth, as Josephus himself notes, was already mentioned in *J. W.* 2 §129 (though not by name). Since it was used for the purificatory baths, it is possible that the novices had their own baths apart from the community during the first year.[186] The white garment given to the novice accords well with Josephus' previous statement in *J. W.* 2 §123 that the Essenes were always dressed in white.[187] While there is no specific mention of these three items in Qumran literature with respect to the novices, all three items and the purposes for their use do fit well with the concern for ritual purity evident at Qumran.

*He must take awesome oaths* (§139). Josephus next describes the "awesome oaths" (ὅρκους ... φρικώδεις) that must be taken before the novice may become a full member of the community and partake of the common meal. He gives an elaborate list of eleven oaths, and concludes by saying "with such oaths as these (τοιούτοις) they secure the allegiance of those who enter (their community)" (2 §142). Apparently, Josephus is implying with the use of τοιούτοις that he has reproduced only the essence of the oaths, and not necessarily the precise wording of all their oaths.

Qumran literature does make mention of an oath taken by those entering the community. It seems to be connected with entrance into the "covenant of God," and its primary focus appears to be obedience to the Law. In the *Manual of Discipline*, the one who joins the community is to "enter into the covenant of God in the presence of all the volunteers, and he shall undertake by a binding oath (*yqm 'l npšw bšbw't 'sr* − see Num 30:3−15) to return to the Law of Moses according to all His commands, with all his heart and all his soul, following all that is revealed of it to the sons of Zadok, the priests who keep the covenant and seek His will, and to the majority of the members of their covenant" (1QS 5:8−9). The ceremony of entrance into the covenant is described in 1QS 1:16−2:18, which begins: "And all who enter the order of the community shall enter into a covenant before God to act according to all that He has commanded and shall not turn back from following Him through any fear or terror or affliction during the reign of Belial" (1QS 1:16−17). While no initiatory oaths are mentioned in this text, those entering the community do express their double "amen" after the blessings and cursings of the priests and Levites (1QS 2:10, 18). This ceremony is patterned after the blessings and curses of Deuteronomy 27−30 which accompanied the giving of the Law. Immediately preceding the ceremony of entrance into the covenant, the opening section of the *Manual of Discipline* (1QS 1:1−15) sets down the basic precepts of the community. While not specifically called an oath, these precepts may have formed the basis for the oath of admission to the community. As will be seen below, this section is remarkably similar to the oaths recorded by Josephus.

There is also a reference to an oath of entrance in the *Damascus Document*. Again, this oath is linked with entrance into the covenant. In CD 15:5−6, the sons who have come of age must "swear by the oath of the covenant." Similarly, the next section states that the one who joins the community from the outside, "on the day that he speaks to the overseer of the Many, shall be examined with the oath of the

covenant which Moses concluded with Israel, (namely,) the covenant
to return to the Law of Moses with all his heart [and all] his soul ...
and let not the ordinances be made known to him until he has
presented himself before the overseer'' (CD 15:7–11).[188] Finally, in
the *Hodayot*, 1QH 7:17 may allude to the oath of entrance as well:
''I have undertaken an oath (*bšbw'h hqymwty 'l npšy*) to sin no more
against Thee.''[189]

In comparing Josephus' Essene oaths with the Qumran references,
two possible discrepancies surface. First, the Qumran oath appears
to be made at the beginning of the initiation period rather than at
the end as Josephus states.[190] The oath is made in conjunction with
entrance into the covenant (1QS 5:8–9), which seems to be associated
with the preliminary stage of entrance, according to 1QS 6:14–15,
not the later stages. But the time sequence of the oath and the stages
of entrance into the community are not clearly spelled out. It is
possible that there were various degrees of entrance into the covenant,
and that the phrase may refer to a preliminary entrance in 1QS
6:14–15 and a final entrance in 1QS 5:8–9. Josephus, in fact, is less
than precise in his chronology of the oath, since he merely states that
the oaths are taken ''before he may touch the common meal'' – he
does not actually specify how long prior to full acceptance into the
community the oaths are taken. G. Vermes speculates that Josephus
may have placed the oaths at the end of his discussion in order ''to
emphasize the secret character of the Essene association.''[191]

A second problem with respect to the oaths is that the Qumran oath
deals primarily with obedience to the Law of Moses, while the Essene
oaths described by Josephus concern the basic tenets of the sect and
not specifically the Mosaic Law. Yet even here the differences between
Qumran and Josephus may be only slight. For even in 1QS 5:8–9,
the novice was to swear to keep the Law of Moses as it was interpreted
by the priests and the community as a whole. This almost certainly
involved far more than a mere literal adherence to the Mosaic Law,
as the esoteric interpretations of Scripture in the *Pesharim* and
elsewhere demonstrate. And Josephus, writing for a non-Jewish
audience, may not have wished to stress the Mosaic Law per se,
though he does mention in the oaths that they are to ''preserve ...
the books of their sect'' (*J.W.* 2 §142), and later stresses their
reverence for their lawgiver (i.e., Moses – see pp.92–4 below).
It is possible, of course, that there were two oaths taken by the novice
– one at the beginning, emphasizing the Law, and one at the end,
stressing the sectarians' teaching, but it seems more likely that

Josephus is referring to the same oath of admission as mentioned in the scrolls, taken at some point prior to full acceptance into the community.

*He will practice piety towards the Deity* (§139). The first oath Josephus lists concerns the sectarian's relationship to God, while the other ten deal with his relations with people, especially fellow community members. Josephus states that the sectarian is "to practice piety towards the Deity" (εὐσεβήσειν τὸ θεῖον). Josephus uses much the same language as in *J. W.* 2 §128, where he remarks that the Essenes "are pious towards the Deity (πρός ... τὸ θεῖον εὐσεβεῖς) in a particular way." Philo also mentions the Essenes' piety towards God: he states that their very name is probably derived from ὁσιότητος, holiness, "because they have shown themselves especially devout in the service of God" (*Every Good Man is Free* 12 §75). He also mentions that they are "trained in piety" (παιδεύονται ... εὐσέβειαν) and that their first of three standards of conduct is "love of God" (φιλοθέῳ – *Every Good Man is Free* 12 §83) (love of virtue and love of human beings are the second and third).

Piety towards God is a major concept in Qumran literature. The opening lines of the *Manual of Discipline* contain these words: "to seek God [with all their heart and all their soul, and] do what is good and right before Him" (1QS 1:1–2). In 1QS 1:16–17, those who are entering the community are to "enter into a covenant before God to act according to all that He has commanded and not to turn back from following Him." And in 1QS 3:9–11, the one who does not scorn God's ordinances is to "order his steps to walk perfectly in all the ways of God according as He has commanded at the fixed times of His revealing (them), and not swerve to right or left and not walk contrary to a single one of all His words." Again, according to 1QS 5:8–10, the one who joins the community is to "undertake with a binding oath to return to the Law of Moses according to all His commands, with all his heart and all his soul" and follow those "who all devote themselves to His truth and to walking in His will." In the hymn at the end of the *Manual of Discipline* (1QS 10:1–11:22), the writer praises God, at one point declaring: "At the beginning of every enterprise of my hands or feet I will bless His name; at the beginning of every activity, when I go out and return, when I sit and rise up and when I retire to bed I will utter cries of joy unto Him" (1QS 10:13–14). Similar expressions of praise to God are found throughout the *Hodayot*. Piety towards God is also expressed in many other portions of Qumran literature, including 1QS 1:8; 6:27–7:1; 9:11, 13;

and 11QTempleᵃ 57:8–9 ("And all the men whom he will choose
[for the royal guard] will be faithful men, fearing God").
*He will cherish justice towards human beings* (§139). The next two
oaths Josephus relates both have to do with the sectarian's concern
for justice: he is to cherish justice (δίκαια φυλάξειν) towards others
and wrong no one, even if ordered. In fact, Josephus continues, the
sectarian is to "hate forever the unjust and fight together with the
just" (μισήσειν δ' ἀεὶ τοὺς ἀδίκους καὶ συναγωνιεῖσθαι τοῖς
δικαίοις). These words indicate a strong concern for justice, in that
the sectarian is even to disobey orders from a superior if it involves
wronging someone else, and is to "hate" unjust persons and actively
fight on the side of the just. Later in the passage Josephus reiterates
the Essene concern for justice: "In their judgments they are most
scrupulous and just, and they administer justice with not less than
a hundred members assembled" (*J. W.* 2 §145). And in *Ant.* 18 §21,
Josephus states that the Essenes do not seek to acquire slaves, since
this practice "leads to injustice." Philo, too, mentions that the
Essenes "are trained in piety, holiness, justice (δικαιοσύνην) ..."
(*Every Good Man is Free* 12 §83).

Justice is stressed in the sectarian writings at Qumran as well. The
opening lines of the *Manual of Discipline* (a section which, as noted
earlier, contains numerous parallels with the oaths mentioned by
Josephus) state that the sectarian is to "cling to all good works, and
to practice truth and righteousness (*ṣdqh*) and justice (*mšpṭ*) on earth"
(1QS 1:5–6).[192] Similar sentiments are expressed in 1QS 2:24 ("For
they shall all be in the community of truth and virtuous humility and
loving charity and righteous intention [*mḥšbt ṣdq*] one towards
another"), 1QS 5:3–4 ("They shall practice truth in common and
humility and righteousness [*ṣdqh*] and justice (*mšpṭ*) and loving
charity and modesty in all their ways"), and 1QS 8:2–3 (the twelve
men and three priests are "to practice truth and righteousness [*ṣdqh*]
and justice [*mšpṭ*] and loving charity and modesty one towards the
other"). Likewise, the opening words of the *Damascus Document*
are addressed to "all you who know justice (*kl ywdʿy ṣdq*) and
comprehend the words of God" (CD 1:1). And in the *Temple Scroll*,
a section based on Deut 16:18–20 states that just judges and administrators are to be appointed in every city. These judges are to render
righteous judgments (*mšpṭ ṣdq*) for the people, and are not to take
bribes or pervert justice in any way (11QTempleᵃ 51:11–18). In fact,
in a provision going beyond Deuteronomy 16, 11QTempleᵃ 51:16–
17 states that "the man who receives a bribe and perverts righteous

judgment shall be put to death." Similarly, in 11QTemple[a] 57:19–21, the king must not take bribes or pervert justice in any way.

There is also evidence at Qumran for the strong hatred towards the unjust mentioned by Josephus. Again in the opening section of the *Manual of Discipline*, the command is "to love all that He has chosen and hate all that He has despised, and to depart from all evil and cling to all good works" (1QS 1:3–5). In 1QS 1:9–10, the sectarians are to "love all the sons of light," but "hate all the sons of darkness." In 1QS 4:23–5, the spirits of truth and perversity battle in man, "and according to each man's share of truth and righteousness, so does he hate perversity." In 1QS 9:14–16, the man of understanding is to "separate and weigh the sons of righteousness[193] according to their spirits ... and as his love is, so shall his hatred be." And 1QS 9:21–2 explains that there should be "eternal hatred (*śn't 'wlm*) for the men of destruction" (compare Josephus' expression μισήσειν δ' ἀεί, "to hate forever"). In the *Damascus Document*, there is also emphasis on distinguishing the righteous from the wicked. CD 1:19–20 declares that God's anger was kindled "because they declared the wicked righteous and the righteous wicked ... and because they threatened the life of the just." And CD 20:20–1 provides the exhortation to "distinguish anew between the just and the wicked" (see also CD 4:7). Finally, the hymn writer in the *Hodayot* exclaims: "I am full of zeal against all evil-doers and men of falsehood ... For thou art righteous and all Thine elect are truth, and all perversity [and ungod]liness Thou wilt destroy forever and Thy righteousness shall be revealed to the eyes of all Thy works" (1QH 14:14–16; see also 1QH 14:26). Thus, both love of justice and a strong hatred of the unjust are important concerns of the Qumran community.

*He will forever show himself trustworthy ... especially to those in authority* (§140). The next two oaths given by Josephus deal with one's attitude towards authority. The Essene is to show himself trustworthy (τὸ πιστὸν ... παρέξειν) to everyone, but especially to those in authority, since God is behind the ruling power.[194] Furthermore, the one entering the community affirms that if he himself becomes a ruling authority, he will not rule or dress arrogantly. Thus, Josephus presents a balanced picture of respect for authority, on the one hand, yet a humble, non-overbearing attitude on the part of those in authority, on the other. Michel and Bauernfeind think that the authorities meant here by Josephus are not the community authorities, since obedience to them had previously been stressed (*J. W.* 2 §129,

134), but rather the ruling authorities in the world.[195] But Josephus often repeats himself, and it seems more likely that the community leaders are the primary group in mind, since the very next oath deals with the attitude that the community leaders should have.[196] Trustworthiness is an important concept in Qumran literature, as has already been discussed (see *J. W.* 2 §135, pp. 66–7). One passage in particular that relates trustworthiness to those in authority is 11QTemple[a] 57:8, in which the royal guard for the king must consist of "trustworthy men" (*'nšy 'mt*). Josephus' statement that "no one achieves his ruling authority apart from God" is also reflected in Qumran literature. In the *Manual of Discipline*, the wise man (*mśkyl*) who instructs the community[197] is told that "he shall do the will (of God) in every enterprise of his hands and in all the exercise of his authority as He has commanded. In all that befalls he shall freely delight, and nothing shall please him except God's will. He shall delight [in all] the words of His mouth, and shall not covet anything which He has not comman[ded]" (1QS 9:23–5). And 1QS 3:15–18 states that "From the God of knowledge comes all that is and shall be, and before (beings) were, He established all their design ... It is He who made man that he might rule over the earth." See further below, pp. 113–14 (*Ant.* 18 §18).

The corresponding oath mentioned by Josephus, that if the sectarian became a ruler himself he would not rule arrogantly or dress in a way to "outshine his subjects," is also in general harmony with Qumran thought, though there is no specific parallel from Qumran literature. In the penal code of the *Manual of Discipline*, the one who "speaks to his fellow arrogantly" is to be punished for six months (1QS 7:5). According to 1QS 11:1–2, the one who instructs the murmurers is also to "answer with humility the proud of spirit, and with a contrite spirit those that brandish a stick, that point the finger and utter wounding words." Furthermore, the *mśkyl* of 1QS 9:21–5 (mentioned above) is to desire nothing beyond the will of God, thus making him a humble, non-self-seeking leader. There is no specific indication in Qumran literature of the leader's attire; so no comparison with Josephus may be made on that point.[198]

*He will forever love the truth and expose liars* (§141). The next oath of the Essene, that "he will forever love the truth (τὴν ἀλήθειαν) and expose (προβάλλεσθαι) liars," is similar in intensity and contrast to the earlier oath, "he will hate forever the unjust and fight together with the just" (*J. W.* 2 §139). Josephus has previously stressed the importance of truth and trustworthiness to the Essenes: in *J. W.* 2 §135 he calls the Essenes "guardians of faithfulness" and explains that they avoid swearing, since their word is stronger than an oath; and a few lines earlier in the oath of admission, the Essene is to "forever show himself trustworthy to all" (*J. W.* 2 §140). But it is in this oath that truth itself (τὴν ἀλήθειαν) is actually mentioned, and the antithesis between the Essene love for truth and hatred for falsehood is clearly brought out. Philo also mentions that the Essenes show their love of God by their truthfulness (τὸ ἀψευδές – lit., "absence of falsehood"), though he does not use strong antithetical language as does Josephus (*Every Good Man is Free* 12 §84).

The concept of truth is deeply rooted in Qumran thought. In those works included in Kuhn's *Konkordanz*, the term *'mt* occurs 140 times, making it the twelfth most frequent noun in Qumran literature.[199] A few examples of its use will suffice. In the opening section of the *Manual of Discipline*, the sectarian is to "cling to all good works and to practice truth and righteousness and justice on earth" (1QS 1:5–6). 1 QS 1:11 further speaks of the "volunteers that cling to His truth," and 1QS 5:3 states that "they shall practice truth in common." Sometimes, "truth" even forms a part of the community's self-designation. For example, 1QS 2:24, 26 speaks of the "community of truth," while 1QS 4:5–6 twice refers to the community as the "sons of truth." In the *War Scroll* 1QM 13:12 and 1QM 17:8 refer to the community as "the lot of Thy truth" and "His sons of truth," respectively.[200]

Also rooted in Qumran thought is the strong antithesis between love for the truth and hatred of liars. In 1QS 1:9, 10, the sectarians are to "love all the sons of light" and "hate all the sons of darkness." This antithesis is most clearly seen in 1QS 3:18–4:26, the section on the two spirits that God put in man: "they are the spirits of truth (*h'mt*) and perversity (*h'wl*) ... The one, God loves everlastingly and delights in all his deeds forever, but the counsel of the other He loathes, and He hates all his ways forever ... An abomination to truth are the deeds of perversity, and an abomination to perversity are all the ways of truth" (1QS 3:18–19, 3:25–4:1; 4:17).[201] In 1QS 5:10–11, those who enter the community are described as "they who volunteer together for His truth and to walk in His will," and they are to "undertake by the covenant to be separated from all perverse men who walk in the way of wickedness." And in 1QS 6:15, the volunteer is brought into the covenant "that he may be converted to the truth and turn away from all perversity." In the *Hodayot*, the writer exclaims, "I am full of zeal against all evil-doers and men of falsehood ... For Thou art righteous and all Thine elect are truth, and all perversity [and ungod]liness Thou wilt destroy forever" (1QH 14:14–16). And in the *Pesharim*, the enemy is called the "Man of the Lie" (*'yš hkzb* – 1QpHab 2:1–2; 5:11; 4QpPs$^a$ 1–10 i 26; 1–10 iv 14; see also 1QpHab 10:9; 4QpNah 3–4 ii 2, 8), while the righteous "rejoice in the inheritance of truth" (4QpPs$^a$ 1–10 iv 12; see also 4 QpPs$^a$ 1–10 iii 16). Further references to the love of truth and hatred of falsehood at Qumran are as follows: 1QS 1:15, 25–6; 6:24–5; 7:3–4; 8:1–2, 5–6; 9:16; 10:19–25; CD 3:13–15; 8:13 (= 19:25–6); 20:15; 1QM 4:6; 1QH 1:26–7; 2:31–2; 7:20; and 10:30–1. Josephus' statement concerning the Essene love of truth, with its strong antithesis between truth and falsehood, thus lies at the heart of Qumran thought as well.

*He will keep his hands pure of stealing* (§141). The next oath is a prohibition of theft (κλοπῆς) and unholy gain (ἀνοσίου κέρδους): the Essene is to keep his hands pure (καθαράν) from the former and his heart (ψυχήν, lit., "soul") from the latter. This oath is in harmony with Josephus' earlier assertion that "they despise riches, and their sharing of goods is admirable ... the possessions of each are mingled together, and there is, as among brothers, one property common to all" (*J. W.* 2 §122 – see discussion above, pp. 43–5).

Qumran literature contains numerous references to stealing and unjust gain. In the *Manual of Discipline*, 1QS 4:10 speaks of the spirit of perversity inciting "abominable deeds committed in the spirit of lust," while in 1QS 10:19 the writer promises that "my soul shall not covet the wealth of violence."[202] In the *Damascus Document*, those who enter the covenant are "to keep themselves from the unclean riches of iniquity (gotten) with a vow or anathema, or from the Temple treasure, or by stealing from the poor of His people" (CD 6:15–16). In CD 8:7 (= 19:19), God will judge those unfaithful sectarians who "acted arrogantly for the sake of riches and unjust gain (*bṣ'*)." And according to CD 9:10–12, the one who knows the thief but does not denounce him shall be guilty. In the *Hodayot*, the writer's language echoes that of Josephus: "[The s]oul of Thy servant has loathed [riches] and unjust gain (*bṣ'*)" (1QH 10:30; see also 1QH 10:22–3). And in the *Temple Scroll*, the royal guard must consist of "trustworthy men, fearing God, hating unjust gain (*śwn'y bṣ'*)" (11QTemple$^a$ 57:8–9). Finally, in the *Commentary on Habakkuk*, the Wicked Priest is depicted as one who abandoned God and "stole and heaped up the riches of violent men who rebel against God" (1QpHab 8:10–12; see also

1QpHab 12:10), while the last priests of Jerusalem are said to "heap up riches and unjust gain (*bṣ'*) by plundering the peoples" (1QpHab 9:5). Thus, throughout Qumran literature stealing and unjust gain are severely condemned.

*He will neither hide anything from the members of his sect nor disclose anything about them to others* (§141). The next oath Josephus mentions is one of openness to fellow sectarians, and secrecy concerning the sect to those outside, even if "tortured to death." This oath is a further enunciation of the close-knit and even exclusive nature of the sect, a fact stated earlier by Josephus (see *J. W.* 2 §119, p. 37), and especially brought out in connection with the common meal (see *J. W.* 2 §129, pp. 57–8). Though Philo mentions the close-knit nature of the Essenes, he does not stress the secrecy of the sect as does Josephus.

There is evidence in the rule books of Qumran for both the openness among members and the secretive nature of the group. In the *Manual of Discipline*, 1QS 8:11–12 states concerning those who have completed their initiation period and become full members, "Let nothing of that which was hidden from Israel, but found by the man who seeks, be hidden from them (the new members) out of fear of the spirit of apostasy." This text is very similar to the first part of the oath reported by Josephus (the sectarian will not "hide anything from the members of his sect"). Likewise, there are several places in the *Manual of Discipline* that stress the importance of secrecy concerning the group's teachings. According to 1QS 4:5–6, among the qualities that belong to the spirit of truth is "humble conduct with all prudence concealing for the sake of truth the secrets of knowledge (*yhb' l'mt rzy d't*)"[203] (see also 1QS 10:24–5: "I will conceal knowledge"). In the penal code, the one who "betrays the truth ... if he returns he shall be punished for two years" (1QS 7:18–19). Furthermore, no one who has been with the community more than ten years and "turns back to the point of betraying the community ... shall return again" (1QS 7:22–4). In addition, there are several exhortations to "be separated" from "perverse men" and study the Law (1QS 8:13–15; 9:19–21; see also CD 6:14–15; 13:14–15). And one passage in the *Damascus Document*, while not mentioning the disclosure of teachings to others, does state that a man who has made an oath "to practice some point of the Law, let him not violate it even at the price of death" (CD 16:7–9 – compare Josephus' phrase, "even if one be tortured to death"). Finally, 1QS 9:16–19, which contains precepts for an instructor of the group (*mśkyl*),[204] is very similar to the oath mentioned by Josephus, stressing both the teaching of sectarians, and hiding their teaching from others: "Let him not rebuke the men of the Pit or dispute with them; let him conceal the counsel of the Law from the midst of the men of perversity. And let him keep true knowledge and right justice for them that have chosen the way. He shall guide each man in knowledge ... and likewise he shall instruct them in the mysteries of wonder and truth."

*He will transmit their teachings ... as he received them* (§142). The next oath given by Josephus is similar to the last: the sectarian promises that "he will transmit (μεταδοῦναι) their teachings to no one in a way other than as he received them," i.e., he will transmit their teachings faithfully.[205] Again Josephus stresses the Essene quality of trustworthiness (see *J.W.* 2 §135, 140, 141, pp. 66–7, 80–3), this time with special reference to transmission of their teachings. In addition to the texts given in the previous paragraph (especially 1QS 9:16–19), several other passages may be mentioned. In *The Rule of the Congregation (for the End-Time)*, all the people are to be gathered together, and "they shall read into [their ears] all the precepts of the covenant and shall instruct them in all their ordinances lest they stray" (1QSa 1:4; see also 1QSa 1:6–7: "From [his] you[th he shall be in]structed in the Book of Meditation and shall be taught the precepts of the covenant"). And in the *Damascus Document*, the overseer of the camp "shall instruct the Many in the works of God and shall teach them His marvellous deeds and shall recount before them the happenings of former times" (CD 13:7–10). Faithful transmission of one's teachings is also stressed in the book of *Enoch* (*1 Enoch* 104:10–13), a work popular at Qumran.[206]

*He will refrain from brigandage* (§142). The next oath given by Josephus, though only three words (ἀφέξεσθαι δὲ λῃστείας, "to refrain from robbery, brigandage"), has engendered the most controversy among scholars concerning its meaning. Since an earlier oath stated that the Essene would not steal (2 §141), why would Josephus again mention robbery only a few lines later? The phrase is all the more noteworthy since it is surrounded by oaths concerning the faithful preservation of the sect's teachings. Scholars have proposed various other understandings of the phrase. Some think the Greek text itself is in error. For example, A. Dupont-Sommer states that the Greek text "should be corrected," and translates the phrase "abstaining from all alteration" − which makes sense in the context, but he gives no indication what Greek word he thinks should be in the text.[207] E. Kutsch regards the source of Josephus' expression as

1QS 8:16–17, which forbids anyone "who has turned aside (*ysyr*) from anything that is commanded, acting with a high hand (*byd rmh*)" from touching "the purity of the men of holiness." He thinks that Josephus misunderstood the Hebrew expression he had in front of him, taking *byd rmh* to mean robbery.[208] But even if Josephus did have some Hebrew document in front of him, it is highly unlikely that he would have misunderstood a Hebrew expression.[209] In addition, much of Josephus' knowledge of the Essenes seems to have been from first-hand contact with them, not from written documents.[210] J.D. Amoussine makes an interesting proposal that since the work was originally written in Hebrew or Aramaic, perhaps one of his collaborators who translated the work into Greek (see *Ag. Ap.* 1.9 §50) mistranslated the Hebrew word *hms* (a word that usually means "to treat violently," but may also have the nuance "to desecrate, alter" with respect to the Law [Ezek 22:26]).[211] Amoussine may be correct, but it seems best to try to treat the text as we have it, rather than assume that Josephus overlooked a collaborator's incorrect translation.

What, then, is the meaning of ληστείας? C. Daniel regards the word as a reference to the Zealots, and thus thinks the oath means not to associate with the Zealot movement.[212] But ληστεία means "robbery" or "brigandage," not "Zealot movement," as a check of the word's usage elsewhere in Josephus indicates.[213] O. Michel thinks the reference is to pillaging community goods, but this seems unlikely because of the injunction against stealing only a few lines earlier.[214] It is likely that Josephus means that the Essenes were to abstain from brigandage, i.e., looting raids against others (especially against the Romans), activities that other Jewish groups were involved in according to Josephus (*Ant.* 14.16, 2 §471–2; *J.W.* 1.18, 1 §347). Josephus himself, in fact, reports that he personally told the Galilean Jews to abstain from the practice of brigandage (ληστείας – *J.W.* 2.20, 7 §581). So it seems likely that it is this same practice of brigandage (and not simply thievery in general) that is forbidden in the Essene oath as well.[215]

There is no specific prohibition against brigandage in Qumran literature, but all the passages cited above (pp. 83–4) in reference to stealing are applicable here. In particular, 1QS 10:19 states that "my soul shall not covet the wealth of violence," and in 1QpHab 9:5, the last priests of Jerusalem are condemned for "plundering the peoples" (*mšll h'mym*; see also CD 6:15–16). In the *War Scroll*, particular officers (*šwlly hšll*) are entrusted with the duty of plundering

(1QM 7:2) and even God is exhorted to "do Your plundering" (1QM 12:11; 19:3), but the context in the *War Scroll* is the eschatological battle, not acts of piracy; thus, there is no conflict with Josephus here.

*He will preserve ... the books of their sect and the names of the angels* (§142). The final oath given by Josephus is that the sectarian will preserve (συντηρήσειν) "both the books of their sect and the names of the angels." This oath again stresses faithful transmission of the teachings of the sect (see *J. W.* 2 §142, above, p. 85), specifically mentioning the sect's books and the angels' names.

There may be specific references in the Qumran literature to their own writings. As mentioned above, the *spr hhgy* ("Book of Meditation") of CD 10.6 and 1QSa 1:7 may be a reference to the *Manual of Discipline* (see *J. W.* 2 §136, pp. 71–2) or to the "sectarian Torah" (Wacholder's name for 11QTemple[a]). The *War Scroll* also seems to speak of sectarian literature: in 1QM 15:4–5, the officials are to "read into their ears the prayer in time of wa[r and all the bo]ok of the rule of that time (*ṣrk 'tw*), with all the words of their hymns of thanksgiving (*hwdwtm*)." Y. Yadin considers the *ṣrk 'tw* to be the "sectarian source on which the author of the [War] scroll based himself," and the words of thanksgiving to be a part of this source.[216] A. Dupont-Sommer, however, thinks the *hwdwtm* ("hymns of thanksgiving") are the *Hodayot* found at Qumran.[217] In any event, if these texts contain references to the sectarian writings, they would provide further evidence of the sect's esteem for their own writings.

While no Qumran text specifically mentions the preservation of their books, if it were not for the sect's careful preservation of their writings, there would not have been any Dead Sea Scrolls in existence today, two thousand years after they were written. In many of the caves, the scrolls were placed in earthenware jars, and in Cave 1 the scrolls were wrapped in linen as well (Cave 4 is an exception to this, where the scrolls were densely piled up, apparently deposited there in a hurry).[218] Preservation of their books is thus clearly a characteristic of the Qumran community.

The last part of the oath, that the sectarian will preserve "the names of the angels," is strikingly illustrated by Qumran literature. In canonical OT writings, names of the angels only occur in the book of Daniel, and there only two names are given (Gabriel in Dan 8:16 and Michael in Dan 10:21); in addition, Raphael is mentioned throughout the deuterocanonical book of Tobit. But in the intertestamental literature, angelology is more developed. In several places in the book of *Enoch* (a work popular at Qumran) various names of the angels are given. In *1 Enoch* 6:3–8, the names of nineteen evil angelic leaders who took wives of men (an old interpretation of the "sons of God" in Gen 6:2) are specifically listed, as well as four good angelic leaders (Michael, Uriel, Raphael, and Gabriel) in *1 Enoch* 9:1. Later in *1 Enoch* 20:1–8, "the names of the holy angels who watch" are given (Uriel, Raphael, Raguel, Michael, Saraqael, Gabriel, and Remiel).[219]

Qumran literature itself is replete with references to angels. In the rule books and the *Hodayot*, mention is made of the "angel of darkness" (1QS 3:20–1), "angel of truth" (1QS 3:24), "angels of destruction" (1QS 4:12; CD 2:6), "angel of hostility" (CD 16:5), "holy angels" (1QSa 2:8–9); 1QH 1:11; CD 15:17, preserved in 4QD[b]),[220] "holy ones" (1QS 11:8), "sons of heaven" (1QS 11:8; 1QH 3:22), "host of the saints" (1QH 3:22; 10:35), "heavenly host" (1QH 3:35), and "angels of Thy presence" (1QH 6:13; 1QSb 4:25–6). According to 1QS 11:7–9, the sectarians are in some way to be united with the angels: "Those whom God has chosen he has given to be an eternal possession and has given them for their inheritance the lot of the holy ones. With the sons of heaven he has united their assembly to be a council of community ..." 1QSa 2:8–9 similarly indicates that "holy angels are in their [Congrega]tion" in the end-time, and for this reason no person with an impurity or blemish may enter the Congregation (1QSa 2:3–10; see also 4QD[b], 4QM[a]).

But it is in the *War Scroll* that Qumran angelology blossoms: as Y. Yadin observes, this scroll "considerably extends our knowledge of Jewish angelology in general and that of the scrolls sect in particular, as the scroll uses every opportunity to explain the activities of the different angels and their names."[221] The numerous designations of the angels used in the *War Scroll* are given by Yadin.[222] Several passages in the *War Scroll* are noteworthy because they depict the angels as fighting side by side with the community. 1QM 1:10–11 speaks of a day appointed by God "on which there shall engage in a great carnage the congregation of angels and the assembly of men, the sons of light and the lot of darkness, fighting each in communion through the might of God." 1QM 7:6 states that no impure man may join in battle, "for holy angels are in communion with their hosts." And 1QM 9:14–16 indicates that the names of the angels Michael, Gabriel, Sariel, and Raphael are written on the shields of the battle towers. Finally, 1QM 12:1–5 shows that the elect sectarians will be together with the angels in heaven, and that they are named, numbered, and organized just like the angels:

For a multitude of holy ones Thou hast in the heavens and hosts of angels in Thy holy habitation [to praise Thy name]. The elect ones of the holy nation Thou didst place for Thyself in [a community; and the enumer]ation of the names of all their host is with Thee in Thy holy abode, and the nu[mber of the ho]ly ones in the habitation of Thy glory. Mercy of blessing [for Thy thousands] and the covenant of peace Thou hast engraved for them with a stylus of life, so as to be king [over them] in all appointed times of eternity and to muster [the hosts of Thine el]ect by their thousands and their myriads together with Thy holy ones [and the host] of Thine angels, for strength of hand in battle.

One final sectarian work found at Qumran, 4QŠirŠabb (the *Angelic Liturgy*), should be mentioned, since it is devoted to angelic worship in heaven. The first fragment concerns the blessings given by the seven chief angels upon the godly both in heaven and on earth. For example, the blessing by the sixth chief angel is as follows: "The sixth of the chief princes will bless in the name of the mighty acts of the godly ones all the mighty ones in understanding with seven words of His wondrous mighty acts, and will bless all the perfect of conduct with seven words of wonder, so that they should be forever with all those who exist eternally" (4QŠirŠabb 1:21–2). A second fragment describes the chariot throne drawn by the Cherubim (see Ezek 1:4–28; 10:1–22; Rev 4:1–11). From these brief fragments, J. Strugnell has compiled "a catalogue of angelic titles" consisting of eighty-two titles or epithets used in the fragments.[223] Such a concatenation of terms for the angels further demonstrates that the Qumran community was indeed concerned with angelology in general, and "the names of the angels" in particular.

Thus, while the oaths listed by Josephus are not specifically mentioned as oaths in Qumran literature, many are set forth in 1QS 1:1–15. Furthermore, as the preceding discussion has shown, all the oaths are in harmony with Qumran thought.

## 7.  J.W. 2.8, 8 §143–4

*Those who are caught in serious offenses they expel from the order* (§143–4). Having treated the requirements for admission into the sect, Josephus next discusses the reverse situation, namely, expulsion from the order. Those who are caught (ἁλόντας, "caught, convicted") in a serious offense are expelled. Josephus does not specify what constitutes a "serious" (ἀξιοχρέοις) offense. But he does dramatically depict the severity of the punishment: since the expelled Essene was still bound by his oaths, he could not partake of any non-Essene prepared food, and hence he would eat only wild herbs until he eventually died. Many at the point of death, however, were received back into the order, thus demonstrating the compassion of the sect.

Josephus' expulsion account is paralleled by Qumran literature at several points. First, the *Manual of Discipline* does record several offenses that are so severe that the members are expelled from the order. In 1QS 7:1–2, the one who blasphemes while reading the book (i.e., the Law) or pronouncing the blessing shall be expelled (*hbdylhw*, lit., "they shall separate him"), "and he shall not return any more to the council of the community." Similarly, in 1QS 7:16–17 the one who slanders the Many "shall be sent away from them and shall not return" (*lšlḥ hw'h m'tm wlw' yšwb 'wd*). 1QS 7:22–5 states that one who betrays the community after ten or more years of membership shall not be permitted to come back, nor will one who mingles with such a person be permitted to remain in the community. And 1QS 8:21–3 indicates that whoever sins against the Mosaic Law "shall be expelled from the council of the community and shall not return." Hence, according to these passages there were at Qumran various "serious offenses" for which a member would be permanently expelled.

Second, with regard to Josephus' account of the sorry plight of the expelled one, it is true that those in the Qumran community were not to eat the food of any outside the sect. 1QS 5:15–16 states: "And let no member of the community answer their [i.e., those who are not counted in His covenant] questions concerning any law or ordinance; and let him neither eat nor drink anything of theirs." But one wonders if Josephus is not exaggerating to some degree at this point, since it would be normal for one expelled from the order to eat food from outsiders (disregarding his former oaths), since he himself was now an outsider as well.[224]

Finally, Josephus reports that many at the point of death (from lack of nourishment) are compassionately received back into the order. The *Manual of Discipline* does contain several references to this practice of readmittance. First, 1QS 7:22–4 states that no one betraying the community who has been a member for ten or more years may return to the community. This regulation implies that those who have been members for a shorter time (less than ten years) may be readmitted into the community if they repent of their actions. In addition, 1QS 8:24–9:2 indicates that the one who has sinned against the Mosaic Law inadvertently (*bšggh*) may be readmitted to the community in two years if his conduct is excellent in the interim. Thus, while some of Josephus' statements may be somewhat over-dramatized, the basic practices of expulsion and (under certain conditions) readmission into the community are found at Qumran.

## 8. J.W. 2.8, 9 §145–9

*In their judgments they are most scrupulous and just* (§145). Perhaps motivated to explain that this process of expulsion is not carelessly carried out, Josephus next turns to the subject of justice and obedience to the law (§145–9). He states that the Essenes are most scrupulous and just (ἀκριβέστατοι καὶ δίκαιοι) in their judicial decisions (κρίσεις), always having a court of at least one hundred members. Earlier in the oath section Josephus indicated the Essene concern for justice: the second oath is "that he will cherish justice towards human beings and will wrong no one, either by his own decision or by (another's) order" (*J.W.* 2 §139).

As discussed earlier in connection with the oath to cherish justice (*J.W.* 2 §139), the Qumran writings indicate a strong concern for justice and the proper judicial procedure. In addition to those passages cited above (*J.W.* 2 §139, pp. 79–80), a number of passages describe the judicial process at Qumran. Both 1QS 6:27 and CD 9:9–10 warn against a person who "metes out justice by his own hand" (alluding to 1 Sam 25:26), and 1QS 6:27 prescribes a one-year punishment for the offense. In fact, 1QS 6:1 mentions the necessity of reproof before witnesses as a part of the judicial process prior to taking the matter to court: "Let no cause be brought before the Many, by one man against another, unless reproof has been made before witnesses" (so also CD 9:2–3). And there is a long section in the *Damascus Document* that specifies the number of witnesses necessary for judgment of various offenses (CD 9:16–10:3).

The composition of the judicial court at Qumran is somewhat unclear. 1QS 8:1–4 states that there was a Community Council consisting of twelve men and three priests who were (among other duties) "to practice justice." The *Damascus Document*, however, indicates a judicial body of only ten men: "And this is the rule concerning the judges of the congregation. (Let them be) to the number of ten men, periodically chosen by the congregation: four for the tribe of Levi and Aaron, and for Israel six. They must be learned in the Book of Meditation and in the constitutions of the covenant, and aged from twenty-five to sixty years old" (CD 10:4–7). Furthermore, a fragment from Cave 4 lists a judicial body of twelve: "Te]n men and two priests, and they shall be judged before these twelve" (4QOrd 2–4 i 3–4). Finally, according to the *Manual of Discipline* (1QS 6:1, 8–23; 8:19–9:2) at least some of the judicial decisions are rendered by the "Many" (*hrbym*), or the "majority" (*rwb*), i.e., either the entire community or a large number of them. 1QS 6:8–13 gives "the rule for an assembly of the Many (*mwšb hrbym*)": the priests have the first position, then the elders, then all the rest of the people.[225] This "assembly of the Many" seems most similar to Josephus' count of "not less than a hundred members assembled."[226] Whether these various judicial bodies mentioned in Qumran literature (twelve men, three priests in 1QS; six Levites, four laymen in CD 10; ten men, two priests in 4QOrd; and the "assembly of the Many" in 1QS) existed at the same time, or (more likely) represent a developing judiciary system over a span of years (and perhaps places as well) is beyond the scope of this analysis.[227] If Josephus' one-hundred-member court is not an exaggeration then he is most likely describing something akin to the "assembly of the Many" at Qumran.

*They have the greatest reverence, after God, for the name of the lawgiver* (§145). Continuing along the lines of law and concern for justice, Josephus mentions the high regard the Essenes have for "the lawgiver"(τοῦ νομοθέτου): they hold him highest in esteem next to God, and blasphemy against him is punishable by death. Josephus mentions the lawgiver again in *J.W.* 2 §152, where the Romans try unsuccessfully to force the Essenes "to blaspheme the lawgiver or eat something forbidden."

Who is "the lawgiver" mentioned by Josephus? Dupont-Sommer regards the lawgiver as the Teacher of Righteousness at Qumran, and notes a similar prohibition among the Pythagoreans from pronouncing the name of Pythagoras.[228] Tempting as this suggestion is, it does not accord well with the evidence from Josephus.[229] The word νομοθέτης ("lawgiver") is used fifty-one times by Josephus in his writings, eleven times in the plural and forty times in the singular. In the forty singular usages, twice the reference is indefinite (*Ant.* 4.8, 47 §319: "Even if a human legislator is a formidable foe …"; *Ag. Ap.* 2.15 §153: "The virtue of a legislator is to have insight"). In the other thirty-eight passages, νομοθέτης refers to Moses in every instance. Sometimes the expression used is "our lawgiver" (ὁ ἡμέτερος νομοθέτης) or "their lawgiver" (ὁ νομοθέτης αὐτῶν), but the usual expression is simply "the lawgiver," as here in *J. W.* 2 §145, 152.[230] Philo uses the same term in introducing his discussion of the Essenes in *Hypothetica* 11.1: "Our lawgiver has trained multitudes of disciples for the life of fellowship, who are called Essenes." Since Philo uses the phrase ὁ ἡμέτερος νομοθέτης, "*our* lawgiver," he too is clearly referring to Moses.

Qumran literature does reveal that Moses (and especially the Law of Moses) was held in high regard by the community, though there is no mention of the death penalty for blasphemy against him. In the *Manual of Discipline*, the opening words instruct the saints to seek God with all their heart and soul and "do what is good and right before Him, as He commanded by the hand of Moses and all His servants the prophets" (1QS 1:1–3). 1QS 5:8 states that the one entering the community is to "undertake with a binding oath to return to the Law of Moses according to all His commands, with all his heart and his soul." In 1QS 8:15, the "way" of Isa 40:3 is interpreted as "the study of the Law which He has promulgated by the hand of Moses." And in 1QS 8:22, the one who "sins against the Law of Moses shall be expelled." The *Damascus Document* also states that adherence to the Law of Moses is necessary for community members: "He shall be examined with the oath of the covenant which Moses concluded with Israel, (namely), the covenant to return to the Law of Moses with all his heart [and all] his soul" (CD 15:8–9; see also CD 15:12–13; CD 16:2: "For this reason a man will undertake to return to the Law of Moses, for by it all things are carefully taught"). According to CD 5:21, Israel strayed because "they preached rebellion against the commandments of God (given) by the hand of Moses." Furthermore, numerous OT citations are introduced by various phrases linking them with Moses: "Moses said" (*mšh 'mr*, CD 5:8, 8:14), "The Lord spoke by the hand of Moses" (*byd mwšh*, 1QM 10:6; 1QH 17:12), and "The Lord spoke to Moses in these words" (4QTestim 1). There are even fragments of a work called the *Words of Moses* at Qumran, consisting of excerpts from the farewell discourses of Moses given in Deuteronomy (1QDM = 1Q22).

With regard to blasphemy against the lawgiver, two passages from Qumran may possibly be relevant. 1QS 6:27–7:2 states: "he who mentions any thing in the Name honored above all (*bšm hnkbd 'l kwl*) [shall be put to death]. But if he has blasphemed from fright or affliction or for any other reason while reading the book or pronouncing the blessings, he shall be excluded." Dupont-Sommer thinks the

"Name honored above all" refers to the name of the Teacher of Righteousness, but this seems highly unlikely, since the reference is almost certainly to God.[231] A second passage, however, may shed some light on Josephus' statement. CD 15:1–3 states that one may swear "neither by Aleph and Lamed [i.e., Elohim] nor by Aleph and Daled [i.e., Adonai], but with an oath of [...] by the curses of the covenant. Even the Law of Moses let him not mention, for [...,] and if he were to swear and then break his oath, he would profane the name." This text indicates that, in addition to the name of God, the Law of Moses was so highly regarded that it was forbidden to swear by it. This practice may be the one Josephus has in mind when he speaks of blasphemy against the lawgiver.

*They ... obey the elders and the majority* (§146). Josephus next states that the Essenes consider it good "to obey the elders (πρεσβυτέροις) and the majority (πλείοσιν)". He gives an example of such obedience: "if ten people are sitting together, one would not speak against the will of the nine." Philo also mentions that respect and care are given to the elders, although πρεσβυτέρων in Philo's context refers to elderly men, and not necessarily community leaders.

As was seen in connection with Josephus' earlier assertion that "they do nothing except by the order of their overseers" (*J.W.* 2 §134), obedience to authority is a major tenet in Qumran thought (see discussion above, pp. 64–5). But what is especially noteworthy in this passage is Josephus' mention of the elders and the majority as the authoritative bodies who are obeyed by the Essene members. In Qumran literature, the usual ranking is priests, Levites, and laity (see, for example, 1QS 2:19–23), but occasionally the elders (*zqnym*) are mentioned. In the *War Scroll*, those who bless the God of Israel and curse Belial are "the priests, the Levites, and all the elders of the army with him" (1QM 13:1).[232] Perhaps more significant is 1QS 6:8–9, which describes the seating for an assembly: "This is the rule for an assembly of the Many. Let each man sit according to his rank. Let the priests sit in the first place, and the elders in the second, and then the rest of all the people; let them sit according to their ranks." Here, the elders are mentioned instead of the Levites (as in 1QS 2:20).[233] Elders are also mentioned in CD 9:4, where a man who accuses someone without witnesses "to his elders in order to dishonor him is a man who takes revenge and bears malice." Here, the elders seem to function as judges (as in Exod 18:21). Probably the elders serve as the lay representatives alongside the priests (though subordinate to them) in the judicial body at Qumran (whether twelve elders, three priests [1QS 8:1–4]; four elders, six priests and Levites [CD 10:4–7]; or ten elders, two priests [4QOrd 2–4 i 3–4] – see *J. W.* 2 §145, pp. 91–2).[234] Josephus may in fact be using the term πρεσβυτέροις to refer to this Qumran judicial body as a whole, comprised of (mostly) elders and (a few) priests.[235]

The second authoritative group mentioned by Josephus is the "majority" (πλείοσιν), a term also found at Qumran (*rwb*) in a similar context of obedience. According to 1QS 5:2–3, those who join the community must "submit to the authority of the sons of Zadok, the priests who keep the covenant, and to the authority of the majority of the men of the community (*rwb 'nšy hyḥd*) who hold fast to the covenant." A similar statement is given in 1QS 5:9 where the expression "the majority of the men of their covenant" (*rwb 'nšy brytm*) is used (see also 1QS 5:22, "the majority of Israel"). Again, 1QS 6:19 states that the applicant may be advanced to the next stage according to "the decision of the priests and the majority of the men of their covenant (*rwb 'nšy brytm*)." This group also seems to be designated by the term *hrbym*, "the Many" (see *J. W.* 2 §145, p. 92). Thus, some decisions appear to have been made jointly by the judicial body (comprised of priests and elders) *and* a majority of the community members (all of whom are seated together in 1QS 6:8–9).

Josephus' example of obedience to the majority ("if ten are sitting together, one would not speak against the will of the nine") reveals the same kind of concern for orderliness in speaking as his earlier statement: "they yield to one another to speak in turn" (*J. W.* 2 §132 – for Qumran parallels, see discussion above, pp. 61–2). Josephus' choice of "ten" people may be significant, since ten seems to have constituted a basic unit at Qumran.[236] As in Exod 18:21, the community was divided into thousands, hundreds, fifties, and tens, according to 1QS 2:21–2. The *War Scroll* also refers to "the chiefs of its tens" (1QM 4:3–5). Particularly interesting is 1QS 6:3–4, which states that "in every place where there are ten persons of the council of the community, let them not lack among them a man who is a priest" (see also 1QS 6:6–7; cf. 1QS 9:7). CD 13:1–3 makes a similar statement: those who are in the camps are to be "in groups of at least ten men, by thousands and hundreds and fifties and tens. And when there are ten of them, let there not lack a man who is a priest learned in the Book of Meditation; they shall all obey his orders." Likewise, *The Rule of the Congregation (for the End-Time)* concludes the discussion of the meal by saying that "they shall proceed according to this rite at every mea[l where] at least ten persons [are as]sembled"

(1QSa 2:21–2). Hence, Josephus' mention of a group of ten may reflect the basic organizational unit at Qumran.

*They avoid spitting* (§147). As an illustration of the Essenes' high regard for obedience to the Law, Josephus mentions their carefulness in bodily functions (spitting, defecating) and their strict adherence to the Sabbath. First, he states that "they avoid spitting in the midst of the group or on the right side." Spitting on the right may have been done for good luck (since the right-hand side was associated with good fortune[237]). A. R. C. Leaney believes that the prohibition may be based on levitical purity (see Lev 15:8).[238] There is a similar prohibition against spitting in the Jerusalem Talmud, but it only concerns spitting during prayer-time (*y. Ber.* 3.5).

Amazingly, Qumran literature also contains a prohibition against spitting. 1QS 7:13 states that "the man who spits into the midst of the assembly of the Many shall be punished for thirty days." The wording is strikingly similar in Josephus and the *Manual of Discipline*, as both speak of spitting "into the midst" of a group (Josephus, πτύσαι εἰς μέσους; 1QS 7:13, *yrwq 'l twk*). It is interesting that the next section in the *Manual of Discipline* (1QS 7:13b–15) may well be describing regulations for relieving oneself, the same topic that Josephus takes up next.[239] The similarity in detail between Josephus and the Qumran sources on such a minor matter as spitting in the midst of a group provides strong evidence for the Essene identification of the Qumran community.[240]

*They are stricter than all Jews in not undertaking work on the seventh day* (§147). The Essenes are depicted by Josephus as strict observers of the Sabbath: "They are stricter than all Jews in not undertaking work on the seventh day, for not only do they prepare their meals on the day before, so as not to kindle a fire on that day, but they do not dare to move a vessel or even to relieve themselves." Philo also mentions the Essene regard for the Sabbath: "For that day has been set apart to be kept holy, and on it they abstain from all other work" and are instructed in their synagogues (*Every Good Man is Free* 12 §81).

Qumran literature also indicates a great deal of concern for the Sabbath. CD 3:14 lists God's "holy Sabbaths" as the first area in which "Israel of old had strayed." CD 6:18 likewise states that the sectarian must "observe the Sabbath according to its exact rules" (*kprwš*).[241] And CD 12:3–6 specifies that one who strays and violates the Sabbath is to be put out of the assembly for seven years, at which time readmission is possible.[242] But by far the longest

portion of Qumran literature dealing with the Sabbath is CD
10:14–11:18, a section containing a long list of activities prohibited
on the Sabbath. Similar laws on the Sabbath appear in *Jubilees*, a
book popular at Qumran (*Jub.* 2:17–31; 50:6–13).[243] The laws in
CD 10:14–11:18 as a whole are quite severe, some even more strict
than the rabbinic law. For example, CD 10:21 states that no man is
to walk "further than a thousand cubits outside his town" on the
Sabbath. This distance comes from Num 35:4, whereas the Rabbis
took their more lenient distance of two thousand cubits from Num
35:5 (*m. Soṭa* 5:3).[244] Several laws in CD 10:14–11:18 are particularly close to Josephus' statements regarding the Sabbath. Corresponding to Josephus' remark that "they prepare their meals on the
day before, so as not to kindle a fire on that day" is CD 10:22: "Let
only that be eaten on the Sabbath day which has been prepared (on
the previous day)." Though there is no mention in CD of kindling
a fire as the reason for preparing the food ahead, the rest is quite
similar in Josephus and CD.[245] And similar to Josephus' assertion
that "they do not dare to move a vessel or even to relieve themselves"
are the commands to "let nothing be carried from the house to the
outside, or from outside to the house. Even if a man is in a hut (*swkh*),
let nothing be taken out of it and nothing be taken in" (CD 11:7–
9).[246] The prohibition in Josephus regarding defecation on the
Sabbath is not recorded in Qumran literature. Relieving oneself is
apparently prohibited because one would need to dig the required pit,
and thus perform work on the Sabbath.[247]

*On the other days they dig a pit* ... (§148–9). Josephus next
explains the elaborate care taken by the Essenes in defecating on days
other than the Sabbath: they dig a pit in an isolated place with the
hatchet given to them when they were initiates; they make sure they
are completely covered "so as not to insult the rays of the Deity";
and finally, after relieving themselves they push the soil back and wash
themselves "as if they were unclean."

Such a detailed description of the defecatory process is not found
at Qumran. Yet, much of what Josephus states is in fact already
contained in Deut 23:13–15,[248] and since the community was "to
return to the Law of Moses according to all His commands, with all
his heart and his soul" (1QS 5:8 – see *J.W.* 2 §145, pp. 92–4),
presumably these commandments were followed at Qumran. In
addition, there are several specific indications of such a practice.
Josephus calls the tool that is used to dig the pit both a "hoe"
(σκαλίς) and a "small hatchet" (ἀξινίδιον here, but ἀξινάριον in

2 §137 – both words are diminuitives of ἀξίνη). In Cave 11 of Qumran, a small hatchet-pick combination tool was found. De Vaux reports that this tool could be used for cutting wood (using the hatchet side) and digging up the ground (using the curved side), and it was light enough to be used with one hand. His conclusion is that Josephus' hatchet-hoe "correspond exactement à la hachette-piochette de la grotte 11."[249]

With regard to the necessity of being covered completely during the excretory process, a rule in the *Manual of Discipline* may refer to a similar situation. 1QS 7:13–14 states that "whoever allows his hand (*ydw*) to protrude from beneath his garment, if this garment is in rags and reveals his nakedness he shall be punished for thirty days." Some commentators take the use of *yd* ("hand") here literally – for instance, both Wernberg-Møller and L. Silberman consider the regulation to be a matter of good table etiquette, i.e., not reaching out for one's food.[250] But since (as Silberman recognizes) the following phrase ("if this garment is in rags and reveals his nakedness") relates so closely to the first, it seems more likely that *yd* is used euphemistically for penis (as in Isa 57:8).[251] If this interpretation is correct, then 1QS 7:13–14 necessitates that the body not be exposed during the excretory process. There is nothing in this passage or elsewhere in Qumran literature that parallels Josephus' reason for being covered, namely, "so as not to insult the rays (αὐγάς) of the Deity." As in *J.W.* 2 §128, it is unlikely that Josephus is representing the Essenes as sun-worshippers (see above, pp. 52–4); rather, αὐγάς is used by Josephus to connote to his readers the radiance, glory, and holiness of God.[252]

Finally, Josephus mentions that for the elaborate defecatory process "they choose the more isolated places" (*J.W.* 2 §149). Two passages from Qumran literature indicate that this may have been the practice at Qumran as well. In the *War Scroll*, 1QM 7:6–7 states that "there shall be a space between all their camps and the place of the 'hand' (*mqwm hyd*), about two thousand cubits, and no unseemly evil thing shall be seen in the vicinity of their encampments." This rule, taken from Deut 23:13–15, establishes a distance of two thousand cubits between the camps and the place of the "hand," i.e., the place for relieving themselves. The Deuteronomy text does not indicate a distance. A similar reworking of Deut 23:13–15 occurs in the *Temple Scroll*: "You will lay out for them a place of the 'hand' outside the city. There they will go, outside to the northwest of the city. You will make latrines there, small structures with pits in the middle into which the excrement will fall. It will not be visible to anyone, since it will be distant from the city by three thousand cubits" (11QTemple[a] 46:13–16). These passages provide striking parallels to Josephus' account of Essene customs on what would appear to be a relatively minor point.[253]

## 9. J.W. 2.8, 10 §150–3

*They are divided … into four groups* (§150). Josephus continues his discussion by noting the discipline of the Essenes. He mentions that they are divided into four groups "according to the duration of their training" (ἀσκήσεως), and that a senior member must wash ceremonially if he comes in contact with a junior. Since Josephus does not name the four groups, various explanations have been proposed. Michel and Bauernfeind believe that the four groups are the priests, Levites, laity, and novices (in harmony with CD 14:3–4: "Let them all be counted by name: the priests first, and the Levites second, and the sons of Israel third, and the proselytes fourth").[254] Yadin seems to take the four classes as age groups (and relates them to the division of warriors according to age in 1QM 6:12–13; 7:1–3: 25–30; 30–45; 40–50; and 50–60).[255] Philo's statement that the Essenes sit in the synagogues "arranged in rows according to their ages, the younger below the elder" (*Every Good Man is Free* 12 §81) also seems to refer to a ranking by age. R. H. Pfeiffer and A. Pelletier, on the other hand, regard the four classes as children, first-stage novices, second-stage novices, and full members.[256] Finally, Lightfoot, Thackeray, and many others regard the four classes as the first-year novices, second-year novices, third-year novices, and full members.[257]

   That the Qumran community was also excessively concerned with "rank" and hierarchy is evident from the numerous groupings mentioned in the scrolls. For example, 1QS 2:19–23 states that each year "the priests shall pass first, in order," then the Levites, "and thirdly, all the people shall pass in order, one after another, by thousands and hundreds and fifties and tens, that every man of Israel may know the place he must occupy in the Community of God, that of the eternal Counsel. And no man shall go down from the place he must occupy, or raise himself above the place to which his lot assigns him." Similarly, 1QS 6:8–9 affirms: "Let each man sit according to his rank. Let the priests sit in the first (place), and the elders in the second, and then the rest of all the people; let them sit according to their ranks." Other "rankings" are given in 1QSa 1:8

(twenty years old, twenty-five, thirty; chiefs of thousands, hundreds, fifties, tens, judges, and officers); 2:11–21 (priest, chiefs of sons of Aaron, Messiah of Israel, chiefs of tribes of Israel, heads of families, wise men of the congregation – "each according to his rank" (*'yš lpy kbwdw*); CD 14:3–6 (priests, Levites, sons of Israel, proselytes); 1QM 2:1–9 (chief priest, chiefs of the priests, courses, Levites, tribes, heads of families) and throughout 1QM; 1QH 12:23; and 11QTemple[a] 21:4–7 (priests, Levites, [...,] all the people from greatest to least).

In view of the multiplicity of ways the sect is categorized in Qumran literature, it does not seem possible to relate Josephus' four groups to any particular ranking with certainty. Michel and Bauernfeind's thesis that the group consists of novices (as mentioned in CD 14:3–4) is interesting, but unlikely, since Josephus specifically states that the division is "according to the time of their training." This phrase makes the final alternative, namely, the first-, second-, and third-year novices, and full members, the most likely division Josephus has in mind. The strictness of contact between seniors and juniors noted by Josephus thus may be a reference to the specific regulations concerning purification, food, and drink at the various stages of initiation into the community (1QS 6:13–23 – see further *J. W.* 2 §137–8, pp. 73–5 above). In any event, concern for rank is abundantly illustrated at Qumran.

*They are long-lived* (§151). Josephus finds evidence of the success of the Essene lifestyle in the fact that "most of them remain alive over a hundred years." This longevity he attributes to the "simplicity (ἁπλότητα) and discipline (εὐταξίαν) of their way of life." Philo also comments on the good health and longevity of the Essenes: the old men "regularly close their life with an exceedingly prosperous and comfortable old age" (*Hypothetica* 11.13). In a different context, Philo stresses the simple, frugal living of the Essenes (they are "lovers of frugality who shun expensive luxury as a disease of both body and soul," *Hypothetica* 11.11) and their disciplined order (*Hypothetica* 11.6–9).

There is a passage in the *Manual of Discipline* that promises a long life for those who live righteously: those who walk in the spirit of truth will be visited with "healing and abundance of peace, with length of days (*b'wrk ymym*) and fruitfulness" (1QS 4:6–7). This concept of longevity as a blessing for obedience is rooted in the OT. For example, in Deut 4:40 there is an exhortation to keep God's commandments "that it may go well with you, and with your children after you, and that you may prolong your days (*ta'ărîk yāmîm*) in the land which the Lord your God gives you forever" (see also Exod 23:26; Deut 6:2; Job 5:26; and Ps 55:23).

While no passage in Qumran literature specifically lists simplicity and discipline as reasons for longevity in the same way as Josephus, these characteristics seem to accord well with one who walks in the spirit of truth (see 1QS 4:2–6). Both qualities are characteristic of the Qumran community. The first term Josephus uses, ἁπλότητα, may be taken in two ways: "simplicity," i.e., plainness or frugality, or "singleness," i.e., a steadfast purpose (see Eph 6:5; Col 3:22). The simple, frugal lifestyle of the Qumran community has been noted previously (see *J. W.* 2 §122, 126, pp. 43–5, 50–1), and needs no further comment. With regard to "singleness," i.e., an undistracted purpose, the first section of the *Manual of Discipline* makes it clear that the sectarians "shall not depart from His precepts of truth to walk either to right or to left" (1QS 1:15).

The second Essene characteristic mentioned by Josephus, εὐταξίαν, is also an integral part of the Qumran community. The word is made up of two parts (εὖ, "good," and τάξις, "order"), and thus may be translated "good order," "discipline," or "regularity." The concern that everything be done in a well-ordered way at Qumran has already been mentioned (see *J. W.* 2 §150, pp. 99–100). But it should also be pointed out that *serek*, the Hebrew word corresponding to Greek τάξις, is an important word in Qumran literature, occurring thirty-four times. Sometimes (especially in the *War Scroll*) the word refers to a military order or division, but in other cases it is used to denote the entire community ("all the elders of the army" [*srk*], 1QM 13:1), or the orderly precepts of the community (as in 1QS 1:16 ["all who decide to enter into the rule of the community"]; 1QS 5:1 ["this is the rule for the members of the community"]; 1QS 6:8; and 1QS 1:1). Hence, both the *War Scroll* and the *Manual of Discipline* reveal the fundamental importance of regulated order and discipline at Qumran.[258]

*They are fearless of danger* (§151). Josephus continues to emphasize the discipline of the Essenes by stressing their endurance over danger, pain, and persecution. Not only are they fearless of danger, but they actually prefer a glorious death to immortality (ἀθανασίας).[259] Philo contains no such statements in his description of the Essenes, but he does indicate that the Jews as a whole had a similar attitude towards death: "One nation only standing apart, the nation of the Jews, was suspected of intending opposition, since it was accustomed to accept death as willingly as if it were immortality (ἀθανασίαν), to save it from submitting to the destruction of any of its ancestral traditions, even the smallest" (*The Embassy to Gaius* 16 §117).

Qumran literature contains numerous references to fearlessness in the face of trials. The first section of the *Manual of Discipline* states that all who decide to enter the community must undertake "to act according to all His commands and not to turn back from Him on account of any fear, or fright, or trial (*mṣrp*[260]) during the dominion of Belial" (1QS 1:16–17). In fact, 1QS 7:1 states that the one who blasphemes "from fright or under the blow of distress" is to be separated from the Council of the Community. 1QS 8:4 specifically mentions among the duties of the Council of the Community that they are "to endure the trial of affliction" (*ṣrt mṣrp*), thus indicating that suffering was an expected part of the life of the righteous at Qumran. In the *Hodayot*, the psalmist writes that "Thou [God] hast delivered my soul from the hand of the mighty, and in the midst of their mockery Thou hast not made me afraid, lest I should forsake Thy service for fear of the cruelties of the wi[ck]ed" (1QH 2:35–6; see also 1QS 10:15–17). Finally, in the *War Scroll* there are numerous exhortations not to be afraid in the battle against Belial and the sons of darkness. For example, in 1QM 17:4–9 the righteous are exhorted to "be ye strong and fear them not ... be ye strong in God's crucible (*bmṣrp 'l*), until He shall lift up His hand and shall complete His testings (*mṣrpyw*)." Similar exhortations are given in 1QM 10:2–8 and 15:6–15. Fearlessness in the face of danger, then, is a highly esteemed concept at Qumran.

*The war with the Romans tested their souls* (§152–3). Josephus next provides an example of the fearlessness of the Essenes under testing, namely, the war with the Romans. Although tormented in every way, Josephus reports, they refused to "blaspheme the lawgiver or eat something forbidden." In fact, they did not even shed a tear, but "gave up their souls cheerfully." Philo mentions nothing about Essene resistance to the Romans, but instead implies that they are pacifists (they refuse to be involved in "any industry concerned with war" – *Every Good Man is Free* 12 §78). Josephus, however, clearly depicts the Essenes as involved in the war, both here and in *J. W.* 2.20, 4 §567 and 3.2, 1–2 §9–12, where John the Essene is mentioned. According to Josephus, John was appointed general of the Jews for northwest Judaea (from Thamna to the Mediterranean) early in the First Revolt, but was killed in an abortive attempt to take Ascalon in A.D. 67. It seems clear from the account of John's exploits that by "the war with the Romans" Josephus is referring to the

First Revolt of A.D. 66–70, i.e., the primary subject of his *Jewish War*.[261]

If the identity of the Qumran community as Essene is correct, then it is probable that Josephus' statement regarding Essene bravery during "the war with the Romans" should be connected with the destruction of Qumran by the Romans in A.D. 68. According to Josephus, in June of A.D. 68, Vespasian took control of Jericho and the Dead Sea region (*J. W.* 4.8, 1–4.9, 2 §440–502). Though the military action against Qumran is not specifically mentioned by Josephus (or any persecution of the community), he states that he is not narrating these events in detail (*J. W.* 4.9, 2 §496),[262] and thus he (or his source) passes over the comparatively insignificant overthrow of Qumran.[263] Further evidence that the destruction of Qumran occurred in A.D. 68 is provided by the coins found at Qumran. De Vaux reports that the latest Jewish coins (found in the level of the destruction) were put into circulation in March, A.D. 68, while the earliest Roman coins (found in the level of the reconstruction) are dated A.D. 67/68.[264] Hence, he concludes that "the year 68, at which the two numismatic sequences meet, marks the destruction of the lower level and the initiation of the higher one."[265]

Evidence from the scrolls also points to the antagonism between the sectarians and the Romans. Numerous passages in the *Pesharim* and the *War Scroll* refer to the Kittim (spelled *ktyym* or *kty'ym*) as a strong, greatly feared military power.[266] The word was first used to describe the inhabitants of Kition in Cyprus, then the inhabitants of the eastern Mediterranean islands, later "all islands and most of the peoples living beyond the sea" (Josephus, *Ant.* 1.6, 1 §128), and finally the greatest world power of the day. Thus, in 1 Macc 1:1 and 8:5 they are Greeks, while in Dan 11:30 they are Romans (the LXX-Daniel even uses the term 'Ρωμαῖοι rather than Κίτιοι in Dan 11:30). In Qumran literature, the Kittim also refer to the Romans. This seems certain from 1QpHab 6:3–5, which indicates that the Kittim "sacrifice to their standards and worship their weapons of war" (as was characteristic of the Roman armies – see Josephus, *J. W.* 6.6, 1 §316), and from 4QpNah 3–4 i 3, which states that the "rulers of the Kittim" arise after "the kings of Greece."[267] The Kittim in the *Pesharim* are described as merciless conquerors, "fear and dread of whom are upon all the nations. By design all their plans are to do evil, and with cunning and deceit they associate with all the peoples" (1QpHab 2:4–6). Similarly, 1QpHab 6:10–12 states that the Kittim "destroy many with the sword – young men, strong men and old men, women and toddlers — and on the fruit of the womb they have no compassion.''[268] But it is in the *War Scroll* that the Kittim are clearly depicted as arch-enemies of the sect, against whom the end-time war must be fought. The opening lines of the *War Scroll* associate the Kittim with the sons of darkness: "The first engagement of the sons of light shall be to attack the lot of the sons of darkness, the army of Belial, the troop of Edom and Moab and the sons of Ammon and the army [of the dwellers of] Philistia and the troops of the Kittim of Asshur, and in league with them the offenders against the covenant" (1QM 1:1–2). Later in the first column of the *War Scroll*, the defeat of the Kittim is described: "And on the day when the Kittim fall (there shall be) battle and rude slaughter before the God of Israel; for this is the day appointed by Him from former times for the war of destruction of the sons of darkness" (1QM 1:9–10; see also 1QM 1:6–7). The fierceness of the battle between them is then described (1QM 1:11–14), and it is in this context (1QM 15:1–3) that the priest exhorts the people: "Be strong! Be hardy! Show yourselves men of valor! Fear not, nor be dismayed ... for they are a wicked congregation and all their works are in darkness ... Gather your strength for the battle of God, for this day is an appointed time of battle" (1QM 15:7–12; see also 1QM 10:2–8; 17:4–9). Such an attitude of hatred and fearlessness towards the Kittim/Romans revealed in the *War Scroll* may well have had an opportunity to be displayed in "the war with the Romans" in A.D. 68 mentioned by Josephus.[269]

There is no specific confirmation in Qumran literature of Josephus' statement that the Romans tried to force the Essenes to "blaspheme the lawgiver or eat something forbidden." For the concept of blasphemy against the lawgiver, see *J. W.* 2 §145 (pp. 92–4). There are a number of passages in Qumran literature that refer to dietary laws. In particular, 1QS 5:15–16 states that a member of the community may not "eat or drink anything of theirs," i.e., anything of those who are not members of the community. Furthermore, CD 3:6 specifically mentions that the Israelites disobeyed God in the wilderness because "they ate blood." And in CD 6:17, one of the obligations of the members of the covenant is "to distinguish between the unclean and the clean." Finally, CD 12:11–15 and 11QTemple[a] 48:1–7 give various dietary regulations. Thus, to "eat something forbidden" was regarded quite seriously at Qumran.

## 10.  J.W. 2.8, 11 §154−8

*Bodies are corruptible ... but ... souls are immortal* (§154−8).
Josephus explains that the fearlessness of the Essenes in the face of
death stems from their belief in the immortality of the soul. In an
extended section, he sets forth the Essene doctrine of the soul.
He states that while bodies are corruptible, souls are immortal.[270]
These souls apparently exist prior to the body ("emanating from the
finest ether"), then are imprisoned in the body, and finally are set
free (upon the death of the body) "and are carried aloft." Good souls
go to a refreshing place "beyond the ocean," while evil souls are
assigned to "a gloomy and tempestuous recess, filled with incessant
punishments." This belief, Josephus twice states, is similar to that
of the Greeks. He attributes to the Greeks a practical motive for the
doctrine, namely, that it encourages the good to be better (because
of the hope of a reward after death) and deters the wicked (for fear
of punishment in the afterlife). Josephus concludes that the Essene
teachings on the soul are "inescapable bait" for those who are
acquainted with their wisdom.

It should be recognized at the outset that Josephus' description
of the Essene view of immortality is highly colored by Greek thought.
As mentioned earlier, Josephus' desire to depict the Jews in a
favorable manner to his Gentile readers sometimes results in an
adaptation of his material to Greek ways of thinking.[271] And in this
discussion of immortality, he even explicitly mentions twice that the
Essene doctrine is similar to the Greeks'. Thus, he is especially
concerned with maximizing the similarities and minimizing the
differences between the Essene and Greek views. In fact, Josephus
treats the Pharisees' doctrine of resurrection in much the same way.
Josephus emphasizes the Pharisees' view of the immortality of the
soul (a doctrine similar to the Greeks'), but does not explicitly mention
their concept of bodily resurrection. Thus, in *Ant.* 18.1, 3 §14,
Josephus states that "they believe that souls have power to survive
death and that there are rewards and punishments under the earth
for those who have led lives of virtue or vice: eternal imprisonment
is the lot of evil souls, while the good souls receive an easy passage
to a new life." No mention at all is made of their belief in a bodily
resurrection. Similarly, Josephus writes in *J. W.* 2.8, 14 §163 that the
Pharisees believe that "every soul is imperishable, but the soul of the
good alone passes into another body, while the souls of the wicked
suffer eternal punishment." Again, rather than bodily resurrection,

Josephus appears to be saying that the Pharisees believe in the Greek doctrine of the reincarnation of the soul.

Even the language Josephus uses in his description of the Essene view of immortality demonstrates the Greek flavor of the section. The "dwelling beyond the ocean" for the good souls, "even a place unoppressed by rain or snow or blazing heat, but cooled by the mild west wind ever blowing from the ocean," which Josephus ascribes to the Essene view, actually owes its origin to Hesiod and Homer. Hesiod's *Works and Days* states that "they live untouched by sorrow in the islands of the blessed along the shore of deep swirling Ocean, happy heroes ..." (170–2). Similarly, in Homer's *Odyssey*, the old man of the sea speaks these words:

> But for yourself, Menelaus, fostered of Zeus, it is not ordained that thou shouldst die and meet thy fate in horse-pasturing Argos, but to the Elysian plain and the bounds of the earth will the immortals convey thee, where dwells fair-haired Rhadamanthus, and where life is easiest for men. No snow is there, or heavy storm, or even rain, but ever does Ocean send up blasts of the shrill-blowing West Wind that they may give cooling to men.                    (4:561–8)

Thus, Josephus' account is here garbed in Greek language and thought.

With respect to Qumran thought regarding immortality, not surprisingly there is no mention in Qumran literature of the pre-existence of the soul or a rigid dichotomy of body and soul, with the body a mere corrupt "prison-house" for the soul. There are, however, a number of passages that refer to "everlasting life," and a few that may speak of resurrection. In the *Manual of Discipline*, 1QS 4:6–8 states that those who walk according to the spirit of truth will receive "healing and abundance of peace, with length of days and fruitfulness, and all blessings without end, and eternal joy in everlasting life (*wśmḥt 'wlmym bḥyy nṣḥ*), and the glorious crown and garment of honor in everlasting light." The first blessings refer to this life, but the later ones (eternal joy, etc.) seem to point to a future eternal existence (see also 4:12–14 [the fate of the wicked]; 4:22–6). In the *Collection of Blessings*, the priests are promised that they will be "in the company of God" and the angels "for everlasting time and for all ages forever" (1QSb 4:24–6). Similarly, the *Damascus Document* states that those who cling to God's commandments are destined "for eternal life" (*lḥyy nṣḥ*) (CD 3:20), and the righteous "will live for a thousand generations" (CD 7:6).

Several Qumran passages may speak of resurrection. In the *War Scroll*, it appears as if the elect ones are now in heaven fighting against Belial alongside the angels (1QM 12:1–4), thus implying resurrection.[272] In the *Hodayot*, the psalmist exclaims:

> I thank Thee, O Lord, for Thou hast released my soul from the grave, and from the abyss of Sheol. Thou hast raised me up to an eternal height, so that I can wander in the plain without limit, and so that I know that there is hope for him whom Thou hast formed out of dust unto an eternal fellowship. And the perverted spirit Thou hast cleansed from the great transgression to stand in the assembly with the host of the saints, and to come into communion with the congregation of the sons of heaven.          (1QH 3:19–22)

The psalmist may simply be using eschatological language to describe his blissful state in the community,[273] but the reference may be to an actual resurrection of the soul and an eternal state.[274] 1QH 6:34 may also speak of resurrection: "they that lie in the dust (*škb 'pr*) raise the banner and the worms of the dead raise the standard." Since in the OT *škb 'pr* only means "to be dead" (Job 7:21; 20:11; 21:26), the use of this phrase in the *Hodayot* may point to resurrection from the dead (see also 1QH 11:12: "to raise from the dust of the worms of the dead to an everlasting fellowship").[275] In the light of these passages, the Qumran community may have believed in some sort of a resurrection, but the evidence from Qumran literature is far from clear.[276]

It should also be recognized that while the doctrine of the immortality of the soul (but not of the body) that Josephus ascribes to the Essenes is not clearly evident in Qumran literature, this doctrine does occur in other intertestamental literature, most notably in some works (such as *Jubilees* and *Enoch*) popular at Qumran. It is true that the resurrection of the body was held by the Pharisees,[277] and is evident in such texts as Dan 12:2; 2 Macc 7:9–23, 36; and probably *1 Enoch* 51:1 and 61:5 as well (in the *Parables* section). But numerous intertestamental texts seem to speak only of the immortality of the soul or spirit. *Jub.* 23:31 states concerning the righteous that "their bones shall rest in the earth, and their spirits shall have much joy." One section in the *Testaments of the Twelve Patriarchs* states that the unrighteous soul is "tormented by the evil spirit" after death, but the righteous soul is led by the angel of peace" into eternal life" (*T. Asher* 6:4–6; see also *T. Judah* 25:4 and *T. Benj.* 10:6–8).[278] The

Wisdom of Solomon similarly speaks of the punishment of the unrighteous and the immortality of the souls of the righteous: "For God created man for incorruption ... but through the devil's envy death entered the world, and those who belong to his party experience it. But the souls of the righteous are in the hand of God, and no torment will ever touch them ... their hope is full of immortality" (Wis 2:23−3:4 − the entire section from 2:23−5:23 deals with this subject; see also 4 Macc, which eliminates the reference to bodily resurrection in 2 Macc 7 and stresses the immortality of the soul [4 Macc 18:23]). Wis 9:15 even speaks of "a perishable body" that "weighs down the soul." These texts from the Wisdom of Solomon seem close to Josephus' description of the Essenes, in that the first seems to refer to the original immortality of the soul (see also *1 Enoch* 69:11), while the second talks about the body as a burden to the soul in much the same way as Josephus. And as P. Grelot has observed, there are numerous passages in *1 Enoch* (outside the *Parables* section − see p. 10 above) that seem to speak of the immortality of the soul or spirit. In *1 Enoch* 9:3, "the souls of [dead − see 8:4] men make their suit" to God, while in 10:15 the Lord commands that "all the spirits of the reprobate" be destroyed. In 22:3, Enoch visits the "spirits of the souls of the dead" in Sheol, where both the spirits of the righteous (22:9) and the sinners (22:13) are awaiting the day of judgment. And *1 Enoch* 103:1−104:13 indicates that "the spirits of you who have died in righteousness shall live and rejoice" (103:4), but as for the sinners, "their souls will be made to descend into Sheol and they shall be wretched in their great tribulation" (103:7−8).[279]

Hence, Josephus' description of the Essene doctrine of immortality, while clearly altered in many respects to conform to the Greek views of the soul, may properly reflect certain Essene tenets: namely, the immortality of the soul, but not the resurrection of the body (perhaps reflecting their general tendency to look down upon the body). Even though these views do not show up clearly in Qumran literature, their abundant attestation elsewhere in intertestamental literature (especially in *Jubilees* and *1 Enoch*, two works of great importance to the community), combined with the testimony of Josephus, make it probable that these views form a part of the thinking of the Qumran sect.

### 11. J.W. 2.8, 12 §159

*Some among them ... profess to foreknow the future* (§159). Following his discussion of the Essene view of future life, Josephus next discusses the Essene ability to foresee the future. He says that some, not all, of the Essenes have this ability, and that it comes from "being educated in holy books and various rites of purification (διαφόροις ἁγνείαις) and sayings of prophets." Furthermore, he notes that "rarely, if ever, do they err in their predictions."

Elsewhere in *Jewish War* and *Antiquities* Josephus cites three examples of Essene prophecy at work. In *J.W.* 1.3, 5 §78–80 (and the parallel passage in *Ant.* 13.11, 2 §311–13) Josephus relates how an Essene named Judas, who never erred in his predictions, was distraught because his prediction that Antigonus would be killed at Strato's Tower seemed to be incorrect. Later, however, it was discovered that there had been some confusion about the location of Strato's Tower, and the prophecy proved to be correct after all. The parallel passage in *Ant.* 13.11, 2 §311–13 also notes that Judas was accompanied by friends who were learning how to prophesy from him.[280] In *J.W.* 2.7, 3 §111–13 (and *Ant.* 17.13, 3 §346–8), Josephus mentions how another Essene named Simon interpreted Archelaus' dream correctly, a dream that the other interpreters could not properly interpret. As R.T. Beckwith notes, both the dream (nine full ears of corn being eaten by oxen) and its interpretation (ears of grain are years of reign) closely parallel the dreams interpreted by Joseph in Genesis 40–1.[281] The third example of Essene prediction given by Josephus is that of Menahem in *Ant.* 15.10, 4–5 §371–9, who made several accurate predictions concerning Herod: (1) when Herod was still young, that he would be king of the Jews; and (2) at the height of Herod's reign, that he would reign for twenty or thirty more years.[282] Josephus mentions that it is because of the virtue (καλοκαγαθία) of Menahem in particular and the Essenes in general that they have been "thought worthy of this acquaintance with divine things."

As mentioned above, Josephus' description of the training of the Essene "prophets" includes three elements: "holy books," "various rites of purification" (διαφόροις ἁγνείαις), and "sayings of prophets." This unusual combination has prompted Dupont-Sommer to emend διαφόροις ἁγνείαις to διαφόροις ἁγίαις, "sacred books," taking διαφόροις in the sense of "writings."[283] However, this suggestion is problematic and unnecessary. First, διαφόροις is used sixty-two times in Josephus and usually means "different" or "various," never "writings." Second, as Vermes notes, purification and asceticism often form a part of the late Jewish concept of prophecy.[284] And more significantly, Josephus shows that the priestly element is an important part of his own thinking on the subject, as he records a dream that he had (and interpreted) in *J. W.* 3.8, 3 §351–2. He states that "he [Josephus] was an interpreter of dreams and skilled in divining the meaning of ambiguous utterances of the Deity; a priest himself and of priestly descent, he was not ignorant of the prophecies in the sacred books" (see also Josephus' dream in *Life* 42 §208). Hence, the text in *J. W.* 2 §159 should be left as it stands.

There is abundant evidence at Qumran concerning the importance of the OT prophets in the sect's thinking and of prophetic reinterpretations of numerous OT passages. The *Manual of Discipline* opens with a statement that expresses the importance of the prophets: the sectarians are to seek God and do what is right "as He commanded by the hand of Moses and all His servants the Prophets" (1QS 1:2–3; see also the similar statement in 8:14–15). A phrase in 1QS 9:11 mentions the "coming of the Prophet and the Anointed Ones of Aaron and Israel," thus apparently alluding to the coming of the prophet promised in Deut 18:15–18 (possibly the Teacher of Righteousness?).[285] Furthermore, CD 7:17–18 indicates that Israel's problem is that she has despised "the books of the prophets" (so also 4QpHos[a] 2:3–5). And the numerous copies of the OT prophetical books as well as the large number of citations from these books in the rest of Qumran literature all furnish proof of the popularity of the prophetical writings at Qumran.[286]

Especially important in this regard are the *pesharim* at Qumran. Dupont-Sommer defines the *pesher* as "an explanation of the hidden significance, a revelation of the secrets concealed in the divine books, which only inspired commentators, prophets, or initiates were able to discover."[287] This definition indicates the *pesher*'s close connection with prophecy itself. Horgan lists three important principles derived from a study of the *pesharim*.[288] First, the sectarians believed that the biblical books contained mysteries that the prophets themselves did not understand. 1QpHab 7:1–2 states that "God told Habakkuk to write down the things that are going to come upon the last generation, but the fulfillment of the end-time he did not make known to him." Second, they believed that these mysteries found in the biblical books actually pertained to the history of their community.

Thus, 1QpHab 2:9−10 speaks of "the words of His servants the prophets, by whose hand God enumerated all that is going to come upon His people and upon His congregation." The following passage in 1QpHab 2:10−13 gives a good example of their method, as Hab 1:6a ("For behold I rouse the Chaldaeans, the bitter and hasty nation") is interpreted to mean "the Kittim [i.e., Romans], who are swift and vigorous in battle, so as to destroy many" (1QpHab 2:10−13; see also 1QM 11:11−16). Prophetic fulfillment of the biblical passage is thus found in the contemporary situation of the community.[289] Finally, the sectarians believed that these prophetic mysteries could be interpreted by the Teacher of Righteousness and others who followed after him. 1QpHab 7:4−5 is most revealing regarding the Teacher of Righteousness' ability to interpret prophecy: "the interpretation of it concerns the Teacher of Righteousness, to whom God made known all the mysteries of the words of His servants the prophets" (so also CD 1:11−12: "He raised up for them a Teacher of Righteousness ... to make known to the last generations what He would do to the last generation, the congregation of traitors").[290] In addition to the Teacher of Righteousness, 1QpHab 2:7−10 also mentions a "priest into whose heart God put understanding to interpret all the words of his servants the prophets." Thus, the prophetic environment at Qumran, with the emphasis on reinterpretation of the prophetic books, seems to fit well with Josephus' picture of certain Essenes who were able to prophesy through their study of "holy books" and "sayings of prophets."

## 12.  J.W. 2.8, 13 §160−1

*There is another order of Essenes, who ... are at variance in their opinion of marriage* (§160−1). Josephus ends his long discussion of the Essenes in *Jewish War* by mentioning a second order of Essenes, who differ from the primary order in that they permit marriage. This surprising admission of diversity within the Essene community may indicate that the entire Essene movement was more fluid than Josephus presents. In any event, Josephus states here (as in *J.W.* 2 §120−1) that the Essenes marry in order to have children and thus preserve their lineage. That they do not marry for self-gratification is evident, Josephus contends, since they marry only those who are able to bear children and they do not have intercourse during pregnancy.

The question of celibacy and marriage at Qumran has previously been addressed (see discussion of *J. W.* 2 §120, pp. 38–9). As was concluded from that discussion, there is abundant evidence for marriage at Qumran. In addition, that the purpose of marriage is for procreation may be indicated by CD 7:6–7, which speaks of those who "live in camps according to the rule of the land, and take a wife and beget children" (see discussion of *J. W.* 2 §121, pp. 41–2). Also, Josephus' statement that the Essenes have no intercourse during pregnancy (demonstrating their self-control and lack of self-gratification in marriage) is entirely in harmony with the self-control commanded of the men of Qumran, who had to be at least twenty years old before they married (1QSa 1:9–10).

Josephus now mentions that the wives are put to the test for three years, and the men marry only those who show, by means of "three periods of purification" (τρὶς καθαρθῶσιν), that they are able to bear children. The precise nature of this test is unclear, and the Qumran scrolls do not refer to it. Some have seen two different tests here: a three-year test, which refers to the normal three-year period of candidacy that the male also went through; and "three purifications," which refers to the purifications after menstruation (see Lev 15:19), and thus a proof of fertility.[291] Dupont-Sommer, on the other hand, alters τριετίᾳ ("three years") to τρίμηνοι ("three months"), and views the entire test as consisting of the three menstrual periods alone.[292] Since the context of Josephus' remarks is that of bearing children, it does seem more likely that there is only one test involved, namely, a regular menstrual cycle that would indicate fertility.[293]

Josephus ends his discussion of the married order of Essenes with the remark that the women wear a garment, while the men wear a loin cloth in the baths. Such propriety in dress is also seen in the Qumran community. 1QS 7:12 states that "whoever goes naked before his fellow without being gravely ill shall be punished for six months" (see also the discussion of Essene care in exercising bodily functions, *J. W.* 2 §147–9, pp. 96–9). As H. Moehring notes, this Essene practice is in marked contrast to the customs of the Greeks, and perhaps that is why Josephus mentions it here.[294]

### C. Ant. 18.1, 2, 5 §11, 18–22

#### 1. Ant. 18.1, 2 §11

*Three philosophies among the Jews* (§11). In addition to the detailed description of the Essenes given by Josephus in *J. W.* 2 §119–61,

Josephus writes again about the Essenes in *Ant*. 18 §11, 18–22. Although this passage is not nearly as detailed as *J. W.* 2 §119–61, and is to a large degree a summary of the earlier section, nonetheless it contains several important statements, not found in the earlier account, which deserve our attention.

As in *J. W.* 2 §119, Josephus describes the Essenes, Sadducees, and Pharisees as the three "philosophies" (φιλοσοφίαι) of the Jews (see also *Life* 1.2 §10; *Ant*. 13.5, 9 §171). Josephus himself mentions that he has talked of these groups in the second book of the *Jewish War*, and so will now only speak of them briefly. His coverage of the three groups is actually far more even here than it was in *J. W.*, where nearly all the space was devoted to the Essenes.[295] See further the discussion of *J. W.* 2 §119 above, pp. 35–6.

## 2. Ant. 18.1, 5 §18–22

*They like to leave all things to God* (§18). The first thing Josephus mentions about the Essenes in this section is that they like to leave all things to God. This deterministic outlook is further highlighted in *Ant*. 13.5, 9 §171–3, where Josephus compares the attitudes of the three sects regarding human actions and fate: the Pharisees say that some events are the work of fate (εἰμαρμένης), but not all; the Essenes believe that "fate is ruler of all things, and that nothing happens to people except it be according to its decree"; while the Sadducees "do away with fate," believing that "all things lie within our own power." As R. Marcus and others have noted, "fate" (εἰμαρμένη) as used in this passage is probably equivalent to divine providence; the term "fate" was probably chosen as a term Josephus' Gentile readership would understand.[296] Philo also notes the Essene belief that "the Deity is the cause of all good things, and nothing bad" (*Every Good Man is Free* 12 §84).

A deterministic attitude is characteristic of the Qumran community as well. In fact, E. Merrill regards the most striking parallel between the Qumran sectarians and the Essenes to be "their common concern with predestination."[297] The community's deterministic outlook may be seen throughout the Dead Sea Scrolls. In the *Manual of Discipline*, 1QS 3:15–16 states that "From the God of knowledge comes all that is and shall be, and before (beings) were, He established all their design. And when they are, they fulfill their task according to their statutes, in accordance with His glorious design, changing nothing in it." 1QS 9:23–4 further indicates the sectarian's total submission to God's will: "He shall do the will (of God) in every enterprise of his hands and in all the exercise of his authority as He has commanded. In all that befalls he shall freely delight, and nothing shall please him except God's will. He shall delight [in all] the words of His mouth, and shall not covet anything which He has not comman[ded]." The *War Scroll* contains similar references to God's control over the affairs of people: for example, 1QM 17:5 states that "[to the God] of Israel belongs all that is and that will be ... Today is His appointed time to subdue and to humble the prince of the domain of wickedness" (see also 1QM 1:10; 6:6; 11:4–5; 13:14–15; 15:1–2; and 18:10).

Finally, the *Hodayot* in particular contains numerous passages that speak of God's control over all things. Merrill considers predestination to be "one of the chief doctrines in 1QH, if not *the* most prominent."[298] The entire section of 1QH 1:7–31 is concerned with this theme. In particular, 1QH 1:7–8 states that "before Thou createdst them Thou knewest all their deeds forever and ever. [Without Thee no]thing is done, and apart from Thy will nothing can be known." Similarly, 1QH 7:31–2 declares that "Thou art a God of eternity, and all Thy ways are established from everlasting to everlasting, and beside Thee there is nothing." And in 1QH 15:12–22, the psalmist exclaims that it is God, not man, who ordains man's way – whether righteous or wicked:

> And I know by Thine insight that it is not by human strength that man can [make straight] his way, and a man cannot guide his step aright; but I know that in Thine hand is the forming of every spirit, [and its work] Thou hast ordained before ever Thou createdst it; and how should any be able to alter Thy words? Thou alone hast [created] the righteous, and from the womb Thou hast prepared him for the appointed time of grace ... but the ungodly Thou has created for [the time of Thy choosing], and from the womb Thou hast ordained them for the day of slaughter.
> (1QH 15:12–15, 17; see also 1QH 3:22; 4:38; 9:29–31; 10:5–7; and 12:32–5)

Such passages as these indicate that the deterministic outlook is an important tenet of the sectarian's theology.[299]

*They regard souls as immortal* (§18). For a discussion of the immortality of the soul, see *J. W.* 2 §154–8, pp. 105–8.

*The path of righteousness is worth striving for* (§18). Josephus next indicates the importance for the Essene of doing what is right (τοῦ δικαίου). Some translate τοῦ δικαίου τὴν πρόσοδον as "the reward of righteousness," and it is true that πρόσοδος sometimes has the sense of revenue or profit.³⁰⁰ But this usage is largely confined to the plural, and in fact a few lines down Josephus uses the plural τῶν προσόδων to mean "revenue" (18 §22). Hence, as Strugnell and Feldman note, πρόσοδος should probably be rendered "approach" or "path" in this context.³⁰¹

The importance of righteousness and justice to the Qumran community has already been mentioned (see discussion of *J. W.* 2 §139, above, pp. 79–80). In addition to those passages cited previously, there are several that are strikingly similar to Josephus' words here (especially if πρόσοδος is understood as "approach" or "path"). In the *Manual of Discipline*, 1QS 4:2 states that the spirit of truth is "to enlighten the heart of man, and to make straight before him all the ways of righteousness" (*drky ṣdq*; see also 1QS 3:20; 5:3–4; 9:17–18). In the *Damascus Document*, CD 1:14–16 speaks condemningly of those who have "departed from the way," and whom the man of mockery caused to depart "from the paths of righteousness" (*mntybwt ṣdq*). Similarly, the psalmist in 1QH 7:14 states that God has established his heart, "and directs my steps towards paths of righteousness" (*lntybwt ṣdqh*). All of these passages serve to underscore the importance of "the path of righteousness" in Qumran thought.

*They offer sacrifices* (§19). Josephus next discusses the Essene attitude towards sacrifice. There is a major textual problem here, as the Epitome and the Latin version reflect the negative οὐκ, "they do not offer sacrifices" (θυσίας οὐκ ἐπιτελοῦσιν) rather than the θυσίας ἐπιτελοῦσιν of the Greek manuscripts. Scholars are divided concerning which reading is correct. My translation follows Niese and Feldman in omitting οὐκ (with the Greek manuscripts), though the matter is not easily decided.³⁰² Josephus, then, is saying that the Essenes send votive offerings to the Temple, but because they have different purification rites, they are excluded³⁰³ from the common court and offer sacrifices by themselves.

Before discussing Josephus's text further, it is well to consider the attitude towards sacrifice displayed in Qumran literature. In the *Manual of Discipline*, the community is described as "an institution of the holy spirit of eternal truth to atone for the guilt of transgression and sinful iniquity and for favor to the land through the flesh of burnt offerings (*mbśr ʿwlwt*), and through the fats of sacrifice (*wmḥlby zbḥ*) and the offering of the lips, for judgment as a fragrant offering of righteousness, and perfection of way as a pleasing freewill offering" (1QS 9:3–5). This passage is subject to several interpretations, depending upon the force of the *min* of *mbśr*. First, the *min* may be taken as a comparative, "more than," in which case the institution has more expiatory value than the flesh of burnt offerings or the fats of sacrifice ("the offering of the lips" is then usually taken as the start of the next clause, to show the contrast between it and the literal offerings). Many Qumran scholars have interpreted the passage in this way.[304] But J. T. Milik and others interpret the *min* as indicating source, i.e., "from" or "by means of."[305] In support of this interpretation, J. Carmignac notes a parallel passage with similar terminology in 1QM 1:5–6: "These shall stand by at the burnt offerings and the sacrifices, to set out the fragrant incense offering for the pleasure of God, to atone for all His congregation, and to bring fat sacrifices before Him perpetually on the table of glory."[306] Furthermore, in a postscript to Carmignac's article, Milik notes that in 4QS[d] the second *min* (on *wmḥlby*) is lacking. Thus, in the variant, all three phrases ("flesh of burnt offerings," "fats of sacrifice," and "offering of the lips") are coordinated by the single *min*, which can no longer be understood as a comparative.[307] For these reasons, the *min* is best taken here as meaning "from" or "through," as reflected in the translation given above. 1QS 9:3–5, therefore, probably indicates a favorable attitude towards literal sacrifices on the part of the Qumran community.

There are three passages in the *Damascus Document* that speak of sacrifice. CD 3:18–4:4, a loose citation of Ezek 44:15, states that "the priests and the Levites and the sons of Zadok who kept the charge of my sanctuary while the children of Israel went astray from me shall come near < to me to serve me and shall stand before me to offer > me fat and blood." This passage and its interpretation seem to indicate approval of sacrifices, though little detail is given. A second passage, CD 6:11–14, speaks of the proper conditions for sacrifice: "And none of those who have entered the Covenant shall enter the Temple to kindle His altar in vain, but they shall close the door; as God said, 'Who among you will close his door? And you shall not light my altar in vain.'" The last phrase is taken from Mal 1:10, where the Lord condemns those who are offering up ritually unclean animals for sacrifice. It is possible that CD 6:11–14 means that none of the sectarians is to enter the Temple at any time for sacrifice.[308] Probably, however, the prohibition is not absolute, but simply says (as CD 6:14

goes on to state) that those bringing the offering should "be careful to act according to the exact tenor of the Law." In other words, CD 6:11–14 seems to be saying that those who offer sacrifices at the Temple must be very careful to do so with utmost ritual purity, or the offerings are invalid.[309]

Another passage from the *Damascus Document* lends support to this intepretation. CD 11:17–22 states:

> Let nothing be offered on the altar on the Sabbath except the Sabbath burnt offering; for it is written, "besides your Sabbaths." Let there be sent to the altar of holocaust neither offering nor incense nor wood by the hand of a man defiled by any defilement whatsoever, permitting him thus to render the altar unclean; for it is written, "The sacrifice of the wicked is an abomination, but the prayer of the just is like a delectable offering." And whoever enters the House of Prostration (*byt hšthwt*), let him not enter in a state of uncleanness; let him wash himself.

The term *byt hšthwt* almost certainly refers to the Temple, where prostrations apparently formed a part of the Temple service.[310] The entire section indicates that a person who was ritually defiled in any way should not bring an offering or even enter the Temple. The passage thus implies that those who were not defiled could do these things. Hence, the evidence from Qumran indicates that at least at one point in the community's history, it was permissible to bring sacrifices to the Temple, but the strictest ritual purity was to be observed in so doing.

Several scholars believe that Josephus' testimony concerning the Essenes and the evidence from Qumran are in direct contradiction regarding the matter of sacrifices. They believe that the Qumran texts encourage Temple sacrifice, while Josephus' statement (and Philo's as well) expressly forbids it. Thus, even prior to the discovery of the Dead Sea Scrolls, R. H. Charles said that the author of the *Fragments of a Zadokite Work* (today known as the *Damascus Document*) could not be Essene, since the *Zadokite Work* "inculcated the duty of animal sacrifice."[311] This position has been echoed more recently by M. Delcor, who believes that the Qumran community cannot possibly be Essene since the sectarians believe in the resurrection and practice sacrifices in the Temple.[312]

As was discussed above, however, Josephus' statement does not necessarily mean that the Essenes sent no offerings to the Temple at all, especially if the οὐκ is not part of the text. Also, Philo's declaration on the subject does not actually rule out sacrifice either. Philo states that the Essenes "have shown themselves especially devout in the service of God, not by offering sacrifices of animals, but by resolving to sanctify their minds" (*Every Good Man is Free* 12 §75). As R. Marcus and others have observed, this does not necessarily imply that the Essenes did not sacrifice, but rather that sacrifice was not the focal point of their worship.[313] Hence, there is no inherent contradiction between Josephus (and Philo) and the Qumran community on the matter of sacrifices.

Scholars who believe that the Qumran sectarians are Essene have suggested several ways of resolving the sacrifice question. Some believe that the "sacrifices" spoken of by Josephus and Qumran literature were not literal but figurative. For example, J. Baumgarten, translating ἐφ' αὐτῶν τὰς θυσίας ἐπιτελοῦσιν (the last phrase in Josephus' statement) as "they conduct their worship separately," suggests that the Essene purifications and communal meals ultimately replaced the Temple worship.[314] Similarly, K. Kuhn states that the Essenes "understood their meals as a substitute for the Temple sacrifices."[315] Yet, as Cross and others have pointed out, Baumgarten's translation of Josephus' words is highly unlikely, since θυσίας ἐπιτελοῦσιν is used by Josephus earlier in the same sentence to refer to literal sacrifices; the same expression thus should be translated similarly in both places.[316]

Josephus' statement, then, seems to point to literal sacrifices by the Essenes. The problem remains, where did they sacrifice? Cross, Steckoll, and others believe that actual sacrifices were conducted at Qumran.[317] Archaeological evidence for this is seen in the animal bone deposits found at Qumran. Because of the careful way bones were set apart, de Vaux concludes that "it is possible that these are the remnants of sacrifices."[318] Furthermore, Steckoll asserts that an altar has been found at Qumran, which would further support the supposition that sacrifices were performed there.[319] Yet, upon closer inspection, neither the bones nor Steckoll's "altar" provide solid evidence for sacrifice at Qumran. Given the Essene concern for ritual purity in everything they did, it is not surprising at all that they treated the animal bones in a careful manner. In themselves, the bones are insufficient evidence for animal sacrifice at Qumran.[320] And Steckoll's "altar" is even more uncertain. It is a cube made from solid stone, approximately ten inches per side. Such a size would seem to be too small for group worship and sacrifice, and, as R. Beckwith notes, the stone itself does not seem to have been affected by fire.[321] Hence, it does not appear that any altar for sacrifice has been found at Qumran.[322]

Other scholars believe that the Essenes did sacrifice at the Jerusalem Temple. Black proposes that the Essenes simply avoided contact with other worshippers in the public precinct. He links this with the gate of the Essenes (mentioned by Josephus in *J. W.* *5*.4, 2 §145), necessary to avoid contact with other Temple worshippers.[323] Baumgarten suggests that the Essenes may have eaten the sacrifices by themselves in an isolated area of the Temple after the priests had offered them on the altar.[324] He notes that according to Josephus, the Essenes certainly had not made a complete break with Jerusalem and the Temple: Judas was teaching in the court of the Temple (*J. W.* 1.3, 5 §78); Menahem talked with Herod in his youth (*Ant.* 15.10, 5 §373); John the Essene was appointed general at a public meeting in the Temple (*J. W.* 2.20, 4 §562–7); and the existence of the gate of the Essenes (*J. W.* 5.4, 2 §145) denotes the Essenes' presence in Jerusalem. Thus, the Essenes may well have sacrificed at Jerusalem, but segregated themselves to eat the sacrifices with ritual purity.

The entire question of sacrifices and the Essenes, however, is not easily settled. Any attempted solution is further complicated by the fact that there may well have been an historical development within the sect regarding their attitude towards the Temple and the sacrifices. In any event, both Josephus and Qumran literature present a picture of a group that did offer sacrifices, though with a great concern for ritual purity in the process.

*They are the noblest men in their way of life* (§19–20). After presenting the Essene view of sacrifice, Josephus speaks of other basic distinctive qualities of the Essenes. Much of his discussion is similar to that of Philo in *Every Good Man is Free* 12 §75–88, though Josephus' account is more condensed. Since most of the subjects Josephus mentions here have already been discussed in connection with his longer account of the Essenes (*J. W.* 2 §119–61), it will be sufficient in many cases simply to refer to the discussion in *J. W.* 2 §119–61.

Josephus states in this section that the Essenes are "the noblest men in their way of life," who are to be admired above all others because of their unhindered pursuit of virtuous qualities. Philo similarly mentions that the Essenes are known by their "love of virtue" (φιλάρετος), demonstrated "by their freedom from the love of either money or reputation or pleasure, by self-mastery and endurance, again by frugality, simple living, contentment, humility, respect for law, steadiness and all similar qualities" (*Every Good Man is Free* 12 §84; see also 13 §88, *Hypothetica* 11.2). Such virtuous qualities have been mentioned more fully in Josephus' long account of the Essenes (*J. W.* 2 §120–3, 135, 139–42), and Qumran parallels are indicated in the discussion of these sections. One passage in particular may be cited to indicate the stress on virtuous qualities at Qumran: 1QS 5:3–4 states that those who enter the community "shall practice truth in common, and humility, and righteousness and justice and loving charity, and modesty in all their ways."

For a discussion of Josephus' statement that the Essenes work "entirely in agriculture," see the treatment of *J. W.* 2 §129 (pp. 54–5).

*They hold their possessions in common* (§20). See discussion of *J. W.* 2 §122 (pp. 44–5). On Josephus' statement that there are over four thousand who live in this way, see *J. W.* 2 §124 (pp. 48–50).

*They neither bring wives into (the community) nor do they seek to acquire slaves* (§21). On the Essene view of marriage, see *J. W.* 2 §120–1 (pp. 38–42). On slavery, Josephus states that the Essenes do not seek to acquire slaves because it leads to injustice, and instead they freely serve one another. Philo's statement is similar: "Not a single slave is to be found among them, but all are free, exchanging services with each other, and they denounce the owners of slaves" because of their injustice to the law and nature itself (*Every Good Man is Free* 12 §79).

Qumran literature is largely silent on the subject of slavery, except for two references in the *Damascus Document*. CD 11:12 states that no one "shall irritate his slave or maidservant or employee on the Sabbath," while CD 12:10–11 states: "Concerning his slave and his maidservant, let no man sell them to them [the Gentiles] because they have entered with him into the covenant of Abraham." Both of these references seem to indicate the presence of slaves within the community. It is possible that Josephus means not that the Essenes did not have any slaves, but that they no longer sought to acquire slaves (though Philo states categorically that they did not have any slaves). The issue might well have been not so much injustice as contamination with the Gentiles.[325] Also, since slaves are only mentioned in the *Damascus Document*, the matter is further complicated by the degree to which that document reflects different stages of the community's development.[326] Possibly slaves might have been accepted into the community initially, but were gradually phased out.

*They elect good men as treasurers ... and priests for the preparation of their bread* (§22). In this section Josephus appears to refer to two distinct groups of elected officials: treasurers and priests.[327] As noted earlier, the treasurers Josephus mentions here are probably the same as the overseers (ἐπιμεληταί) described by Josephus in *J. W.* 2 §123, 129, and 134. They seem to function as the financial guardians of the community. For further discussion, see pp. 46–7 above. The priests whom Josephus describes here may actually have been the baker and the cook, or possibly may have supervised the work done by the (lay) baker and cook. See further pp. 58–60 above.

*They live ... most similarly to those who among the Dacians are called Ctistae* (§22). The text and meaning of Josephus' statement is unclear. The Greek manuscripts state that the Essenes live most similarly to "those called the majority of the Dacians" (Δακῶν τοῖς πλείστοις λεγομένοις), but this makes little sense. Dupont-Sommer suggests that Δακῶν be emended to Σαδδουκαίων, and the phrase be translated as "those of the Sadducees who are called the Many." He regards πλείστοις as a translation of Hebrew *hrbym* ("the Many"), a term used often in the Dead Sea Scrolls to refer to the Qumran community. Thus, according to Dupont-Sommer, Josephus is saying that the various Essene groups conformed to the model of the Qumran community (the "sons of Zadok," designated here as the "Sadducees who are called the Many").[328] But this suggestion is unlikely, on two grounds. First, Josephus has already spoken of the classical Sadducees in the section immediately preceding his discussion of the Essenes (*Ant.* 18.1, 4 §16–17), and it would be odd for him to use the same term to designate a different group without some sort of explanation. Second, the emendation of Δακῶν to Σαδδουκαίων is palaeographically unlikely.[329] J. Carmignac proposes that Δακῶν be emended to αὐτῶν ("of them"), in which case the phrase would read "those of them called the great ones." Carmignac prefers "the great ones" or "chiefs" for πλείστοις (rather than Dupont-Sommer's "the Many") because he believes that the Hebrew term *rbym* used at Qumran refers to the leaders of the community, who were to be venerated by the others. He finds support in this understanding of *rbym* from the Aramaic meaning of *rb* ("great").[330] While Carmignac's emendation seems more plausible than Dupont-Sommer's, it still must be asked why Josephus would say that the Essene way of life was most similar to the Essene leaders at Qumran: this would seem to be a self-evident point, not worth stating. S. Isser builds on Carmignac's emendation of Δακῶν to αὐτῶν, and continues by emending πλείστοις to παλαιοῖς: "those called their ancients." According to Isser's suggestion, Josephus would be denoting once again the conservative nature of the Essenes by mentioning that they follow the ancients.[331] But this would require the emendation of two words, and, while possible, it does not seem likely that Josephus would bring up such a matter at the end of his discussion of the Essenes.

Other scholars have sought to solve the problem by emending only πλείστοις. Some have changed πλείστοις to Πολισταῖς, "city founders." But this word is not attested elsewhere in extant Greek literature, and is rejected by the grammarian Pollux.[332] L. Feldman follows the suggestion of Ortelius and others to emend πλείστοις to Κτίσταις, "Ctistae," a word that means "Founders."[333] The Ctistae are a group of Thracians mentioned by Strabo (citing Poseidonius) who live a peaceable, god-fearing life and, in particular, "live apart from women" (Strabo, *Geography* 7.3, 3 §296). This would fit well with the preceding section in Josephus which specifically mentions that the Essenes do not bring wives into their community (*Ant.* 18 §21). However, it still is unusual that Josephus would single out this group for comparison with the Essenes, especially after saying that the virtues of the Essenes did not compare with those of the Greeks or barbarians (*Ant.* 18 §20). Nonetheless, this emendation is at least as plausible as the other suggestions, and has been followed in our text of Josephus. The Qumran scrolls do not shed any light on this passage (unless, of course, Dupont-Sommer's or Carmignac's suggestions are adopted), and the Ctistae remain obscure except for the reference in Strabo.

# 4

## CONCLUSION

As was mentioned at the outset, the purpose of this study has been to provide a commentary on Josephus' description of the Essenes wherein the relevant passages from the Dead Sea Scrolls are compared with Josephus' text. With the commentary now complete, it remains to summarize the parallels and discrepancies found between Josephus' description and the scrolls, and briefly to consider the reliability of Josephus' account. The parallels and discrepancies between Josephus and Qumran will be summarized in four categories: parallels between Josephus and Qumran; probable parallels between Josephus and Qumran (where some problems of correlation still remain); statements made by Josephus with no known Qumran parallel; and apparent discrepancies between Josephus and Qumran.

### Parallels between Josephus and Qumran

The following sections in Josephus' description of the Essenes are closely paralleled in Qumran literature. For further discussion of the Qumran parallels, see the appropriate section in the commentary.

1. Jews by birth (*J. W.* 2 §119). 1QS 6:13–14.
2. More mutual affection (*J. W.* 2 §119); each one gives what he has to one in need (*J. W.* 2 §127). 1QS 1:9; 2:24–5; CD 6:20–7:1.
3. They turn aside from pleasures as an evil (*J. W.* 2 §120); self-control (*J. W.* 2 §120). 1QS 4:9–11.
4. They despise riches (*J. W.* 2 §122). 1QS 9:21–4; 10:18–19; 11:1–2.
5. They replace neither clothing nor sandals (*J. W.* 2 §126). 1QS 7:13–14.
6. Girding themselves with linen wraps, they bathe their bodies (*J. W.* 2 §129). (Both Josephus and Qumran speak of purificatory washings.) 1QS 3:4–5; 5:13–14.

7.    They go into the dining-room ... (*J. W.* 2 §129). (Both speak of a common meal.) 1QS 6:2–5.

8.    The priest prays before the meal (*J. W.* 2 §131). 1QS 6:4–5; 1QSa 2:17–21.

9.    The silence of those within ... (*J. W.* 2 §132–3). 1QS 6:10–13.

10.   They do nothing except by the order of their overseers (*J. W.* 2 §134). 1QS 5:2–3; 6:11–13; 7:17.

11.   Masters of their temper (*J. W.* 2 §135); they are the noblest men ... (*Ant.* 18 §19–20). 1QS 4:3, 10; 5:25; 6:25–7; 11:1–2.

12.   Guardians of faithfulness (*J. W.* 2 §135); he will forever show himself trustworthy (*J. W.* 2 §140). 1QS 8:1–3; 10:24–5.

13.   Ministers of peace (*J. W.* 2 §135). 1QS 4:6–7 (but cf. 1QM).

14.   Zealous in (studying) the writings of the ancients (*J.W.* 2 §136); educated in holy books (*J. W.* 2 §159). 1QS 6:6–8; CD 16:1–5.

15.   He will practice piety towards the Deity (*J.W.* 2 §139). 1QS 1:1–2, 16–17, etc.

16.   He will cherish justice towards human beings (*J. W.* 2 §139); the path of righteousness is worth striving for (*Ant.* 18 §18). 1QS 1:5–6; 5:3–4; 8:2–3.

17.   He will forever love the truth and expose liars (*J. W.* 2 §141). 1QS 1:9–11; 5:3.

18.   He will keep his hands pure of stealing (*J. W.* 2 §141). 1QS 4:10; 10:19.

19.   He will neither hide anything from the members of his sect nor disclose anything about them to others (*J. W.* 2 §141); he will transmit their teachings ... as he received them (*J. W.* 2 §142). 1QS 8:11–12; 4:5–6; 7:22–4.

20.   He will preserve ... the books of their sect and the names of the angels (*J. W.* 2 §142). 1QM, *1 Enoch*, etc.

21.   They avoid spitting (*J. W.* 2 §147). 1QS 7:13.

22.   On the other days they dig a pit ... (*J. W.* 2 §148–9). (Both Josephus and Qumran mention that they choose isolated places.) 1QM 7:6–7; 11QTemple[a] 46:13–16.

23.   They are fearless of danger (*J. W.* 2 §151). 1QS 1:16–17.

24.   The war with the Romans tested their souls (*J. W.* 2 §152–3). *Kittim* in the *Pesharim*; War Scroll.

25.   Some among them ... profess to foreknow the future (*J. W.* 2 §159). *Pesharim*.

26.   They like to leave all things to God (*Ant.* 18 §18). 1QS 3:15–16; 9:23–4.

Admittedly, many of the parallels mentioned above are rather general qualities that might fit many groups (mutual affection, self-control, despising riches, etc.), and thus are not particularly helpful in deciding whether the Qumran community was Essene or not. But the sheer number of parallels is striking, and puts the burden of proof upon those who would insist that the Qumran community was *not* Essene.

Furthermore, numerous parallels in the above list are quite unusual, and point rather clearly to the identity of the Qumran community as Essene. For example, not only do both Josephus and Qumran literature mention the common meal (parallel 7), but they also mention that a priest prays before each meal (parallel 8). This is not a major point, and thus it is surprising that both sources mention it. In addition, the oaths mentioned by Josephus (parallels 15–20) are not only parallel in thought to Qumran literature, but they are also quite similar to the opening passage in the *Manual of Discipline*, 1QS 1:1–15. And in my opinion, the most amazing parallel of all is that both mention that they do not spit in the midst of a group (parallel 21) – a trivial point, to be sure, but astonishing that both Josephus and Qumran literature should mention it. Similar in this respect is the agreement of Josephus and Qumran texts regarding the custom of the sect to go to a remote place for defecation (parallel 22). All of these parallels point strongly to the conclusion that the Qumran community was Essene.

### Probable parallels between Josephus and Qumran

In addition to those parallels mentioned above, there are numerous sections in Josephus' description that appear to be paralleled in Qumran literature, but some problems of correlation remain. In some instances there are minor discrepancies between Josephus and a portion of the Qumran evidence; in others, there is not enough evidence at Qumran to illustrate a particular statement by Josephus, though there is a general correlation. Thus, I have categorized them as "probable" parallels.

1.      Marriage they regard with contempt (*J. W.* 2 §120); they do not reject marriage (*J. W.* 2 §121); there is another order of Essenes, who ... are at variance in their opinion of marriage (*J. W.* 2 §160–1). 1QSa 1:4, 9–12; CD 4:19–5:2, 6–7; 11QTemple[a] 57:15–19 speak of marriage, but cemetery shows all male skeletons in one portion.

2. Licentious allurements of women (*J. W.* 2 §121). (Supported by 4Q*184*?)

3. One property common to all (*J. W.* 2 §122); they hold their possessions in common (*Ant.* 18 §20). (Supported by 1QS 1:11–12; 5:1–2; 6:17–22, but not by CD 9:10–16; 14:12–13.)

4. They regard oil as a defilement (*J. W.* 2 §123). CD 12:15–17; 11QTemple[a] 21:12–22:16.

5. Always being dressed in white (*J. W.*2 §123). 1QM 7:9–10.

6. Elected overseers (*J. W.* 2 §123); they elect good men ... (*Ant.* 18 §22). 1QS 6:12, 20; CD 9:18–22; 13:7–8, 11; etc.

7. Many settle in each city (*J. W.* 2 §124). CD 7:6–7; etc.

8. Before the rising of the sun they ... direct certain ancestral prayers towards it (*J. W.* 2 §128). (High regard for the sun at Qumran as well.) 1QS 9:26–10:8.

9. They labor earnestly until the fifth hour (*J. W.* 2 §129). 1QS 9:22.

10. Succor and mercy (*J. W.* 2 §134). (1QS supports voluntary charity, but CD indicates that overseers handled it.) 1QS 10:26; CD 6:20–1; 14:12–16.

11. Healing of diseases (*J. W.* 2 §136). 1QapGen 20:19–20; *1 Enoch*.

12. Entrance is not immediate (*J. W.* 2 §137–8). (Very similar stages of entrance into the community, but 1QS 6:13–23 states that the novice can touch the meal after one year, while Josephus seems to indicate a two-year waiting period.)

13. He must take awesome oaths (*J. W.* 2 §139). (Similar to 1QS 5:8–9, but there is question concerning when oaths are taken, and whether they were limited to the Mosaic Law or broader in scope.)

14. Those who are caught in serious offenses they expel from the order (*J. W.* 2 §143–4). (Similar in expulsion, but Josephus says the expelled one is still bound by his oaths, and thus wastes away.) 1QS 7:1–2, 16–17; 7:22–5; 8:21–3.

15. In their judgments they are most scrupulous and just (*J. W.* 2 §145). (Similar to 1QS 6:27; CD 9:9–10, but Qumran literature does not mention a one-hundred-member court.)

16. They have the greatest reverence, after God, for the name of the lawgiver (*J. W.* 2 §145). (Reverence is indicated by Qumran literature [cf. 1QS 1:1–3; 5:8], but not blasphemy of his name.)

17.    They ... obey the elders and the majority (*J. W.* 2 §146).
        (Information from Qumran is unclear − cf. 1QS 2:19−23.)
18.    They are stricter than all Jews in not undertaking work on
        the seventh day (*J. W.* 2 §147). CD 3:14; 6:18.
19.    They are divided ... into four groups (*J. W.* 2 §150). (Qumran
        literature is unclear − see 1QS 2:19−23; CD 14:3−4.)
20.    They are long-lived (*J. W.* 2 §151). 1QS 4:6−7.
21.    They offer sacrifices (*Ant.* 18 §19). (Neither Josephus nor
        Qumran is entirely clear − cf. 1QS 9:3−5; etc.)

Among the sections mentioned above are some of the most difficult problems in correlating Josephus' statements with Qumran literature: the question of marriage at Qumran, common ownership of possessions, the governmental structure, the sect's regard for the sun, the stages of entrance into the community, and the question of sacrifices. Yet, in many cases the problem is not so much comparing what Josephus says with the Qumran data, but rather interpreting the Qumran evidence itself. Sometimes (as in many of the topics listed above) specific information from Qumran on a particular custom Josephus mentions is not available, and thus while a general parallel may be discerned, confirmation of the particulars is impossible. This makes it difficult to determine, for example, whether Josephus is simply exaggerating when he says that the Essenes did not relieve themselves on the Sabbath, or whether in fact this custom did exist at Qumran.

In other instances, the *Manual of Discipline* and the *Damascus Document* may differ on a particular issue (for example, parallel 3), and thus comparison with Josephus becomes problematic. As has been mentioned numerous times, it is quite possible that these documents represent different stages in the community's development, and this may well account for some of the discrepancies not only between the Qumran documents but also between these documents and Josephus. On the whole it appears that Josephus' description of the Essenes more closely parallels the *Manual of Discipline* than the *Damascus Document*.

Yet, despite these difficulties in establishing a precise correlation between Josephus and Qumran literature on the passages given above, the fact remains that there *is* a high degree of correlation, indeed more correlation than its opposite. Certainly more work needs to be done, especially in obtaining a better understanding of the customs and theology of the Qumran community, and gaining further insight into the history of the group and its writings. Perhaps some of the unpublished fragments from Cave 4 and elsewhere will be of help as well. But there are very few actual discrepancies between the scrolls and Josephus and many similarities. Given the current state of knowledge, then, we regard the above parallels as "probable," and thus as further evidence of the identification of the Qumran community as Essene.

### Statements made by Josephus with no known Qumran parallel

Certain statements made by Josephus concerning the Essenes have no known parallel in Qumran literature. These statements do not contradict anything in Qumran literature, but are simply not mentioned there. The more important details that have no known Qumran parallel are given below.

1. Adopting other persons' children (*J. W.* 2 §120).
2. When they journey (*J. W.* 2 §124–5). (Essene hospitality towards visitors.)
3. The baker serves the loaves in order (*J. W.* 2 §130). (Some details of the common meal, such as the baker, cook, etc., are not mentioned in Qumran literature.)
4. He will refrain from brigandage (*J. W.* 2 §142). (No specific prohibition against brigandage in Qumran literature.)
5. Those who are caught in serious offenses they expel from the order (*J. W.* 2 §143). (Details of the expelled one still bound to his oaths not found in Qumran literature.)
6. They are stricter than all Jews in not undertaking work on the seventh day (*J. W.* 2 §147). (Details of not relieving themselves on the Sabbath not mentioned by Qumran.)
7. On the other days they dig a pit ... (*J. W.* 2 §148–9).
8. Bodies are corruptible ... but ... souls are immortal (*J. W.* 2 §154–8). (No mention of pre-existence of the soul or dichotomy of body and soul in Qumran literature.)
9. There is another order of Essenes, who ... are at variance in their opinion of marriage (*J. W.* 2 §160–1). (No mention at Qumran of wives being put to the test for three years.)
10. They live ... most similarly to ... the ... Ctistae (*Ant.* 18 §22).

Because of the lack of concrete data from Qumran on the above topics, it is not possible to correlate Josephus' statements with the practices of the Qumran community.

### Apparent discrepancies between Josephus and Qumran

The following sections in Josephus' description contain statements that are apparently contradicted by portions of Qumran literature. In most cases these sections are largely parallel to the Qumran data (and thus have been listed above as "probable" parallels), yet they contain portions that are at odds with the Qumran evidence.

1. One property common to all (*J. W.* 2 §122). (CD indicates ownership.)
2. Succor and mercy (*J. W.* 2 §134). (CD indicates that overseers handled charity, not volunteers.)
3. They avoid swearing (*J. W.* 2 §135). (CD permits oaths.)
4. Entrance is not immediate (*J. W.* 2 §137–8). (Josephus says that a novice cannot touch the meal for two years, but 1QS indicates only a one-year wait for the meal.)
5. He must take awesome oaths (*J. W.* 2 §139). (Josephus implies that the oath is at the end of the initiation period, and is largely concerned with sectarian tenets, while 1QS indicates that the oath is at the beginning, and is concerned with the Mosaic Law.)
6. They neither bring wives into (the community) nor do they seek to acquire slaves (*Ant.* 18 §21). (CD seems to permit slaves.)

A few comments regarding the above list of apparent discrepancies are in order. First, the number of actual discrepancies is surprisingly small, especially in light of the large number of parallels and "probable" parallels. Second, the discrepancies are not major but involve comparatively minor points. Third, some of the discrepancies are between the *Damascus Document* and the *Manual of Discipline* (numbers 1 and 2), and thus the Qumran data are not consistent. Finally, most of the discrepancies involve the *Damascus Document*, not the *Manual of Discipline*; those discrepancies that involve the *Manual of Discipline* (numbers 4 and 5) seem fairly easy to resolve (see discussion of *J. W.* 2 §137–9 above). None of the above apparent discrepancies is serious enough to put into question the identification of the Qumran community with Josephus' Essenes.

## Reliability of Josephus' account

In conclusion, if the identity of the Essenes and the Qumran sectarians is assumed, what may be said regarding the reliability of Josephus' account? While my findings here must be tentative, given the uncertainty of the Qumran data, nonetheless it seems that Josephus' account is quite trustworthy in general (since otherwise we would have encountered many more discrepancies). Two tendencies, however, are apparent in his writings. First, at times he appears to go beyond the facts and exaggerate somewhat (a tendency common to many historians, no doubt!). This may be suggested in the following instances: the amount of time he spent personally with the Essenes (*Life* 1.2 §10–12); the assertion that "many" Essenes settle in each city (*J.W.* 2 §124–5); the Essene avoidance of oaths (*J.W.* 2 §135); the expelled Essene who is still bound by his oath, and thus "wastes away from hunger until he dies" (*J.W.* 2 §143); the Essene court of no less than one hundred members (*J.W.* 2 §145); the punishment of death to the one who "blasphemes" Moses (*J.W.* 2 §145); and such strict observance of the Sabbath that they could not relieve themselves (*J.W.* 2 §147).

A second tendency evident in Josephus' description of the Essenes is his appeal to Greek modes of thought, and hence his attempt to make Essenism more understandable to his Gentile readers. Thus, in *J.W.* 2 §119 the Pharisees, Sadducees, and Essenes are three "philosophical classes." Further, in *J.W.* 2 §154–8, Josephus describes the Essene view of the afterlife in terms of Greek thought. And again, in *Ant.* 15.10, 4 §371 Josephus says that the Essenes practice a way of life "introduced to the Greeks by Pythagoras." It is possible that the high regard for the sun mentioned by Josephus (*J.W.* 2 §128) is further evidence of accommodation to Greek thought.

All in all, however, Josephus has given us a trustworthy account of one of the major Jewish sects prevalent in early NT times. Now illustrated by the Dead Sea Scrolls, we may read with enlightened eyes about this unusual Jewish community, the Essenes of Qumran.

# APPENDIX

## Other passages that mention the Essenes

Listed below are the other (minor) passages in Josephus' writings in which the Essenes are mentioned. The text and translation of these passages are given in Chapter 2 (pp. 24–33). Most of these passages have already been discussed in conjunction with the commentary in Chapter 3, and thus it will suffice simply to refer to that discussion. For the others, brief comments will be given here.

1. *Judas' Prophecy of Antigonus' Death* (*J. W.* 1.3, 5 §78–80 and *Ant.* 13.11, 2 §311–13). For discussion of these passages, see *J. W.* 2 §159 (p. 109).

2. *Simon's Interpretation of Archelaus' Dream* (*J. W.* 2.7, 3 §111–13 and *Ant.* 17.13, 3 §346–8). For discussion of these passages, see *J. W.* 2 §159 (p. 109).

3. *John the Essene's Military Exploits* (*J. W.* 2.20, 4 §566–8 and *J. W.* 3.2, 1 §9–12). On the Essene attitude towards war, see *J. W.* 2 §135 (pp. 67–8) and especially *J. W.* 2 §152–3 (pp. 102–4).

4. *The Gate of the Essenes* (*J. W.* 5.4, 2 §142–5). In describing the western part of the First Wall in Jerusalem, Josephus mentions two items: a place called Βηθσώ, and the Essene gate farther south. Josephus' geographical notation is the only record of such an Essene gate, and its exact location has been debated. Since the discovery of the *Temple Scroll*, however, Y. Yadin's hypothesis concerning the location of the gate has gained wide acceptance. Yadin suggests (as had others before him) that the place Josephus mentions prior to the Essene gate, Βηθσώ, may well be a Greek transliteration of the Hebrew *bet ṣo'a*, "latrine." Now 11QTemple[a] 46:13–16 states that latrines were to be dug 3,000 cubits outside the city to the northwest. Hence, Yadin believes that Βηθσώ is to be identified with the location of these latrines, on the northwest side of Jerusalem. The Essene gate would then be located farther south, along the southwestern corner of the wall. Presumably the gate was used by the Essenes to leave the city in order to relieve themselves at Βηθσώ. Perhaps the gate then became unofficially named after them.[1]

5. *Fate is Ruler of All Things* (*Ant.* 13.5, 9 §171–2). For discussion of this passage, see *Ant.* 18.1, 5 §18 (pp. 113–14).

6. *Reference to the Three Sects* (*Ant.* 13.10, 6 §298). In this passage, Josephus refers back to his discussion of the Jewish sects in *J. W.* 2 §119–61.

7. *Menahem's Prophecy* (*Ant.* 15.10, 4–5 §371–9). For discussion of Menahem's prophecies concerning Herod, see *J. W.* 2 §159 (p. 109).[2]

Prior to his discussion of Menahem and Herod, Josephus makes an intriguing statement about the Essenes that deserves some comment here.

He says that the Essene sect "practices a way of life introduced to the Greeks by Pythagoras" (*Ant.* 15.10,4 §371). This statement has prompted some scholars, including Zeller, Schürer, Lévy, Lagrange, and Dupont-Sommer, to posit that Essenism was an offspring of Pythagorean thought.[3]

Alleged similarities between the Essenes and Pythagoreanism include the prayer to the sun (*J.W.* 2 §128), practiced at the beginning and end of each day by the Pythagoreans; the prohibition of sacrifice among the Essenes (*Ant.* 18.1,5 §19) and among some Pythagoreans; similarities in their calendar and numerical systems; the immortality of the soul (*J.W.* 2 §154–7); and various similar cultic rituals (wearing of white, baths, secrecy, etc.).[4]

Direct evidence of Essenism upon Pythagorean thought, however, is unlikely. Some of the alleged similarities break down under closer scrutiny. For example, whatever Josephus means by the Essene prayers "to" the sun (see discussion on *J.W.* 2 §128, pp. 52–4), it is highly doubtful that the Essenes actually worshipped the sun, as the Pythagoreans did. The sacrifice issue is complex, but in my view the Essenes did not actually prohibit sacrifice, and thus there is no parallel here with the Pythagoreans (see discussion on *Ant.* 18 §19, pp. 187–93). Similarly, the *nun* found in 1QS 10:4, which Dupont-Sommer takes to be a reference to the sacred Pythagorean number, fifty, seems to be a scribal error (as seen by the Cave 4 variants of the *Manual of Discipline*, 4QS^b and 4QS^d).[5] And the Essene doctrine of the immortality of the soul as presented by Josephus is similar not only to Pythagorean but to Greek doctrine as a whole – hence, this proves little in the way of Pythagorean influence. Finally, with respect to other similar rituals, many of these are common to any cult-type group, such as swearing one to secrecy, etc., and thus do not necessarily indicate any connection between the Essenes and the followers of Pythagoras.

How, then, shall we evaluate Josephus' statement linking the Essenes with Pythagoras? While there are undoubtedly some similarities between the two groups, any Pythagorean influence on the Essenes seems to be no greater than its influence on Palestinian Judaism in general.[6] It seems that Josephus depicts the Essenes as particularly influenced by the Pythagoreans largely to appeal to his Hellenistic readers. In the same manner, in *J.W.* 2 §119 he introduces the three Jewish sects as three "philosophical classes." Similarly, in *Life* 1.2 §12 he calls the Pharisees a sect "which nearly resembles that called Stoic among the Greeks." As G. Vermes observes, it is largely in Josephus' writings that the similarities between the Essenes and the Pythagoreans are emphasized, not in Qumran literature itself.[7] Thus, Josephus has probably exaggerated the Pythagorean features of Essenism in order to appeal to his readership.

# NOTES

## 1 Introduction

1 For a helpful compendium of ancient texts dealing with the Essenes, see A. Adam, *Antike Berichte über die Essener*, Kleine Texte für Vorlesungen und Übungen 182, 2nd edn (Berlin: de Gruyter, 1972).

2 Citations of Philo in this study will be from F. H. Colson and G. H. Whitaker, trans., *Philo*, LCL (10 vols., Cambridge, Mass.: Harvard University Press, 1929–62).

3 G. A. Williamson, *The World of Josephus* (Boston: Little, Brown, 1964), 274–86.

4 H. St. J. Thackeray, *Josephus: The Man and the Historian* (New York: KTAV, 1967), 47. See Williamson (*World of Josephus*, 274–83) for examples of this tendency in Josephus.

5 Williamson, *World of Josephus*, 283–4. So also T. Rajak, *Josephus: The Historian and His Society* (Philadelphia: Fortress, 1984), 228.

6 M. Black, *The Essene Problem* (London: Heffer and Sons, 1961), 2–3; J. A. Sanders, "The Dead Sea Scrolls – A Quarter Century of Study," *BA* 36 (1973), 126; H. W. Attridge, *The Interpretation of Biblical History in the Antiquitates Judaicae of Flavius Josephus*, HDR 7 (Missoula: Scholars, 1976), 5; J. Strugnell, "Flavius Josephus and the Essenes: *Antiquities* XVIII.18–22," *JBL* 77 (1958), 108.

7 Thackeray, *Josephus*, 5.

8 Williamson, *World of Josephus*, 293–4.

9 Thus M. Burrows, *The Dead Sea Scrolls* (New York: Viking, 1955), 285: "We cannot tell how accurately the beliefs of the Essenes are reported in our sources."

10 Josephus first mentions the Essenes in connection with Jonathan Maccabaeus in the mid second century B.C. (*Ant.* 13.5,9 §171), and attests to their continued existence in his own lifetime (*Life* 1.2 §10–12). The dates for Jonathan's rule are usually given as *ca.* 160–143 B.C.

11 R. de Vaux, *Archaeology and the Dead Sea Scrolls* (London: Oxford University Press, 1973), 1–45. De Vaux believes that the site was abandoned from 31–4 B.C. (pp. 20–4), while J. T. Milik (*Ten Years of Discovery in the Wilderness of Judaea*, SBT 26 [London: SCM, 1959], 53–4) thinks that there was at least some Essene occupation during this period. Cf. E.-M. Laperrousaz (*Qoumrân:*

*L'établissement essénien des bords de la Mer Morte. Histoire et archéologie du site* [Paris: A. & J. Picard, 1976], 33—56) for an alternative dating of periods 1b and 2.

12  See P. W. Lapp, *Palestinian Ceramic Chronology 200 B.C. – A.D. 70* (New Haven: American Schools of Oriental Research, 1961), 137—220.

13  De Vaux, *Archaeology*, 102.

14  Ibid., 126—33; R. de Vaux, "Une hachette essénienne?", *VT* 9 (1959), 399—407.

15  S. A. Birnbaum, *The Hebrew Scripts. Part One: The Text* (Leiden: Brill, 1971), 127. See also S. A. Birnbaum, *The Qumrân (Dead Sea) Scrolls and Palaeography*, *BASOR* Supplementary Studies, 13—14 (New Haven: American Schools of Oriental Research, 1952); F. M. Cross, "The Oldest Manuscript from Qumran," *JBL* 74 (1955), 147—72; F. M. Cross, "The Development of the Jewish Script," *The Bible and the Ancient Near East: Essays in Honor of William Foxwell Albright*, ed. G. E. Wright (New York: Doubleday, 1961), 133—202; and N. Avigad, "The Palaeography of the Dead Sea Scrolls and Related Documents," *Aspects of the Dead Sea Scrolls*, Scripta Hierosolymitana 4 (Jerusalem: Magnes, 1957), 56—87.

16  De Vaux, *Archaeology*, 98. On the precise date of the fall of Masada, see W. Eck, "Die Eroberung von Masada und eine neue Inschrift des L. Flavius Silva Nonius Bassus," *ZNW* 60 (1969), 282—9.

17  J. A. Fitzmyer, "The Date of the Qumran Scrolls," *America* 104 (1961), 780—1; de Vaux, *Archaeology*, 101.

18  D. Burton, J. B. Poole, and R. Reed, "A New Approach to the Dating of the Dead Sea Scrolls," *Nature* 184 (1959), 533—4.

19  De Vaux, *Archaeology*, 134. Though J.-P. Audet ("Qumrân et la notice de Pline sur les Esséniens," *RB* 68 [1961], 346—87) maintains that "infra hos" refers to the mountains overlooking Engedi, Laperrousaz ("'Infra hos Engedda', Notes à propos d'un article récent," *RB* 69 [1962], 369—80) and C. Burchard ("Pline et les Esséniens. A propos d'un article récent," *RB* 69 [1962], 533—69) have effectively countered Audet's arguments.

20  De Vaux, *Archaeology*, 134. Excavation at Feshkha has revealed a shed that was probably used as a drying-house for dates. In addition, palm-wood beams, palm-leaves, and dates have been found in the ruins of Khirbet Qumran and the caves (ibid., pp. 73—4).

21  Ibid., p. 134. Likewise G. Vermes (*The Dead Sea Scrolls: Qumran in Perspective* [Cleveland: Collins and World, 1978], 127) states that "in the absence of a rival archaeological site, Pliny's evidence offers a powerful argument in favor of the Essene thesis"; F. Cross ("The Early History of the Qumran Community," *New Directions in Biblical Archaeology*, ed. D. N. Freedman and J. C. Greenfield [Garden City: Doubleday, 1969], 68) affirms that the evidence from Pliny "is virtually decisive" in establishing the identification of the Qumran community with the Essenes; and M. Burrows (*The Dead Sea Scrolls*, 280) concurs that "the geographic connection remains

the strongest reason for regarding the Qumran sectarians as Essenes. If they were not the same, there was hardly room for both Essenes and covenanters in the vicinity of the Wady Qumran."

22  For a good discussion of the parallels, see A. Dupont-Sommer, *The Essene Writings from Qumran* (Gloucester, Mass.: Peter Smith, 1973 [orig. French edn, 1961]), 21–67.

23  Cross, "Early History of the Qumran Community," 68–9. There are, of course, still a small number of scholars who hold that the Qumran community should be identified with a group other than the Essenes: the Zealots, the Pharisees, and even the Karaites and Ebionites have been proposed. For a brief summary of these alternative views, see Sanders, "Dead Sea Scrolls – A Quarter Century," 121–3. See also the publications by Driver, Hoenig, del Medico, Roth, Teicher, and Zeitlin listed in the Bibliography.

24  Dupont-Sommer, *Essene Writings*, 68–412.

25  Strugnell, "Josephus and the Essenes," 107.

26  *J. W.* 1.3,5 §78–80; 2.7,3 §111–13; 2.20,4 §566–8; 3.2,1 §9–12; 5.4,2 §142–5.

27  The other passages are: *Ant.* 13.5,9 §171–2; 13.10,6 §298; 13.11,2 §311–13; 15.10,4–5 §371–9; 17.13,3 §346–8; 18.1,2 §11.

28  B. Niese, *Flavii Josephi opera*, 2nd edn (7 vols., Berlin: Weidmann, 1955 [orig. pub. 1887–95]). See also O. Michel and O. Bauernfeind, eds., *De bello judaico: Der jüdische Krieg* (Darmstadt: Wissenschaftliche Buchgesellschaft; Munich: Kösel, 1960–9); A. Pelletier, *Josèphe: Guerre des Juifs*, Collection des Universités de France (Paris: Belles Lettres, vol. 1, 1975, vol. 2, 1980); and A. Pelletier, *Flavius Josèphe: Autobiographie*, Collection des Universités de France (Paris: Belles Lettres, 1959).

29  There are also ten fragments of the *Manual of Discipline* from Cave 4 (as yet unpublished), and one from Cave 5 (= 5Q*11*). See further J. T. Milik, Review of P. Wernberg-Møller, *The Manual of Discipline Translated and Annotated*, *RB* 67 (1960), 410–16.

30  Cross, "Development of Jewish Script," 198.

31  See especially J. Murphy-O'Connor, "La genèse littéraire de la règle de la communauté," *RB* 76 (1969), 528–49; also, J. H. Charlesworth, "The Origin and Subsequent History of the Authors of the Dead Sea Scrolls: Four Transitional Phases among the Qumran Essenes," *RQ* 10 (1979–81), 213–33. Cf. J. Pouilly, *La règle de la communauté de Qumrân: son évolution littéraire*, Cahiers de la Revue Biblique 17 (Paris: Gabalda, 1976).

32  See P. Wernberg-Møller, *The Manual of Discipline Translated and Annotated*, STDJ 1 (Leiden: Brill, 1957); Vermes, *Dead Sea Scrolls*, 45–6.

33  5QD corresponds to CD 9:7–10, while 6QD corresponds to CD 4:19–21; 5:13–14; 5:18–6:2; 6:20–7:1; and a fragment not found in CD.

34  Milik, *Ten Years*, 151–2.

35  See the following articles by J. Murphy-O'Connor: "An Essene Missionary Document? CD II,14 – VI,1," *RB* 77 (1970), 201–29;

"The Translation of Damascus Document VI,11–14," *RQ* 7 (1971),
553–6; "A Literary Analysis of Damascus Document
VI,2 – VIII,3," *RB* 78 (1971), 210–32; "The Critique of the Princes
of Judah (CD VIII,3–19)," *RB* 79 (1972), 200–16; and "A Literary
Analysis of Damascus Document XIX,33 – XX,34," *RB* 79 (1972),
544–64. So also P. R. Davies, *The Damascus Covenant*, JSOT
Supplement Series 25 (Sheffield: University of Sheffield, 1982).
Note further J. A. Fitzmyer's observation: "Both rule books grew by
accretion and reflect different stages of community development"
(S. Schechter, *Documents of Jewish Sectaries*, with prolegomenon
by J. A. Fitzmyer [2 vols. in one, New York: KTAV, 1970], 17).

36 Dupont-Sommer, *Essene Writings*, 120, 143–4.

37 Davies, *Damascus Covenant*, 2.

38 Y. Yadin, *The Scroll of the War of the Sons of Light Against the
Sons of Darkness* (Oxford: Oxford University Press, 1962), 245–6;
also Dupont-Sommer, *Essene Writings*, 167.

39 See 4QpNah 3–4 i 2–3; 1QpHab 2:12–15; Dupont-Sommer, *Essene
Writings*, 166–7.

40 For a more detailed outline, see J. A. Fitzmyer, *The Dead Sea
Scrolls: Major Publications and Tools for Study*, SBLSBS 8
(Missoula, MT: Scholars, 1977), 95–6.

41 In addition 1Q*35* (Barthélemy and Milik, *Qumrân Cave I*, 136–8)
also forms a part of the *Hodayot*.

42 For an alternative ordering of columns and fragments, see the
following articles by J. Carmignac: "Remarques sur le texte des
Hymnes de Qumrân," *Biblica* 39 (1958), 139–55; and "Localisation
des fragments 15, 18 et 22 des Hymnes," *RQ* 1 (1958–9), 425–30.
Cf. S. Holm-Nielsen, *Hodayot: Psalms from Qumran*, Acta
Theologica Danica 2 (Aarhus: Universitetsforlaget, 1960), 9–13;
B. Kittel, *The Hymns of Qumran: Translation and Commentary*,
SBLDS 50 (Chico, CA: Scholars, 1981).

43 "Le travail d'édition des fragments manuscrits de Qumrân," *RB*
63 (1956), 64 (Communication de J. Strugnell).

44 M. P. Horgan, *Pesharim: Qumran Interpretations of Biblical Books*,
CBQMS 8 (Washington, D.C.: The Catholic Biblical Association
of America, 1979), 1. See also W. H. Brownlee, *The Midrash Pesher
of Habakkuk*, SBLMS 24 (Missoula, MT: Scholars, 1979).

45 Dupont-Sommer, *Essene Writings*, 256.

46 Y. Yadin, *The Temple Scroll* (3 vols., Jerusalem: Israel Exploration
Society, The Institute of Archaeology of the Hebrew University of
Jerusalem, The Shrine of the Book, 1983 [Hebrew edn, 1977]),
1:390.

47 See further B. Z. Wacholder, *The Dawn of Qumran: The Sectarian
Torah and the Teacher of Righteousness* (Cincinnati: Hebrew Union
College, 1983). Wacholder considers this scroll to be the "sectarian
Torah," a text that is "even more faithful to the word of God and
more authoritative than its Mosaic archetype" (p. 4) for the Qumran
community. So also D. Rokéah, "The Temple Scroll, Philo,
Josephus, and the Talmud," *JTS* 34 (1983), 515–26.

48  A. Caquot, "Le Rouleau du Temple de Qoumrân," *ETR* 53 (1978), 449.
49  Yadin, *Temple Scroll*, 1:398–9; Caquot, "Le Rouleau du Temple de Qoumrân," 446–7.
50  See M. A. Knibb, *The Ethiopic Book of Enoch: A New Edition in the Light of the Aramaic Dead Sea Fragments* (2 vols., Oxford: Clarendon Press, 1978); cf. the review of it by J. A. Fitzmyer, *JBL* 99 (1980), 631–6.
51  See nn. 31 and 35 above.

## 3  Commentary on Josephus' major Essene passages

1  Only the book and Niese numbers will be given for references to the major passages (*J. W.* 2.8,2–13 §119–61 and *Ant.* 18.1,2,5 §11,18–22), for sake of simplicity. The complete references are as follows: *J. W.* 2.8,2 §119–21; *J. W.* 2.8,3 §122–3; *J. W.* 2.8,4 §124–7; *J. W.* 2.8,5 §128–33; *J. W.* 2.8,6 §134–6; §2.8,7 §137–42; *J. W.* 2.8,8 §143–4; *J. W.* 2.8,9 §145–9; *J. W.* 2.8,10 §150–3; *J. W.* 2.8,11 §154–8; *J. W.* 2.8,12 §159; *J. W.* 2.8,13 §160–1; *Ant.* 18.1,2 §11; *Ant.* 18.1,5 §18–22.
2  Black, *Essene Problem*, 3–4.
3  Rajak, *Josephus*, 35.
4  Adam, *Antike Berichte über die Essener*, 37; cf. C. Burchard, Review of A. Adam, *Antike Berichte über die Essener*, *RQ* 5 (1964–6), 133.
5  Strangely, in *Ant.* 18.1,6 §23, after explaining the three philosophical classes mentioned in *Ant.* 18.1,2, Josephus mentions a fourth group, but does not identify it.
6  C. D. Ginsburg (*The Essenes: Their History and Doctrines* [London: Longman, Green, Longman, Roberts, and Green, 1864], 27–30) gives nineteen different explanations of the name current in his day; G. Vermes ("The Etymology of 'Essenes,'" *RQ* 2 [1959–60], 427–43) provides a more recent summary of the various views, along with his own proposal.
7  "Their name which is, I think, a variation, though the form of the Greek is inexact, of 'holiness,' is given them, because they have shown themselves especially devout in the service of God" (*Every Good Man is Free* 12 §75).
8  Vermes, "Etymology," 429; Dupont-Sommer, *Essene Writings*, 27 n. 6.
9  See Pelletier, *Josèphe: Guerre des Juifs*, 2:31, 206n. Compare Josephus' use of the word in *Life* 49 §258, where it means "dignity" or "propriety."
10  Josephus uses Ἐσσηνοί fourteen times in his writings and Ἐσσαῖοι sixteen times.
11  E. Schürer, *Geschichte des jüdischen Volkes im Zeitalter Jesu Christi*, 4th edn (4 vols., Leipzig: J. C. Hinrichs'sche Buchhandlung, 1907), 2:654–6; F. M. Cross, *The Ancient Library of Qumran and Modern Biblical Studies*, rev. edn (Grand Rapids: Baker, 1980), 51–2; Milik, *Ten Years*, 80 n. 1.

12  P. Benoit, J. T. Milik, et R. de Vaux, *Les Grottes de Murabba'at*, DJD 2 (2 vols: part 1: Texte, part 2: Planches, Oxford: Clarendon, 1961), 163−4; Milik, *Ten Years*, 80 n. 1. Milik, however, gives no evidence in support of his identification of the site of *mṣd ḥsdyn* with Qumran.

13  Dupont-Sommer, *Essene Writings*, 43.

14  Vermes, "Etymology," 434; Cross, *Ancient Library*, 51−2.

15  S. Goranson, "'Essenes': Etymology from 'śh," *RQ* 11 (1982−4), 488−98.

16  See Ginsburg, *Essenes*, 29.

17  Vermes, "Etymology," 435−43; see also G. Vermes, "Essenes and Therapeutai," *RQ* 3 (1961−2), 495−504. See further *J. W.* 2 §136 (pp. 72−3).

18  Cross, *Ancient Library*, 52n.

19  Thus, O. Michel and O. Bauernfeind translate the term in 2 §120 with "sinnlichen Freuden" (*De bello judaico*, 205). Josephus uses the term seven other times in the plural: one time the meaning is neutral (*Ant.* 16.1,2 §9), while the other six times the meaning is negative, referring to some sort of excess. Three of these six cases clearly denote sexual pleasure (sexual pleasure: *Ant.* 15.2,6 §27; 15.2,6 §29; *Ag. Ap.* 2.37 §275; other excess: *Ant.* 2.9,1 §201; 19.1,16 §130; 19.2,5 §207).

20  Pliny also mentions Essene celibacy: the Essene tribe "is remarkable beyond all the other tribes in the whole world, as it has no women and has renounced all sexual desire" (*Natural History* 5.15 §73).

21  W. Bauer, "Essener," *PWSup* 4 (1924), 414. (Bauer's article predates the Qumran finds.)

22  R. Marcus, "The Qumrân Scrolls and Early Judaism," *Biblical Research* 1 (1956), 28−9. So also Black, *Essene Problem*, 19: "One wonders if Josephus is not guilty of selecting the exceptions and making them the rule."

23  Black (*Essene Problem*, 16) conjectures that perhaps it was "this abnormal postponement of marriage" which led to the impression that the sect despised marriage.

24  The precise interpretation of this text has been debated, primarily because of the phrase *bḥyyhm*, "in their [masc.] lifetime." J. Murphy-O'Connor ("Essene Missionary Document," 220) retains the masculine suffix and interprets the text as a prohibition of two marriages in the man's lifetime, thus ruling out any type of second marriage. G. Vermes ("Sectarian Matrimonial Halakhah in the Damascus Rule," *JJS* 25 [1974], 197−202) regards the debate over *bḥyyhm* as of lesser importance than the context of the biblical citations, which he thinks supports the prohibition of polygamy alone (see also L. Ginzberg, *An Unknown Jewish Sect* [New York: Jewish Theological Seminary of America, 1976], 20). Finally, many scholars, including Y. Yadin ("L'attitude essénienne envers la polygamie et le divorce," *RB* 79 [1972], 98−9) and J. A. Fitzmyer ("The Matthean Divorce Texts and Some New Palestinian Evidence," *TS* 37 [1976], 197−226) regard the prohibition to be

against both polygamy and remarriage after divorce. Yadin considers the masculine suffix to be a scribal error (reading instead *bḥyyhn*), while Fitzmyer understands the masculine suffix to refer to both the man and the woman. Either of the last two interpretations mentioned (prohibition against polygamy or prohibition against polygamy and remarriage after divorce) seems more plausible than the first (prohibition against any second marriage), in the light of the evidence from 11QTemple[a] 57:17–19 (see Yadin, "L'attitude essénienne," 98–9; cf. J. Murphy-O'Connor, "Remarques sur l'exposé du Professeur Y. Yadin," *RB* 79 [1972], 99–100). So also A. Tosato ("The Law of Leviticus 18:18: A Re-examination," *CBQ* 46 [1984], 199–214), who argues that both Lev 18:18 and CD 4:20–1 are prohibitions against polygamy and divorce.

25  According to M. Baillet (*Qumrân Grotte 4: III*, pp. 81–105 and pls. XXIX–XXXIV), 4Q*502* describes a marriage ritual, and thus indicates marriage at Qumran. The text, however, is quite fragmentary, and precludes a definitive interpretation.

26  De Vaux, *Archaeology*, 47. See also S. H. Steckoll, "Preliminary Excavation Report in the Qumran Cemetery," *RQ* 6 (1967–9), 323–6 (cf. de Vaux's comments on Steckoll [*Archaeology*, 48]).

27  Milik, *Ten Years*, 96.

28  J. Allegro (*Mystery of the Dead Sea Scrolls Revealed* [New York: Gramercy, 1981], 116–17) holds that 4Q*159* 2–4 i 8–10 supports Essene celibacy, since Exod 22:16–17 "requires a man seducing an unbetrothed virgin to marry her and pay her father an appropriate dowry," while the Qumran text says that he should be fined two minas "and be expelled from the community for life." But this interpretation is almost certainly incorrect. The Qumran passage is based upon Deut 22:16–21, a situation quite different from Exodus 22: it is a question of a man who accuses a woman of not being a virgin at the time of their *marriage*. If the man is correct, the woman is put to death; but if he has falsely borne testimony against her (reading *w'm bš[qr] 'nh bh* with Strugnell ["Notes en marge," 178]), then he shall be fined two minas, and he shall not cast her out all his days (reading [*wlw'*]/*yšlḥ kwl ymyw* with Strugnell ["Notes en marge," 178], rather than Allegro's *wšlḥ kwl ymyw*, "and he shall be expelled all his life" [*Qumrân Cave 4*, 8]. The same expression [*šlḥ* followed by *kwl ymyw*] occurs in Deut 22:19). Hence, 4Q*159* 2–4 i 8–10 is simply a restatement of Deut 22:16–21, which presupposes a married, not a celibate, state.

29  For example, according to K. Kuhn (*Konkordanz zu den Qumrantexten* [Göttingen: Vandenhoeck & Ruprecht, 1960]), the noun *yld* does not occur in the Qumran literature included in his concordance (1QS, 1QSa, 1QSb, 1QM, 1QH, CD, plus many of the *Pesharim* and other smaller writings), while *n'r* and *ṭp* occur only three times each.

30  It is probably best to equate "all your creatures" (*kwl m'śyeh* – 1QH 9:36) with "all the children of your truth" (*lkwl bny 'mtkh*); see further Holm-Nielsen, *Hodayot*, 165 n. 160.

31  Holm-Nielsen, *Hodayot*, 164 n. 158.

32 In fact, if J. Murphy-O'Connor is correct, the first part of the *Damascus Document* (CD 2:14–6:1) is really a missionary appeal for outsiders to join with the Essene community. See further Murphy-O'Connor, "Essene Missionary Document," 201–29.

33 See, however, 1QS 4:7 (the spirit of truth causes "healing and abundance of peace, with length of days and fruitfulness [*wprwt zr'*]with all everlasting blessings"), which some take as an indication of marriage.

34 The importance of descendants is also indicated by the following Qumran texts: 1QS 4:7 (see n. 33 above); 1QH 17:14 (those who hope in God's laws will be delivered, that "their seed [*zr'm*] may be before you forever"); 4QpPs^a 1–10 iii 1–2 (to the penitents of the desert "will be all man's inheritance, and to their seed [*wzr'm*] forever"); and 1QSb 3:2,4.

35 Cross, *Ancient Library*, 96; Marcus, "Qumrân Scrolls," 28; G. Vermes, *Jesus the Jew* (New York: Macmillan, 1974), 99–100.

36 G. W. Buchanan, "The Role of Purity in the Structure of the Essene Sect," *RQ* 4 (1963–4), 402–5. Buchanan states that "it seems unreasonable to believe that this lack of trust referred to marital loyalty" and holds that lack of πίστις is really a mistranslation of Hebrew *n'mnwt*, which means "trustworthy" in a ritualistic purity sense. But the context of Josephus' remarks ("the licentious allurements of women," etc.) indicates that marital loyalty is precisely the issue, not ritualistic purity.

37 A. Marx, "Les racines du célibat essénien," *RQ* 7 (1969–71), 341.

38 J. Coppens, "Le célibat essénien," *Qumrân: Sa piété, sa théologie et son milieu*, ed. M. Delcor, BETL 46 (Leuven: Leuven University Press, 1978), 303.

39 Cross, *Ancient Library*, 98–9; thus also Black, *Essene Problem*, 16–19.

40 Strugnell, "Josephus and the Essenes," 110.

41 See Prov 2:16–19; 6:24–9; 7:5–27; 9:13–18; 19:13; 21:9, 19; 25:24; 27:15; 30:20; 31:3.

42 J. Allegro, "The Wiles of the Wicked Woman: A Sapiential Work from Qumran's Fourth Cave," *PEQ* 96 (1964), 53–5.

43 Allegro, "Wiles," 53. Strugnell ("Notes en marge," 266) and Dupont-Sommer ("Le Psaume CLI dans 11QPs^a et le problème de son origine essénienne," *Sem* 14 [1964], 54) dismiss Allegro's suggestion of Rome.

44 Dupont-Sommer, "Le Psaume CLI," 54–5.

45 J. Carmignac, "Poème allégorique sur la secte rivale," *RQ* 5 (1964–6), 373–4.

46 Strugnell, "Notes en marge," 266–7.

47 In the Qumran literature included in Kuhn's concordance (see n. 29 above), *hwn* ("riches, property") occurs fifty times. In twenty-two instances, the connotation of *hwn* is clearly negative; while twenty-seven times, the meaning is neutral (i.e., "property"). The text of 1QSb 3:19 is too fragmentary to determine the nuance of *hwn*.

48  The expression *hwn rš 'h* ("riches of iniquity") does not refer to ill-gotten gain, but rather to riches that may lead to iniquity (because of self-sufficient pride). In the NT, μαμωνᾶς ἀδικίας ("unrighteous mammon") is apparently used in the same way (Luke 16:9, 11).

49  See further L. E. Keck, "The Poor among the Saints in Jewish Christianity and Qumran," *ZNW* 57 (1966), 66–77; J. A. Fitzmyer, "The Qumran Scrolls, the Ebionites and their Literature," *Essays on the Semitic Background of the New Testament* (London: Geoffrey Chapman, 1971), 446 n. 22; and Fitzmyer, "Jewish Christianity in Acts in the Light of the Qumran Scrolls," *Essays on the Semitic Background of the New Testament* (London, Geoffrey Chapman, 1971), 284–8.

50  Dupont-Sommer (*Essene Writings*, 86 n. 3; see also his *The Jewish Sect of Qumran and the Essenes*, 2nd edn [London: Valentine, Mitchell & Co., 1954], 65) states that the expression "mingling of property" is a "technical term meaning common ownership," which is behind Josephus' use of ἀναμεμιγμένων in this passage. C. Rabin (*Qumran Studies* [London: Oxford University Press, 1957], 27–31) argues, however, that the term *'rb* should not be translated "mingle, mix" as in Mishnaic Hebrew, but rather "to be in contact with, to do business with," as in 2 Kgs 18:23 (= Isa 36:8). With this conclusion M. Black (*The Scrolls and Christian Origins: Studies in the Jewish Background of the New Testament* [London: Nelson, 1961], 38) agrees, and even states that "Josephus (or his source) appears to be familiar with the Hebrew *hith'arebh*, but so far from understanding its meaning, he distorts it to mean something completely different, namely a total community of possessions, which had in fact no relation to the real situation." Black's conclusion, however, goes beyond the evidence: is he suggesting that Josephus had a copy of the *Manual of Discipline* in front of him as he wrote this section? It is true that *'rb* may sometimes be better rendered as "to do business with," but that hardly seems to be the meaning of the word in the context of 1QS 6:17–22.

51  1QS 7:24–5 speaks of one who "mingles with him in his purification and possessions," but the rest of the text is too fragmentary to be certain of the interpretation of the passage. Compare the different translations of Dupont-Sommer (*Essene Writings*, 90), W. H. Brownlee (*The Dead Sea Manual of Discipline: Translation and Notes*, BASOR Supplementary Studies, 10–12 [New Haven: American Schools of Oriental Research, 1951], 30), and A. Leaney (*The Rule of Qumran and Its Meaning: Introduction, Translation and Commentary* [Philadelphia: Westminster, 1966], 199).

52  It is also possible that all personal property was handed over to the community, but a certain portion of the community's money was then allocated to individuals for their personal use. See Milik, *Ten Years*, 102.

53  See Chapter 1 above, pp. 8–9, 11.

54  De Vaux, *Archaeology*, 129. In particular, mention should be made of three pots containing silver Tyrian coins buried below the level

of Period 2 and above that of Period 1a. These three pots contained a total of 561 coins. De Vaux concludes that "the treasure can be considered as comprising a single hoard" (p. 34).

55 Ginsburg, *Essenes*, 42 n. 26; see also G. R. Driver, *The Judean Scrolls: The Problem and a Solution* (Oxford: Blackwell, 1965), 102–3.

56 *Šmn*, rather than *šmw*, is the correct reading. The final *nun* is clear from the photographs (see S. Zeitlin, *The Zadokite Fragments*, JQRMS 1 [Philadelphia: The Dropsie College for Hebrew and Cognate Learning, 1952]). Schechter (*Documents of Jewish Sectaries*, 1:51) and C. Rabin (*The Zadokite Documents: I. The Admonition; II. The Laws* [Oxford: Clarendon Press, 1954]) both have *šmw*, though Schechter himself recognizes the possibility of a final *nun* in a textual note (1:51 n. 25). L. Rost (*Die Damaskusschrift* [Berlin: De Gruyter, 1933], 23), Dupont-Sommer (*Essene Writings*, 155 n. 4), J. Baumgarten ("The Essene Avoidance of Oil and the Laws of Purity," *RQ* 6 [1967–9], 183), and J. Carmignac (Review of S. Schechter, *Documents of Jewish Sectaries*, *RQ* 7 [1969–71], 608) all support *šmn* as the correct reading. In addition, with Baumgarten I read the next word as *bhm*, not *khm*, though this is not critical to the understanding of the passage (see, for example, Dupont-Sommer's translation using *khm* [*Essene Writings*, 155]).

57 Baumgarten, "Essene Avoidance of Oil," 183–91. See also 1QM 9:8 for an example of this principle at Qumran.

58 Yadin, *Temple Scroll*, 1:140–2, 399; 2:101 (vol. 1 contains the discussion, while vol. 2 gives the reconstruction of the text). So also Caquot, "Le Rouleau du Temple de Qoumrân," 447. However, Yadin's reconstruction is far from certain: the parallels cited (2 Kgs 18:32 and Lev 26:20) are not convincing to me. Cf. J. M. Baumgarten's negative assessment of Yadin's proposal (Review of Y. Yadin, *Megillat ha-Miqdaš, The Temple Scroll*, *JBL* 97 [1978], 587) and Yadin's counter discussion (*Temple Scroll*, 1:410).

59 Possibly the extreme heat of the region provided a practical reason for the Essene preference for white as well.

60 *Šēs, bād*, and *bûṣ* (a later synonym of *šēš* from the root *bûṣ*, "to be white") all apparently mean fine white linen. See further W. Ewing, "Linen," *A Dictionary of the Bible*, ed. J. Hastings (4 vols., New York: Scribners, 1901), 3:124–5; A. Hurvitz, "The Usage of *Šēs* and *bûṣ* in the Bible and Its Implication for the date of P," *HTR* 60 (1967), 117–21.

61 Yadin, *Scroll of the War*, 219.

62 The reading ἀδιαίρετοι ("without exception"; lit., "undivided") is original, not αἵρετοι ("chosen," in Thackeray's Loeb edition). The latter reading was thought by Bekker to be the reading of Codex Vossianus (fifteenth century), but Niese denies it (*Flavii Josephi opera*, 1:xlix). Apparently, as Pelletier explains, the first three letters of ἀδιαίρετοι were erased at a later date, thus producing αἵρετοι (Pelletier, *Guerre des Juifs*, 2:206).

63  In his account of the Essenes, Philo describes a treasurer (ταμίας), who is undoubtedly the same person as Josephus' overseer: "Each branch when it has received the wages of these so different occupations gives it to one person who has been appointed as treasurer. He takes it and at once buys what is necessary and provides food in abundance and anything else which human life requires" (*Hypothetica* 11.10).

64  Thus Cross, *Ancient Library*, 232 n. 80; Milik, *Ten Years*, 100; Burrows, *Dead Sea Scrolls*, 281; Brownlee, *Manual of Discipline*, 25; and R. H. Charles, ed., *APOT*, 2:824 (with reference to CD 10:10). The etymology of the words supports this interpretation: ἐπιμέλομαι is from ἐπί + μέλομαι, "to have a concern over," "care for," while *mĕbaqqēr* is from *bqr*, "attend to, bestow care on" (KB 144). The parallel term *pāqîd* (see discussion below) is from *pqd*, "take care of," "care for" (KB 773).

65  There is also mentioned in CD 14:8−12 a *mĕbaqqēr* over all the camps, a man between the ages of 30 and 50 who knows mens' secrets and their languages and settles disputes. This man is probably to be distinguished from the *mĕbaqqēr* mentioned in the other CD texts who functions more within a given camp (see below, pp. 46−7). Thus Rabin, *Zadokite Documents*, 47; B. Reike, "The Constitution of the Primitive Church in the Light of Jewish Documents," *The Scrolls and the New Testament*, ed. K. Stendahl (New York: Harper & Bros., 1957), 154; T. Gaster, *The Dead Sea Scriptures*, 3rd edn (Garden City: Doubleday, 1976), 554; and J. Priest, "Mebaqqer, Paqid, and the Messiah," *JBL* 81 (1962), 58.

66  See Cross, *Ancient Library*, 233n.

67  See further Priest, "Mebaqqer," 58−61. He points out that this division of authority is evident in 1QS 5:2−9, where the one entering the community is under the authority of both the priests and the "majority of the members of the community." Perhaps Josephus is aware of this division as well, since he mentions election of both lay persons and priests in *Ant*. 18 §22. See below, p. 121.

68  Priest, "Mebaqqer," 59−60. One of Priest's arguments is that the verb in CD 13:11 (a passage speaking about the *mĕbaqqēr*) is *ypqdhw*, which may be a reflection of a function originally fulfilled by the *pāqîd*, not the *mĕbaqqēr*.

69  Pelletier (*Guerre des Juifs*, 2:206) notes that the verb μετοικέω used by Josephus may well signify that the Essenes were not considered an integral part of the community in the cities in which they lived. In classical and Hellenistic Greek, μετοικέω often denoted resident aliens.

70  See Vermes, *Dead Sea Scrolls*, 128−9.

71  There are at least five different views about the meaning of "Damascus" in the *Damascus Document*. (1) Damascus (literally): M. H. Segal, "The Habakkuk 'Commentary' and the Damascus Fragments," *JBL* 70 (1951), 131−47; Milik, *Ten Years*, 91 n. 2; Dupont-Sommer, *Essene Writings*, 118−20; C. T. Fritsch, "Herod the Great and the Qumran Community," *JBL* 74 (1955), 178−9;

H. H. Rowley, *The Zadokite Fragments and the Dead Sea Scrolls* (Oxford: Blackwell, 1956), 75. (2) Babylon (as the historic place of Jewish exile after 586 B.C.): I. Rabinovitz, "A Reconsideration of 'Damascus' and '390 Years' in the 'Damascus' ('Zadokite') Fragments," *JBL* 73 (1954), 11–35. (3) Babylon (as the place from which the Essenes came in the second century B.C.): J. Murphy-O'Connor, "The Essenes and Their History," *RB* 81 (1974), 215–44; S. Iwry, "Was There a Migration to Damascus? The Problem of *šby yśr'l*," *W. F. Albright Volume* (*Eretz-Israel* 9 [1969]), 80–8; W. F. Albright, *From the Stone Age to Christianity*, 2nd edn (Baltimore: Johns Hopkins, 1957), 376. (4) Jerusalem: G. Vermes, *Scripture and Tradition in Judaism*, SPB 4, 2nd edn (Leiden: Brill, 1973), 43–9. (5) Qumran: Cross, *Ancient Library*, 81–3; R. North, "The Damascus of Qumran Geography," *PEQ* 87 (1955), 33–48 (North says that Qumran was under Nabatean control at the time); A. Jaubert, "Le pays de Damas," *RB* 65 (1958), 214–48; De Vaux, *Archaeology*, 113; and M. Burrows, *More Light on the Dead Sea Scrolls* (New York: Viking, 1958), 227. F. F. Bruce (*Second Thoughts on the Dead Sea Scrolls*, 2nd edn [Grand Rapids: Eerdmans, 1961], 121) states simply that the Damascus references are "an allegorical way of describing the community's withdrawal to the wilderness under the Teacher of Righteousness," but he is unsure precisely where the community went.

72  For a helpful synopsis of the views, see Charlesworth, "Origin and Subsequent History of the Authors of the Dead Sea Scrolls," 213–33.

73  Murphy-O'Connor, "Essenes and Their History," 215–44; see also his "The Essenes in Palestine," *BA* 40 (1977), 100–24.

74  Murphy-O'Connor, "Essenes and Their History," 235–6.

75  See Cross, *Ancient Library*, 51–160.

76  Ibid., 80; W. H. Brownlee, "A Comparison of the Covenanters of the Dead Sea Scrolls with Pre-Christian Jewish Sects," *BA* 13 (1950), 57–8.

77  Thus Dupont-Sommer, *Essene Writings*, 155. Dupont-Sommer thinks the "towns" correspond to Philo's towns (*Hypothetica* 11.1), while the "camps" correspond to the "villages" in Philo. Cf. Cross, *Ancient Library*, 81.

78  S. Goranson ("On the Hypothesis that Essenes lived on Mt. Carmel," *RQ* 9 [1977–8], 563–7) specifically argues that Mt Carmel was the site of one of the Essene camps, while B. Pinner (*An Essene Quarter on Mount Zion?* [Jerusalem: Franciscan Printing, 1976]) makes a case for an Essene camp on Mt Zion. See below, p. 131 (*J. W.* 5.4, 2). See also F. D. Weinert, "4Q159: Legislation for an Essene Community Outside Qumran?," *JSJ* 5 (1974), 179–207.

79  Cross, *Ancient Library*, 79.

80  Philo presents the Essenes as total pacifists (*Every Good Man is Free* 9 §78), and thus it is not surprising that he does not speak of traveling Essenes carrying arms for protection.

81  G. W. Buchanan ("Role of Purity," 398) mentions another practical

reason for the practice of hospitality described by Josephus and Philo. Since the sect was "so exclusive in its regulations that its members could not accept the food or other provisions supplied either by Gentiles or other sects within Judaism," a traveling Essene might have starved were it not for the practical hospitality of his fellow Essenes.

82  Σχῆμα is a versatile word whose basic meaning is "outward form or structure" (J. Schneider, "Σχῆμα, μετασχηματίζω," *TDNT* 7 [1971], 954). Josephus uses the word variously, including "form" (*Ant.* 1.12, 1 §207; 8.3, 9 §96), "estate, rank" (*Ant.* 5.1, 28 §115), "attitude, demeanor" (*Ant.* 10.1, 3 §11), and even "clothing" (*Ant.* 4.8, 23 §257; 7.8, 4 §182; 8.11, 1 §266).

83  M. Jastrow, *A Dictionary of the Targumim, the Talmud Babli and Yerushalmi, and the Midrashic Literature* (2 vols., New York: Putnams, 1903), 2:1152.

84  Brownlee, *Manual of Discipline*, 31 n. 28; Leaney, *Rule of Qumran*, 207; Wernberg-Møller, *Manual of Discipline*, 118 n. 31; R. Marcus, 'Textual Notes on the Dead Sea Manual of Discipline," *JNES* 11 (1952), 209; Burrows, *Dead Sea Scrolls*, 380; Dupont-Sommer, *Essene Writings*, 89. Cf. J. van der Ploeg, "Le 'Manuel de Discipline' des rouleaux de la Mer Morte," *BO* 8 (1951), 122 n. 77; J. T. Milik, "Manuale disciplinae," *Verbum domini* 29 (1951), 148 (who simply translates *pwḥ* as *efflat*).

85  For a good summary of the various views on this passage, see L. H. Silberman, "Manus Velatae: The Significance of 1QS 7:13–14, 15," *JANESCU* 5 (1973), 383–8. See further the discussion of *J.W.* 2 §148, p. 98.

86  A. Dupont-Sommer, "Le problème des influences étrangères sur la secte juive de Qoumrân," *RHPR* 35 (1955), 87–8. On the complex question of the relationship of Pythagoreanism to Essene doctrine and practices, see below, pp. 131–2 (*Ant.* 15 §371).

87  None of the other ancient sources mentions any such heterodox practice. In the parallel section of the *Philosophuma*, Hippolytus simply mentions that the Essenes "always pray at dawn, not speaking before they have praised God" (9:21). And Philo mentions that the Therapeutae (an Essene-like group in Egypt) pray twice a day, "at dawn and at eventide; at sunrise they pray for a fine bright day, fine and bright in the true sense of the heavenly daylight which they pray may fill their minds" (*On the Contemplative Life* 3 §27).

88  Leaney, *Rule of Qumran*, 78.

89  E. Schürer, *The History of the Jewish People in the Age of Jesus Christ (175 B.C.–A.D. 135)*, rev. English edn, ed. G. Vermes, F. Millar, and M. Black (Edinburgh: T. & T. Clark [vol. 1, 1973, vol. 2, 1979]), 2:573. M. Hengel (*Judaism and Hellenism* [2 vols., London: SCM, 1974], 1:236) states that this passage "probably refers to the Shema prayer before sunrise." In *m. Ber.* 1:2 the time of the reflection of the morning *Shema'* is linked with the appearance of the sun, so that the end of the prayer should coincide with the time when "the sun first shines forth."

90  S. Talmon, "The 'Manual of Benedictions' of the Sect of the Judaean Desert," *RQ* 2 (1959–60), 494–5. Thus also E. A. Abbott, *Notes on New Testament Criticism* (London: A. & C. Black, 1907), 190.

91  J. Daniélou, "La communauté de Qumran et l'organisation de l'église ancienne," *RHPR* 35 (1955), 104–15; Strugnell, "Josephus and the Essenes," 112–13; Cross, *Ancient Library*, 105–6.

92  Strugnell, "Josephus and the Essenes," 112–13. I have adopted Strugnell's proposal in my translation.

93  Daniélou, "La communauté de Qumran," 108.

94  M. Burrows describes this section as "perhaps the most obscure passage in the document" ("The Discipline Manual of the Judaean Covenanters," *OTS* 8 [1950], 165). For various interpretations, see A. Dupont-Sommer, "Contribution à l'exégèse du Manuel de discipline x 1–8," *VT* 2 (1952), 229–43; W. H. Brownlee, "Light on the Manual of Discipline (DSD) from the Book of Jubilees," *BASOR* 123 (1951), 30–2; Brownlee, *Manual of Discipline*, 38–41, 50–1 (Brownlee sees an acrostic *'mn* in lines 1 and 4); Leaney, *Rule of Qumran*, 237–45; Wernberg-Møller, *Manual of Discipline*, 36–7, 139–44.

95  Thus Leaney, *Rule of Qumran*, 239; Dupont-Sommer, "Contribution," 234. See, however, S. Talmon ("Manual of Benedictions," 481), who argues for six times of prayer, three in the daylight and three in the evening.

96  S. Talmon ("The Calendar Reckoning of the Sect from the Judaean Desert," *Aspects of the Dead Sea Scrolls*, Scripta Hierosolymitana 4 [Jerusalem: Magnes, 1957], 187–90) argues both from the order of prayer indicated in 1QS 10:10 and the reversal of the order of the clauses in the paraphrase of Deut 6:7 in 1QS 10:14 that the sectarians reckoned the day from sunrise to sunrise, contrary to normal Jewish practice. If true, this might be further evidence of the influence of the sun in the sectarians' thought (see the discussion of the solar calendar below). See, however, J. Baumgarten's analysis ("The Beginning of the Day in the Calendar of Jubilees," *Studies in Qumran Law*, SJLA 24 [Leiden: Brill, 1977], 125) in which he points out that CD 10:14–15 seems to contradict Talmon's theory.

97  Mention should also be made of 4Q503, recently published by M. Baillet (*Qumran Grotte 4: III*, pp. 105–36 and pls. XXXV, XXXVII, XXXIX, XLI, XLIII, XLV, and XLVII), which contains formulae of morning and evening prayers for each day of the month.

98  A. Dupont-Sommer, "Le Livre des Hymnes découvert près de la mer Morte (1QH)," *Sem* 7 (1957), 42. English translation from *Essene Writings*, 211. See further J. A. Fitzmyer, "Glory Reflected on the Face of Christ (2 Cor 3:7–4:6) and a Palestinian Jewish Motif," *TS* 42 (1981), 640. Fitzmyer (reading *l'wrtym*) translates the phrase, "you have appeared to me for enlightenment." Dupont-Sommer also reads *l'wrtym* instead of *l'wrtwm* in 1QH 18:29 (which he translates, "in the everlasting place where shines the eternal light of the dawn"), again linking contemplation of the "light of the

dawn" with the Essene prayer to the sun ("Livre des Hymnes," 103; *Essene Writings*, 253).

99 See further Milik, *Books of Enoch*, 273—97; Fitzmyer, "Implications of the New Enoch Literature," 341—2. Fragments from *Jubilees* have also been found at Qumran: 1QJub[a],[b]; 2QJub[a],[b]; 4QJub[a–f]. 1Q and 2Q fragments have been published in DJD 1 and DJD 3 respectively. 4QJub[f] has been partially published by Milik, "Fragment d'une source du Psautier (4QPs 89)," *RB* 73 (1966), 104. The respect that *Jubilees* enjoyed at Qumran may also be seen by CD 16:2—4, which praises the book. Strugnell reports that fragments of a work similar to *Jubilees* have been found in Cave 4, a work possibly written to defend a different view of the calendar (M. Baillet et al., "Le travail d'édition des fragments manuscrits de Qumrân," *RB* 63 [1956], 65).

100 The fragments are partially published in J. T. Milik, "Le travail d'édition des manuscrits du Desert de Juda," *Volume du Congrès, Strasbourg, 1956*, VTSup 4 (Leiden, Brill, 1957), 24—5. See also the analysis of this text by Talmon, "Calendar Reckoning," 169—76. Vermes sees additional evidence for the solar calendar in 1QS 10:5 (*Dead Sea Scrolls*, 176). For further references to the calendar in Qumran literature, see 1QS 1:14—15; 10:3—8; 1QH 1:15—20; CD 3:13—15; 6:18—19; 16:1—5; 1QpHab 11:4—8; Leaney, *Rule of Qumran*, 80—90; D. Barthélemy, "Notes en marge de publications récentes sur les manuscrits de Qumrân," *RB* 59 (1952), 200—2; A. Jaubert, "Le calendrier des Jubilés et de la secte de Qumrân: Ses origines bibliques," *VT* 3 (1953), 250—64; and K. Schubert, *The Dead Sea Community: Its Origin and Teachings* (New York: Harper, 1959), 57—8.

101 See also J. Baumgarten, "Qumran Studies," *Studies in Qumran Law*, 10—11 n. 18; Cross, *Ancient Library*, 103—4. Schubert (*Dead Sea Community*, 77) notes that in the large cemetery east of Qumran all the bodies were buried in a north—south position "with the head in the direction of the sun," a custom that he believes points to "a high regard for the sun" in the Qumran community. For a more plausible explanation of this burial practice, however, see J. T. Milik, "Hénoch au pays des aromates (ch. 27—32). Fragments araméens de la grotte 4 de Qumran," *RB* 65 (1958), 77; Milik, *Ten Years*, 47, 104.

102 S. Talmon ("A Further Link Between the Judean Covenanters and the Essenes," *HTR* 56 [1963], 313—19) believes that this simultaneous cessation of work prior to their assembly is reflected in CD 11:22b—12:1a, which he translates as follows: "And when the trumpets for assembly sound — and one should not do so earlier or later — they shall cease all work. This is a holy testimony." While his suggestion is intriguing, it is based on the unlikely assumption that a medieval copyist "misplaced" the negation *wl'* in the passage (p. 318).

103 Philo's claim that the Essenes were total pacifists seems to be in error. See *J. W.* 2 §125 ("they are armed on account of robbers"); the

accounts of John the Essene's exploits against the Romans (*J. W.* 2.20, 4 §567; 3.2, 1 §11–12); and, at Qumran, 1QM (the *War Scroll*).

104   De Vaux, *Archaeology*, 15–17, 28–9, 60–83.

105   De Vaux, *Archaeology*, 85; W. R. Farmer, "The Economic Basis of the Qumran Community," *TZ* 11 (1955), 297–308, esp. 298–9; see also E. W. G. Masterman, "'Ain el-Feshkhah, el-Ḥajar el-Aṣbaḥ, and Khurbet Ḳumrân," *PEFQS* (1902), 160–7; and "Observations on the Dead Sea Level," *PEFQS* (1904), 83–95 (esp. 91–5).

106   De Vaux, *Archaeology*, 84, 86.

107   I have taken ψυχροῖς ὕδασιν as a dative of place, i.e., they bathe (wash) their bodies "in cold water," but it is also possible to understand the phrase as a dative of instrument, "with cold water." See further E. F. Sutcliffe, "Baptism and Baptismal Rites at Qumran?" *HeyJ* 1 (1960), 187.

108   Since the same word (ἁγνείαν, "purification") is used in *J. W.* 2 §138 as in *J. W.* 2 §129, it is likely that the reference in 2 §138 is to the daily washings of the Essenes, not to some one-time initiatory baptismal rite (cf. Cross, *Ancient Library*, 234; Black, *Scrolls*, 96–7). The plural form (which I have translated as "rites of purification") occurs in *J. W.* 2 §159 and *Ant.* 18 §19, and does not seem to refer exclusively (if at all) to the daily washings of the Essenes. See J. Strugnell, "Josephus and the Essenes," 115 n. 39. Cf. L. Cerfaux, "Le baptême des Esséniens," *Recueil Lucien Cerfaux*, BETL 6–7 (Gembloux: Duculot, 1954), 327.

109   H. Gottstein ("Anti-Essene Traits in the Dead Sea Scrolls," *VT* 4 [1954], 145–6) uses these passages to show that the Qumran community "abhorred" the concept of baptism for ritual purity and thus could not have been Essene, but he is reading too much into the text.

110   Thus S. Lieberman, "The Discipline in the So-Called Dead Sea Manual of Discipline," *JBL* 71 (1952), 203; J. M. Baumgarten, "Sacrifice and Worship among the Jewish Sectarians of the Dead Sea (Qumran) Scrolls," *Studies in Qumran Law*, 46 n. 23; Vermes, *Dead Sea Scrolls*, 95–6; Wernberg-Møller, *Manual of Discipline*, 96 n. 52; Cross, *Ancient Library*, 86 n. 59; Black, *Scrolls*, 100 (Black thinks it refers specifically to the "sacred meal"). K. G. Kuhn ("The Lord's Supper and the Communal Meal at Qumran," *The Scrolls and the New Testament*, ed. Stendahl, 67–8), however, considers ṭhrh as a technical term for the bath of immersion; thus also Dupont-Sommer, *Essene Writings*, 83, and *Jewish Sect*, 90 (though on p. 88 of *Jewish Sect* he calls it "the name given to the communal centre"). Yet, as Baumgarten points out (p. 46 n. 23), 1QS 5:13 clearly distinguishes the purificatory bath from the ṭhrh. Because of my interpretation of ṭhrh, the other passages that use this term (1QS 6:16–17, 22, 24–5; 7:2–3, 15–16, 18–20; 8:16–17; CD 9:21, 23) are discussed in connection with the common meal (see pp. 57–8 below), rather than with the purificatory baths.

111   1QM 14:2–3 may also refer to a purificatory washing: "After they

have gone up from among the slain to return to the camp, they will intone the hymn of return. In the morning they will wash their garments and cleanse themselves of the blood of the sinners' corpses."

112 Thus, for example, O. Cullmann, "Die neuentdeckten Qumrantexte und das Judenchristentum der Pseudoklementinen," *BZNW* 21 (1954), 44; Dupont-Sommer, *Jewish Sect*, 167–8.

113 See R. A. S. Macalister, *The Excavation of Gezer* (3 vols., London: John Murray, 1912), 1:274–6; 3: pl.54; R.P. Benoit and R. B. Boismard, "Un ancien sanctuaire chrétien a Béthanie," *RB* 58 (1951), 200–6; De Vaux, *Archaeology*, 131–2; Fitzmyer, "Qumran Scrolls," 471; Cross, *Ancient Library*, 67.

114 De Vaux, *Archaeology*, 132 (see pl. xxxix, §68, 138); Cross, *Ancient Library*, 67–8.

115 Kuhn, "Lord's Supper," 68. Thus also J. Gnilka, "Das Gemeinschaftsmahl der Essener," *BZ* 5 (1961), 43; S. H. Hooke, "Symbolism in the Dead Sea Scrolls," *SE* (1959), 607; and (tentatively) J. Thomas, *Le mouvement baptiste en Palestine et Syrie (150 v. J.-C.–300 apr. J.-C.)* (Gembloux: Duculot, 1935), 18–19 (Thomas' work antedates the discovery of the scrolls).

116 See Sutcliffe, "Baptism," 179–88.

117 In *J. W.* 2 §139, as well, Josephus writes that only a full member of the community may touch the common meal (see pp. 75–8).

118 Philo does, however, describe the feast which the Therapeutae (see n. 87 above) celebrate in great detail (*On the Contemplative Life* 8–11 §65–90). But this feast occurred only once a year, presumably at Pentecost ("the chief feast which Fifty takes for its own, Fifty the most sacred of numbers," *On the Contemplative Life* 8 §65), while the Essene meals described by Josephus and Philo were daily.

119 Cross, in fact, views this passage as setting forth the common meal of the community as "a liturgical anticipation of the Messianic banquet" (*Ancient Library*, 90). So also L. H. Schiffman, "Communal Meals at Qumran," *RQ* 10 (1979–81), 45–56; Vermes, *Dead Sea Scrolls*, 182.

120 De Vaux, *Archaeology*, 11–12.

121 For this understanding of *ṭhrt* ("purity") as referring to ritually pure food, see p. 56 and p. 148 n. 110 above.

122 So Wernberg-Møller, *Manual of Discipline*, 110 n. 65; Leaney, *Rule of Qumran*, 191–5; Brownlee, *Manual of Discipline*, 26, 27 n. 43; Vermes, *Dead Sea Scrolls*, 96. Some scholars, however, believe that *mšqh* refers to the common meal: thus Dupont-Sommer, *Essene Writings*, 87 (translating *mšqh* as "Banquet"); Gaster, *Dead Sea Scriptures*, 56 (translating "common board"); Cross, *Ancient Library*, 86, esp. n. 59; Milik, *Ten Years*, 102; Burrows, "Discipline Manual," 163–4. E. F. Sutcliffe ("Sacred Meals at Qumran?," *HeyJ* 1 [1960], 53–4) argues that both prohibitions are directed only at the preparation (stressing *yg'*, "he shall not touch") of food (*ṭhrt*) and drink (*mšqh*), not at participation in the meal itself.

123 Lieberman, "Discipline," 203; Leaney, *Rule of Qumran*, 194;

Sutcliffe, "Sacred Meals," 53–4; Vermes, *Dead Sea Scrolls*, 95. See also Lev 11:34, 37–8. See further pp. 45–6 (*J. W.* 2 §123).

124 The expression μεθ' ἡσυχίας may be translated either as "quietly" or "in silence." I have chosen the former, since the context indicates that they probably did not observe silence like the Trappists of later centuries (see *J. W.* 2 §133), and the other usages of the expression in Josephus do not seem to refer to absolute silence (*J. W.* 2.15, 5 §325; 3.5, 3 §85; 4.6, 2 §372; *Ant.* 8.11, 2 §275).

125 Thus Dupont-Sommer, *Essene Writings*, 108; Vermes, *Dead Sea Scrolls*, 185; K. G. Kuhn, "The Two Messiahs of Aaron and Israel," *The Scrolls and the New Testament*, 55; Cross, *Ancient Library*, 219–20; Milik, *Ten Years*, 124–7; R. E. Brown, "The Messianism of Qumran," *CBQ* 19 (1957), 56. The text itself does not equate them. Others dispute that the "priest" mentioned in 1QSa should be equated with a "Messiah of Aaron": see Black, *Scrolls*, 146–8; A. J. B. Higgins, "The Priestly Messiah," *NTS* 13 (1966–7), 216–19; C. T. Fritsch, "The So-called 'Priestly Messiah' of the Essenes," *JEOL* 6 (1959–66), 242–8. J. F. Priest ("The Messiah and the Meal in 1QSa," *JBL* 82 [1963], 95–100) thinks that 1QSa speaks of only one Messiah, but reflects a growing projection of the "priest" into the messianic realm (a process completed by the time of 1QS).

126 This expression (*'yš lpy kbwdw*) is used four times in this passage, both with respect to the assembly (1QSa 2:14–17) and the meal (1QSa 2:21).

127 1QS 6:24–5 states that the one who lies knowingly shall be deprived of a quarter of his rations (*rby'yt lḥmw*). This seems to imply equality of food allotments. The frugality of the meal must have made this punishment quite severe.

128 Sutcliffe, "Sacred Meals," 51.

129 Milik, *Ten Years*, 105–6.

130 Vermes, *Dead Sea Scrolls*, 94, 111; Sutcliffe, "Sacred Meals," 50–1; Leaney, *Rule of Qumran*, 184.

131 11QTemple[a] 21:7–8 reads: "They [i.e., all the people] will begin to drink the new wine (*yyn ḥdš*) [and they will not eat] any unripe grape from the vines for on this [day they will expia]te for the new wine (*htyrwš*)." See further, Yadin, *Temple Scroll*, 1:140–2.

132 CD 8:9, 10 cites Deut 32:33, which mentions *yyn*, and then interprets the *yyn* as the (evil) ways of the kings. That *yyn* is used symbolically for something evil does not necessarily indicate that the community considered *yyn* itself evil, but it may point in that direction. The *Temple Scroll*, however, mentions *yyn* eleven times with no negative connotation attached (11QTemple[a] 13:12; 14:14; 18:6; 19:14, 15; 21:7, 10; 43:7, 15; 47:6; 49:12).

133 Sutcliffe, "Sacred Meals," 62.

134 J. van der Ploeg, "The Meals of the Essenes," *JSS* 2 (1957), 169.

135 It is possible that the setting of Josephus' discussion of Essene quietness is a general one, rather than strictly at meal time. But the mention of the meal immediately prior to this section and the

statement of their sobriety with respect to food and drink seem to place the discussion of quietness specifically in the context of the meal.

136  As Philo states (with respect to the Therapeutae), this sobriety is in marked contrast to the luxurious Greek and Roman banquets: "When they are quite exhausted, their bellies crammed up to the gullet, but their lust still ravenous, impotent for eating (they turn to the drink) ... One may well pray for what men most pray to escape, hunger and thirst, rather than for the lavish profusion of food and drink found in festivities of this kind" (*On the Contemplative Life* 6 §55–6).

137  Dupont-Sommer translates the phrase ὡς ἱεράς "since they are sacred garments" (*Essene Writings*, 29), but as M. Delcor notes, the translation of ὡς should be the same as in the parallel construction (ὡς μυστήριον) a few lines down, where ὡς clearly means "as if" and not "since" ("Repas cultuels esséniens et thérapeutes, Thiases et Haburoth," *RQ* 6 [1967–9], 402–3; thus also van der Ploeg, "Meals," 167–8).

138  As van der Ploeg states, "Josephus is explaining the customs of the Essenes to Greek readers and tries to magnify them in their eyes; he compares their customs with those his readers know: entering in 'holy' clothes into a sacred precinct and taking care that nobody who is outside hears the *arcana verba* which are pronounced inside. In this and similar descriptions the style of Josephus belongs to a very special *genre littéraire* which is well recognized" ("Meals," 167). Thus also Sutcliffe, "Sacred Meals," 59–62. It should be noted further that if Josephus is describing a sacred meal, then *all* the meals are sacred according to him, since at the evening meal they dine "in like manner." M. Black thinks that Josephus' description of the meal rests largely upon his imagination: "the refectory as a sacred shrine and the awful silence are not difficult to conjecture. The fact that he is quite vague about the contents of the meal and simply describes an everyday meal in quite general terms betrays an almost complete ignorance of the actual sacral meal of the sect" (*Essene Problem*, 13). But Black's judgment on Josephus seems overly harsh in the light of our own general lack of information on the Qumran meal.

139  Kuhn, "Lord's Supper," 68, 77; Allegro (*Dead Sea Scrolls*, 130–1) translates "table" in 1QSa 2:17–21 with "communion table."

140  As the discussion on pp. 59–60 above (*J.W.* 2 §130) shows, the terms *lḥm* ("bread") and *tyrwš* ("sweet wine") do not have special sacramental significance.

141  Thus Cross, *Ancient Library*, 90; Schiffman, "Communal Meals," 53–6; Milik, *Ten Years*, 106.

142  G. Vermes, *Discovery in the Judean Desert* (New York: Desclée, 1956), 56; Delcor, "Repas," 402–3; Kuhn, "Lord's Supper," 260 n. 15; Gnilka, "Das Gemeinschaftsmahl," 42–3; Yadin, *Scroll of the War*, 200.

143  De Vaux, *Archaeology*, 12–14.

144 Sutcliffe, "Sacred Meals," 57–8. See also J. Bowman, "Did the Qumran Sect Burn the Red Heifer?," *RQ* 1 (1958–9), 73–84.
145 Van der Ploeg, "Meals," 173.
146 Burrows, *More Light*, 367.
147 Thus Burrows, *More Light*, 372; Kuhn, "Lord's Supper," 68.
148 As, for example, Kuhn, "Lord's Supper," 85, 92–3; Allegro, *Dead Sea Scrolls*, 130–1, 164–5.
149 By stressing that it is only the "deserving" who are to be helped, Josephus may be deliberately excluding those who have been expelled from the order (see *J. W.* 2 §143, pp. 89–91).
150 It is possible that Josephus, in seeking to emphasize the Essenes' charity, is simply idealizing the situation; thus, he presents the Essenes as strictly obedient, except in acts of charity where they are free to use their own discretion. Then, lest someone think that this charity be directed primarily to family members, Josephus quickly shows that it is community charity that is meant, by adding the rule about relatives. There is no evidence for this rule about relatives at Qumran, so it is difficult to know whether or not Josephus' depiction is accurate.
151 Thackeray translates the phrase, "holding righteous indignation in reserve" (*Josephus*, 2:375), but δίκαιοι agrees with ταμίαι, not ὀργῆς.
152 K. H. Rengstorf, *A Complete Concordance to Flavius Josephus* (4 vols., Leiden: Brill, 1973–83), 3:414.
153 Truth, in fact, is a central teaching of the community (see below, *J. W.* 2 §141, pp. 81–3).
154 In the Qumran literature surveyed by Kuhn (*Konkordanz*, 17) the various forms of *'mn* occur thirty-five times, with a wide range of meanings.
155 This restoration was suggested by Dupont-Sommer (*Essene Writings*, 242).
156 Yadin, *Scroll of the War*, 15.
157 See above, pp. 9, 136 n. 39.
158 Milik, *Ten Years*, 123.
159 So Vermes (*Dead Sea Scrolls*, 51), who states: "The work is nevertheless not a military manual, but a theological consideration of a perpetual struggle between good and evil in which the opposing forces are of equal strength and to which only God's intervention can bring an end."
160 The Essene love for truth, alluded to in Josephus' previous statement ("guardians of faithfulness") and mentioned here, is discussed below (pp. 81–3) in connection with *J. W.* 2 §141.
161 Compare Philo's opinion that "to swear not at all is the best course and most profitable to life ... to swear truly is only, as people say, a 'second-best voyage,'" and perjury is the worst of all (*The Decalogue* 17–19 §84–93).
162 1QS 6:27–7:2 speaks of blasphemy, and is discussed in connection with *J. W.* 2 §145 below (pp. 93–4).
163 The latter view seems more likely in light of the agreement between

Josephus' statements and the *Manual of Discipline*. Cf. Jesus' statements on oaths in Matt 5:33−7.

164 See also Acts 15:21.

165 Michel and Bauernfeind (*De bello judaico*, 434 n. 56) mention only the biblical books here, but Pelletier (*Guerre des Juifs*, 2:207 n. 2) rightly expands the reference. Παλαιοί is used in a broad sense in *J.W.* 3.10, 8 §513 as well, and is never used in Josephus to refer exclusively to the biblical writers. The expression used in *J.W.* 2 §159 ("holy books" − βίβλοις ἱεραῖς) may well refer strictly to the biblical books. See discussion below, pp. 109−11.

166 See p. 136 n. 47 above.

167 For the most complete list of material published at Qumran, see Fitzmyer, *Dead Sea Scrolls: Major Publications*, 11−39.

168 This is a reference to the title of *Jubilees*, which begins: "This is the history of the division of the days of the law and of the testimony, of the events of the years, of their weeks, of their jubilees, throughout all the years of the world."

169 Mastema as a proper name occurs only here, in *Jubilees* (*Jub.* 10:8; 11:5; 17:16; 18:9, 12; 48:2, 9, 12, 15; 49:2), and in *Acts of Philip* 13 (where it is spelled *mansēmat*), a fourth- or fifth-century work (see E. Hennecke, *New Testament Apocrypha* [2 vols., Philadelphia: Westminster, 1963−5], 2:577; R. A. Lipsius and M. Bonnet, *Acta apostolorum apocrypha post Constantinum Tischendorf* [2 vols., Lipsiae: Mendelssohn, 1891−8], 2/2:7).

170 Dupont-Sommer, *Essene Writings*, 70; cited by Burrows, *More Light*, 325; Rabin, *Zadokite Documents*, 50 n. 3; Vermes, *Dead Sea Scrolls*, 113.

171 Dupont-Sommer, *Essene Writings*, 205.

172 Thus J. A. Fitzmyer, "The Aramaic Language and the Study of the New Testament," *JBL* 99 (1980), 15−16. But Dupont-Sommer (*Essene Writings*, 322) considers *lh* as an expletive, and translates the phrase "an exorcist forgave my sins." See also G. Vermes, *The Dead Sea Scrolls in English*, 2nd edn (Harmondsworth, Middlesex: Penguin, 1975), 229. J. T. Milik takes *šbq* to mean "to grant," corrects *lh* to *ly*, and translates the phrase, "[But when I confessed my sins] and faults, (God) granted me a diviner" ("'Prière de Nabonide,'" 408).

173 Dupont-Sommer, *Essene Writings*, 324−5.

174 In Tobit, it is also Raphael who teaches Tobiah how to exorcize Sarah's demon (Tob 6:17−18; 12:12−15). Fragments of Tobit have been found at Qumran (4QTob ar^a-d and 4QTob hebr^a − see J. T. Milik, "La patrie de Tobie," *RB* 73 (1966), 522 n. 3.

175 There may have been numerous other writings known to the Essenes that we do not possess. Josephus himself reports the tradition that Solomon practiced exorcism and healing: "There was no form of nature with which he was not acquainted or which he passed over without examining, but he studied them all philosophically and revealed the most complete knowledge of their several properties (τῶν ἰδιωμάτων, as in *J.W.* 2 §136). And God granted him

knowledge of the art used against demons for the benefit and healing of men. He also composed incantations by which illnesses are relieved, and left behind forms of exorcisms with which those possessed by demons drive them out, never to return" (*Ant.* 8.2, 5 §44–5).

In the same passage, Josephus states that a contemporary Jew named Eleazar was practicing exorcism by means of "one of the roots prescribed by Solomon" (*Ant.* 8.2, 5 §47). Thus, although Eleazar is not named by Josephus as an Essene, perhaps among the writings studied by the Essenes were those containing such "medicinal roots" and other remedies prescribed by Solomon (see R. Marcus' bold statement that the Essenes "possessed books of medicine attributed to Solomon" [Thackeray et al., *Josephus*, 5:595]). On the tradition of Solomon's healing powers in Jewish and Arabic literature, see M. W. Montgomery and M. Seligsohn, "Solomon," *The Jewish Encyclopedia* 6 (1905), 436–48.

176  On Essene self-control, see the discussion of *J.W.* 2 §120, above (pp. 37–8).

177  So Dupont-Sommer, *Essene Writings*, 30; Brownlee, *Manual of Discipline*, 25 n. 33; Rabin, *Qumran Studies*, 10–11; Burrows, "Discipline Manual," 174–5; Black, *Scrolls*, 96. But A. R. C. Leaney regards Josephus' "purer waters" as the equivalent of "the purity of the many" (1QS 6:16–17), i.e., "objects not capable of transmitting uncleanness" (*Rule of Qumran*, 192–3).

178  Thackeray translates συμβίωσις as "the meetings of the community" (*Josephus*, 2:377), but in view of the specific mention of the "common food" two sentences later (2 §139), it is more likely that συμβίωσις refers either specifically to the common meal or to all community activities, including the common meal, deliberations, etc. So Pelletier, *Guerre des Juifs*, 2:108 n. 7. But E. F. Sutcliffe thinks the term means that the novices did not mix freely with the others, and does not exclude their presence at community prayers and meals ("Sacred Meals," 63).

179  Most likely Josephus means that the novice was previously forbidden to partake of the common meal, but Sutcliffe argues from the use of ἄψασθαι that the novice was only forbidden to "touch" it, i.e., participate in its preparation ("Sacred Meals," 63–4).

180  See discussion of *ṭhrt* above, pp. 56, 148 n. 110.

181  See discussion of *mšqh* above, pp. 58, 149 n. 122.

182  Michel and Bauernfeind, *De bello judaico*, 435 n. 59; so also Brownlee, *Manual of Discipline*, 25 n. 32.

183  This interpretation assumes that *ṭhrt* does not refer to the purificatory baths. See pp. 56, 148 n. 110. See also Rabin, *Qumran Studies*, 7–8.

184  See discussion of *J.W.* 2 §139, pp. 75–8.

185  The general correspondence between Josephus and 1QS as outlined in this paragraph is supported by Milik, *Ten Years*, 101–3; Vermes, *Dead Sea Scrolls*, 95–6; Brownlee, *Manual of Discipline*, 25–6, esp. nn. 32, 37; Schubert, *Dead Sea Community*, 44–5; Burrows,

*Dead Sea Scrolls*, 281; and Gaster, *Dead Sea Scriptures*, 106 n. 61. Cross, however, considering *ṭhrt* a reference to the purificatory bath, matches the first year Josephus mentions (the one outside the community, where the novice could not yet enter into the "purer waters for purification") with the first one-year period actually named as such in the *Manual of Discipline* (in which the novice was not permitted to touch the "purity of the Many," i.e. [according to Cross], the purificatory bath). Then he matches the second and third year mentioned by Josephus (in which the novice could not partake of the common meal) with the second year of 1QS 6:20–1 (in which he could not "touch the drink of the Many," i.e., the common meal). Aside from the difficulties this interpretation presents with regard to the understanding of *ṭhrt* ("purity") and *mšqh* ("drink" – see pp. 56, 58, 148 n. 110, and 149 n. 122), it also creates an additional discrepancy between Josephus and 1QS – namely, Josephus represents as two years what 1QS clearly states as only one. Cross thinks that "Josephus here errs in interpreting his source ... [he]conflated a first degree and a two-year total into a three-year period" (*Ancient Library*, 86 n. 61). Leaney suggests another way of reconciling the two accounts, by taking the phrase "a second year" (*šnh šnyt*) in 1QS 6:21 to mean "two years," but as he himself admits, this explanation is not very satisfactory (*Rule of Qumran*, 192). The correlation between Josephus and 1QS adopted in the text eliminates the apparent discrepancy.

186 Thus A. Dupont-Sommer, "Culpabilité et rites de purification dans la secte juive de Qoumrân," *Sem* 15 (1965), 63 n. 1.

187 See discussion above, p. 46 (2 §123). J. Daniélou's statement that "the practice of dressing the newly baptized in a white robe inevitably recalls the description in Josephus of the white garments worn by those who were newly admitted to the Essenian community" (*The Dead Sea Scrolls and Primitive Christianity* [Baltimore: Helicon, 1958], 42) ignores the fact that according to Josephus *all* Essenes wore white, not simply the novices.

188 Dupont-Sommer suggests that since the preparatory stages as described in the *Manual of Discipline* are not mentioned here, perhaps CD 15:7–11 describes an "archaic procedure" used prior to the establishment of the various stages (*Essene Writings*, 161 n. 4).

189 Thus Dupont-Sommer, *Essene Writings*, 244 n. 4; Holm-Nielsen, *Hodayot*, 221 n. 19.

190 So Rabin, *Qumran Studies*, 6, 10–11; Vermes, *Dead Sea Scrolls*, 128.

191 Vermes, *Dead Sea Scrolls*, 129.

192 The δικαι word group used by Josephus and Philo is used in the LXX to translate both *ṣdq* (*ca.* 464 times) and *mšpṭ* (*ca.* 52 times).

193 The text of 1QS 9:14 actually has *bny hṣdwq*, which Leaney (*Rule of Qumran*, 228) translates as "sons of Zadok." But none of the occurrences of *bny ṣdwq* contain the article on *ṣdwq* (1QS 5:2, 9; 1QSa 1:2, 24; 2:3; 4QFlor 1:17; CD 4:1, 3). Furthermore, Milik reports that 4QS^e reads simply *hṣdq*, not *hṣdwq* ("Review," 414).

194 In *Ant.* 15.10, 5 §374, the words that the Essene Menahem utters to Herod in his youth echo the same concept: "But you shall indeed be king, and you shall exercise the reign well, for you have been found worthy by God." Compare Paul's words in Rom 13:1.

195 Michel and Bauernfeind, *De bello judaico*, 435 n. 61.

196 So Pelletier, *Guerre des Juifs*, 2:208 n. 10; Y. M. Grintz, "Die Männer des Yaḥad-Essener. Zusammenfassungen, Erläuterungen und Bemerkungen zu den Rollen vom Toten Meer," *Zur Josephus-Forschung*, ed. Abraham Schalit (Darmstadt: Wissenschaftliche Buchgesellschaft, 1973), 310 n. 20.

197 The term *maśkyl* (occurring in 1QS 3:13; 9:12, 21; 1QSb 1:1; 3:22; 5:20; CD 12:21; 13:22) means "wise one" or "teacher" (see Dan 11:33, 35; 12:3, 10), and apparently designates an official of the community whose task is instructing the community (see 1QS 9:13, 18, 20). Thus Dupont-Sommer, *Essene Writings*, 95 n. 1; Leaney, *Rule of Qumran*, 229–30; Vermes, *Dead Sea Scrolls in English*, 22–5. Wernberg-Møller, however, regards the term as simply referring to a member of the pious community (*Manual of Discipline*, 66 n. 39). The relationship of the *maśkyl* to the other community officials is uncertain, though Vermes identifies him with the *mebaqqēr* and the *pāqîd* (*Dead Sea Scrolls in English*, 19–25). The term *maśkyl* is also used in the introductions to thirteen OT psalms (Pss 32, 42, 44, 45, 52–5, 74, 78, 88–9, 142), where its meaning is unclear. It may mean a didactic psalm, though this understanding does not seem to fit all the psalms to which *maśkyl* is attached.

198 K. Schubert does point out that in the large cemetery east of Qumran no ornaments whatsoever were found next to the body (*Dead Sea Community*, 47; see de Vaux, *Archaeology*, 47). Thus, at least in their burial, there is no evidence of any special ornamentation for the leaders.

199 The only nouns that occur more frequently in the Qumran literature included in Kuhn's *Konkordanz* are *'yš*, *'l*, *bn*, *bryt*, *dbr*, *yd*, *ywm*, *mšpt*, *'wlm*, *ph*, and *rwḥ*. By contrast, *'mt* occurs only 126 times in the entire MT.

200 For further study of the concept of truth at Qumran, see J. Murphy-O'Connor, "Truth: Paul and Qumran," *Paul and Qumran*, ed. J. Murphy-O'Connor (London: Chapman, 1968), 179–230, esp. 85.

201 On the interpretation of the two spirits in Qumran theology, see Leaney, *Rule of Qumran*, 37–56; H. Ringgren, *The Faith of Qumran: Theology of the Dead Sea Scrolls* (Philadelphia: Fortress, 1963), 68–80; P. Wernberg-Møller, "A Reconsideration of the Two Spirits in the Rule of the Community," *RQ* 3 (1961–2), 413–41; J. H. Charlesworth, "A Critical Comparison of the Dualism in 1QS 3:13–4:26 and the 'Dualism' contained in the Fourth Gospel," *NTS* 15 (1969), 389–418; J. Licht, "An Analysis of the Treatise of the Two Spirits in DSD," *Aspects of the Dead Sea Scrolls*, Scripta Heirosolymitana 4 (Jerusalem: Magnes, 1957), 88–100; and O. J. F. Seitz, "Two Spirits in Man: An Essay in Biblical Exegesis," *NTS* 6 (1959–60), 82–94.

202  It is possible that the phrase "wealth of violence" (*hwn ḥms*) should
     be understood as the wealth that leads to violence, as opposed to
     ill-gotten gain (as in Luke 16:9, "mammon of unrighteousness" –
     see further J. A. Fitzmyer, "The Story of the Dishonest Manager
     (Lk 16:1–13)," *Essays on the Semitic Background of the New
     Testament*, 169 n. 15.
203  For this understanding of the phrase, see Leaney, *Rule of Qumran*,
     144, 151; Wernberg-Møller, *Manual of Discipline*, 78 n. 20 (though
     he translates the phrase "concealing the truth of the mysteries of
     knowledge," considering the *lamed* of *l'mt* to be taken by analogy
     from Isa 42:3).
204  See note 197 above.
205  It is interesting that Paul uses another word in the δίδωμι family,
     παραδίδωμι, to indicate the transmission of the early Christian
     traditions (which he calls παραδόσεις, 1 Cor 11:2; 2 Thess 3:6;
     παράδοσις, 2 Thess 3:6) in 1 Cor 11:2, 23 and 15:3. See further
     B. Gerhardsson, *Memory and Manuscript*, ASNU 22 (Uppsala:
     Gleerup, 1961), 288–305.
206  See p. 147 n. 99 above. A portion of this passage (*1 Enoch* 104:13)
     has been found at Qumran (4QEnᶜ 5:20–1). See Milik, *Books of
     Enoch*, 206–8.
207  Dupont-Sommer, *Essene Writings*, 31.
208  E. Kutsch, "Der Eid der Essener. Ein Beitrag zum Problem des
     Textes von Josephus Bell. jud. 2, 8, 7 (§142)," *TLZ* 81 (1956), 497.
209  Thus, J. D. Amoussine, "Observatiunculae Qumraneae," *RQ* 7
     (1969–71), 539–40.
210  So E. Gross, "Noch einmal: Der Essenereid bei Josephus," *TLZ*
     82 (1957), 73–4.
211  Amoussine, "Observatiunculae Qumraneae," 542–5.
212  C. Daniel, "Les 'Hérodiens' du Nouveau Testament sont-ils des
     Esséniens?," *RQ* 6 (1967–9), 31–53.
213  The word is found sixteen other times in Josephus: *J. W.* 1.18, 1
     §347; 1.18, 2 §349; 2.12, 5 §238; 2.14, 1 §273; 2.20, 7 §581; 4.3,
     2 §134; *Ant.* 1.2, 2 §61, 66; 14.8, 4 §142; 14.16, 2 §471, 472; 15.5,
     1 §120; 15.10, 1 §348; 17.2, 2 §26; 18.8, 4 §274; and *Ag. Ap.*
     1.12 §62.
214  O. Michel, "Der Schwur der Essener," *TLZ* 81 (1956), 189–90.
215  So Pelletier (*Guerre des Juifs*, 2:208 n. 1), who thinks that there may
     have been a danger in the Essenes joining up with various armed
     bands in a "holy war."
216  Yadin, *Scroll of the War*, 17.
217  Dupont-Sommer, *Essene Writings*, 191 n. 4.
218  De Vaux, *Archaeology*, 101–2; Milik, *Ten Years*, 20–1. Dupont-
     Sommer (*Essene Writings*, 3) writes of Cave 1: "Cave 1 was a
     genuine hiding-place where a certain number of books had been
     concealed to keep them safe. This is proved by the fact that originally
     the cave had only one opening, extremely narrow and near to the
     roof. It was certainly not habitable."
219  The Book of Parables (*1 Enoch* 37–71), not found at Qumran, also

contains numerous references to angels. For example, in *1 Enoch* 69:2–15 there is another list of the fallen angels, while the four archangels are mentioned in *1 Enoch* 40:9; 54:6; and 71:8, 9. And *1 Enoch* 43:1 specifically mentions that God calls the angels by name: "And I saw other lightnings and the stars of heaven, and I saw how He called them all by their names and they hearkened unto Him."

220 Milik, *Ten Years*, 114.
221 Yadin, *Scroll of the War*, 229.
222 Ibid., 230–42, esp. 230–2.
223 Strugnell, "Angelic Liturgy," 330–4. The text of 4QŠirŠabb has not yet been fully published.
224 Thus also Leaney, *Rule of Qumran*, 201.
225 *The Rule of the Congregation (for the End-Time)* similarly describes a gathering of "the whole assembly to dispense justice" (1QSa 1:25). Earlier, in 1QSa 1:13–14, the age qualifications for being a judge are given ("At the age of thirty years he may be promoted to arbitrate at lawsuits and trials"). For a discussion of the "majority" (*rwb*), see *J. W.* 2 §146, pp. 94–6.
226 Milik, in fact, states categorically that "Josephus' 'tribunal' (*War* 2, 8, 145) is clearly identical with this body [described in 1QS 6:8]" (*Ten Years*, 101 n. 2).
227 See discussion above, pp. 9, 135–6 n. 35.
228 Dupont-Sommer, *Essene Writings*, 31 n. 3, 358.
229 For additional arguments against Dupont-Sommer's interpretation, see M. Delcor, "Contribution à l'étude de la législation," *RB* 61 (1954), 550–3.
230 "Our lawgiver" (using either ἡμέτερος or ἡμῶν) occurs thirteen times: *Ant.* 1. Proem, 3 §15; 1. Proem, 4 §18, 23; *Ag. Ap.* 2.15 §154, 156; 2.16 §161, 165, 169; 2.17 §173; 2.36 §257; 2.38 §279 (τῆς ἀρετῆς ἡμῶν τοῦ νομοθέτου, "the excellence of our lawgiver"); 2.39 §286 (τῶν αὐτῶν τιμῶντες νομοθέτην, "in honoring our own lawgiver"); 2.40 §290. "Their lawgiver" occurs twice: *Ant.* 1.15 §240 and 4.2, 1 §13. "The lawgiver" occurs twenty-three times: *J. W.* 2.8, 9 §145; 2.8, 10 §152; 5.9, 4 §401; *Ant.* 1. Proem, 2 §6; 1. Proem, 4 §20, 24; 1.3, 6 §95; 3.7, 7 §180, 187 (τὴν ἀρετὴν τοῦ νομοθέτου, "the virtues of the lawgiver"); 4.1, 1 §6; 4.6, 12 §150; 4.6, 13 §156; 4.8, 24 §263; 4.8, 48 §322; 8.7, 5 §192; 11.4, 1 §77; 12.2, 14 §110; 18.8, 2 §264; *Ag. Ap.* 1.35 §316; 2.21 §186; 2.28 §209; 2.30 §218; and 2.33 §237. That Josephus himself regards Moses highly is seen in these passages – note especially those passages cited more fully above. Also, *Ag. Ap.* 2.40 §290 speaks harshly of those who "reviled our lawmaker as an insignificant person; whereas God from of old has borne witness to his virtuous conduct, and after that, time itself has testified likewise." These statements by Josephus and the Qumran passages discussed below seem to discredit B. Z. Wacholder's thesis that 11QTempleᵃ was "more authoritative than the Mosaic archetype" for the Qumran community (*Dawn of Qumran*, p. 4).

231 Dupont-Sommer, *Essene Writings*, 87 n. 2. He supports his interpretation by referring to the words of Josephus regarding blasphemy against the lawgiver.

232 "Him" probably refers to the chief priest (presumably mentioned in col. 12, the end of which is not preserved).

233 See further Wernberg-Møller, *Manual of Discipline*, 56n; Leaney, *Rule of Qumran*, 188.

234 G. Bornkamm, "πρέσβυς," *TDNT* 6 (1968), 660. See also Mark 15:1: "the chief priests, with the elders and scribes, and the whole council."

235 Thus Michel and Bauernfeind, *De bello judaico*, 437 n. 71.

236 Dupont-Sommer, *Essene Writings*, 85 n. 2.

237 See Schürer (Vermes), *History*, 2:570 n. 51.

238 Leaney, *Rule of Qumran*, 206. Leaney also notes that spitting was associated with the saying of a magical formula to heal a wound. This practice was forbidden in the Talmud (*b. Sanh.* 101a; *y. Sanh.* 28b). It seems doubtful, however, that the context of Josephus' statement involves healing.

239 Yadin, *Scroll of the War*, 75 n. 1; Leaney, *Rule of Qumran*, 207. See further *J. W.* 2 §148, pp. 97–9.

240 M. Burrows considers this detail on spitting "perhaps the most astonishing coincidence in what Josephus says of the Essenes and what we find in DSD [i.e., 1QS] ..., a slight and even amusing item, significant only because one cannot believe that Josephus could have invented it" ("Discipline Manual," 176). So also Cross, *Ancient Library*, 96; Brownlee, "Comparison," 62.

241 See the discussion of *prwš* by L. H. Schiffman, *The Halakhah at Qumran*, SJLA 16 (Leiden: Brill, 1975), 37–40, 77. Schiffman notes that the use of *prwš* in CD 6:18 "emphasizes that this is the particular Sabbath law of the sect, as opposed to the (in their view) mistaken practices of the general Jewish community" (p. 77).

242 The text is probably speaking of an unintentional violation of the Sabbath, since an intentional violation was punishable by death according to Num 15:35 (Schiffman, *Halakhah*, 78). Dupont-Sommer regards the violation as that of celebrating the Sabbath (and the feasts) on dates not conforming to the sect's calendar (*Essene Writings*, 154 n. 6). Cf. Rabin, *Qumran Studies*, 86.

243 CD 16:2–4 praises the book of *Jubilees*. See further p. 147 n. 99.

244 See Schiffman, *Halakhah*, 91–8.

245 The prohibition is also found in *Jub.* 2:29 ("they should not prepare thereon anything to be eaten or drunk") and *Jub.* 50:9 ("ye shall do no work whatever on the Sabbath day save what ye have prepared for yourselves on the sixth day").

246 See also *Jub.* 2:30 ("And they shall not bring in or take out from house to house on that day") and *Jub.* 50:8 ("whoever takes up any burden to carry it out of his tent or out of his house shall die"). These laws are based on Jer 17:21–2. See further Schiffman, *Halakhah*, 113–15.

247 Since 1QM 7:6–7 states that the latrines had to be two thousand

cubits away from the camp, and CD 10:11 (discussed above) gives the maximum distance a person could walk on the Sabbath as one thousand cubits, this may be evidence that the sectarians did, in fact, refrain from relieving themselves on the Sabbath, as Josephus states. But it is also possible that this particular (and needful!) activity was excluded from the general ban on travel in excess of one thousand cubits. See further Schiffman, *Halakhah*, 93–4; Yadin, *Scroll of the War*, 73–5.

248 "You shall have a place (*yd*) outside the camp and you shall go out to it; and you shall have a stick with your weapons; and when you sit down outside, you shall dig a hole with it, and turn back and cover your excrement. Because the Lord your God walks in the midst of your camp ... therefore your camp must be holy, that he may not see anything indecent among you, and turn away from you" (Deut 23:13–15 [Heb.; Eng. 23:12–14]).

249 De Vaux, "Une hachette essénienne?," 401.

250 Wernberg-Møller, *Manual of Discipline*, 118 n. 30; Silberman, *Manus Velatae*, 387.

251 Thus Dupont-Sommer, *Essene Writings*, 89 n. 2; Yadin, *Scroll of the War*, 75 n. 1; Leaney, *Rule of Qumran*, 207; Marcus, "Textual Notes," 209; Van der Ploeg, "Manuel de Discipline," 122 n. 77.

252 See further Strugnell, "Josephus and the Essenes," 113 n. 30. The terminology used by Josephus may, in fact, be derived from the original command in Deut 23:14, where the reason for covering their excrement is "that he [God] may not *see* anything indecent among you" (my italics).

253 Thus Charlesworth remarks that "the provisions for a latrine situated 3,000 meters [sic] from the city, described in column XLVI [of the *Temple Scroll*], are strikingly reminiscent of the peculiar habits of the Essenes as described by Josephus" ("Origin and Subsequent History of the Authors of the Dead Sea Scrolls," 216). Yadin likewise remarks that the facts that the Essenes chose desolate places for relieving themselves and (since relieving themselves involved digging) they did not do so on the Sabbath both fit the description in the *War Scroll*, and thus serve "as strong supporting evidence for the identification of the sect with the Essenes, or at least for their having identical customs" (*Scroll of the War*, 75). See also Y. Yadin, "The Gate of the Essenes and the Temple Scroll," *Jerusalem Revealed: Archaeology in the Holy City 1968–1974*, ed. Y. Yadin (New Haven: Yale University Press, 1976), 90–1; Yadin, *The Temple Scroll*, 1:294–304.

254 Michel and Bauernfeind, *De bello judaico*, 437 n. 76. Yet, "novices" and "proselytes" do not necessarily indicate the same group.

255 Yadin, *Scroll of the War*, 75–9.

256 R. H. Pfeiffer, *History of New Testament Times* (New York: Harper & Row, 1949), 56; Pelletier, *Guerre des Juifs*, 2:36 n. 3.

257 J. B. Lightfoot, *Saint Paul's Epistles to the Colossians and to Philemon*, rev. edn (London: Macmillan, 1879), 363n; Thackeray, *Josephus*, 2:381; Schürer (Vermes), *History*, 2:565; and Burrows, "Discipline Manual," 174.

258  See further Yadin, *Scroll of the War*, 148–50; Leaney, *Rule of Qumran*, 124–5.

259  G. Cornfeld translates the last phrase of *J. W.* 2 §151 as "death, if it comes with honor, they prefer to an easy death" (*Josephus: The Jewish War* [Grand Rapids: Zondervan, 1982], 152), but ἀθανασία means "immortality," not "easy death." Perhaps he is proposing εὐθανασίας instead of ἀθανασίας. What Josephus apparently means is that the Essenes prefer a glorious death to a mere perpetuation of (bodily) living. Josephus later explains that this preference for a "glorious death" is rooted in the belief that while the body may die, the all-important soul is immortal (*J. W.* 2 §153–8).

260  *Mṣrp* means "furnace" or "refiner's fire," as in Prov 17:3; 27:21. This fire will destroy the wicked on the one hand, yet purify the righteous through testing (1QS 1:17; 8:4; 1QM 17:1, 9; 1QH 5:16; and CD 20:27). See further Leaney, *Rule of Qumran*, 126–7.

261  This conclusion is strengthened by the fact that elsewhere where the phrase "the war with the Romans" (ὁ πρὸς Ῥωμαίους πόλεμος) is used in Josephus it refers to the First Revolt (*J. W.* 2.17,2 §409; 3.8,8 §392; 7.8,1 §257; 7.8,7 §369; *Ant.* 1.Proem, 1 §4). Cf. Dupont-Sommer, *Essene Writings*, 33 n. 2.

262  Josephus does, however, mention that Vespasian tested the buoyancy of the Dead Sea by tossing bound prisoners into the sea to see if they would float! (*J. W.* 4.8,4 §476–7). So Vespasian must have been in the vicinity of Qumran.

263  Thus de Vaux, *Archaeology*, 40.

264  Ibid., 36–41.

265  Ibid., 41. De Vaux concludes that "since this explanation is in accordance with the historical data ... I consider it certain that Khirbet Qumran was destroyed by the Romans in June 68 of our era."

266  1QpHab 2:12, 14; 3:4, 9; 4:5, 10; 6:1, 10; 9:7; 1QpPs 9:[4]; 4QpIsaᵃ 7–10 iii 7–12; 4QpNah 3–4 i 3; 1QM 1:2, 4, 6, 9, 12; 11:11; 15:2; 16:3, 6, 8, 9; 17:12, 14, 15; 18:2, 4; 19:10, 13.

267  See further Dupont-Sommer, *Essene Writings*, 341–51; Vermes, *Dead Sea Scrolls*, 148–9; Cross, *Ancient Writings*, 124n; Burrows, *More Light*, 191–203.

268  In the light of these passages, it is difficult to agree with Vermes' assessment that "in the Habakkuk Commentary, the portrait of the Kittim is neutral, as in Maccabees and Daniel" (*Dead Sea Scrolls*, 148). Perhaps the hatred of the Kittim is not quite as developed as in the *War Scroll*, but it is there nonetheless.

269  Thus Milik (*Ten Years*, 123) states that "one would not be surprised to find that the leaders of the Jewish Revolt had considered the *Rule for the War* as an excellent piece of propaganda, nor that at the signal for the outburst of the Revolt the Essenes ... joined the ranks of those who were fighting the Romans (the Kittim of our texts), who were the 'Sons of Belial' *par excellence*." See also Schürer (Vermes), *History*, 2:588.

270 Hippolytus' description of the Essenes, while generally following
Josephus, contains an interesting variation at this point: "The
doctrine of the resurrection is firmly established among them. They
declare, in fact, that flesh will rise again and be immortal, just as
the soul is already immortal" (*Refutation* 9.27,1). Hence, according
to Hippolytus, the Essenes did believe in the resurrection of the body.
Probably Hippolytus is presenting a somewhat "Christianized" ver-
sion of the Essenes (thus C. Burchard, "Die Essener bei Hippolyt,"
*JSJ* 8 [1977], 1–41), though Morton Smith concludes that
Hippolytus' text is more accurate on this point than Josephus ("The
Description of the Essenes in Josephus and the Philosophumena,"
*HUCA* 29 [1958], 284). See also M. Black, "The Account of the
Essenes in Hippolytus and Josephus," *The Background of the New
Testament and its Eschatology*, ed. W. D. Davies and D. Daube
(Cambridge, 1956), 172–5.

271 See discussion above, pp. 2–3. An amusing example of this tendency
occurs in *Ant.* 2.15,4 §346 (and again in *Ant.* 4.7,44 §303), where
Josephus writes that Moses composed a poem "in hexameter verse"!

272 So Yadin, *Scroll of the War*, 241–2.

273 So G. W. E. Nickelsburg, "Future Life in Intertestamental
Literature," *IDBSup* (1976), 350; R. B. Laurin, "The Question of
Immortality in the Qumran *Hodayot*," *JSS* 3 (1958), 344–55;
Holm-Nielsen, *Hodayot*, 66–7.

274 J. van der Ploeg, "The Belief in Immortality in the Writings of
Qumran," *BO* 18 (1961), 122.

275 See further Holm-Nielsen, *Hodayot*, 121 nn. 172–3.

276 So Vermes, *Dead Sea Scrolls*, 187; van der Ploeg, "Belief," 118–24.

277 Van der Ploeg, "Belief," 118.

278 Fragments of the *Testaments of the Twelve Patriarchs* have been
found at Qumran: 1QTLevi ar (= 1Q*21* in *DJD* 1); 4QTLevi ar[a]
(see Milik, *Books of Enoch*, 23–4; J. T. Milik, "Le Testament de
Lévi en araméen: Fragment de la grotte 4 de Qumrân," *RB* 62
[1955], 398–406); 4QTNapht (Milik, *Books of Enoch*, 198);
4QTJud; and 4QTJos (for 4QTJud and 4QTJos, see J. T. Milik,
"Ecrits préesséniens de Qumrân: d'Hénoch à Amram," *Qumrân:
Sa piété, sa théologie et son milieu*, ed. M. Delcor, BETL 46
[Leuven: Leuven University Press, 1978], 97–102). The *Testaments
of the Twelve Patriarchs* must be used with caution, since it is
apparent that the work contains numerous Christian interpolations
(see J. H. Charlesworth, ed., *The Old Testament Pseudepigrapha*,
vol. 1, *Apocalyptic Literature and Testaments* [Garden City, NY:
Doubleday, 1983], 776–8).

279 See further P. Grelot, "L'eschatologie des Esséniens et le livre
d'Hénoch," *RQ* 1 (1958–9), 113–31, esp. 117–23. There may be
some references to bodily resurrection in the *Parables* section of
*1 Enoch* (51:1 and 61:5), a portion not found at Qumran and
possibly written later than the rest of *1 Enoch* (Milik even believes
it is of Christian origin – see further Milik, *Books of Enoch*, 89–98;
Dupont-Sommer, *Essene Writings*, 298–300).

280 See further J. Carmignac, "Qui était le Docteur de Justice?," *RQ* 10 (1980), 235–46.

281 R. T. Beckwith, "The Significance of the Calendar for Interpreting Essene Chronology and Eschatology," *RQ* 10 (1980), 201.

282 Beckwith thinks that two different methods of Essene foretelling are at work in these three examples given by Josephus: interpretation of OT prophecies and casting of horoscopes (the latter possibly supported at Qumran by 4Q*186* 2:8, 9: "And this is the time of birth on which he is brought forth – on the festival of Taurus. He will be poor; and this is his beast – Taurus"). Beckwith sees the first method (interpretation of OT prophecies) at work in Simon's interpretation of Archelaus' dream (utilizing Genesis 40–1) and in Menahem's second prediction that Herod would not reign more than thirty years (since according to the Essene interpretation of Daniel's prophecy of the seventy weeks, the Messiahs were expected in the last "week," i.e., between 10 and 6 B.C.; hence, Herod could rule only until the Messiahs came). The second method (casting of horoscopes) he sees at work in Judas' prediction of Antigonus' death and Menahem's first prediction that Herod would be king. See further Beckwith, "Significance of the Calendar," 200–2.

283 Dupont-Sommer, *Essene Writings*, 34 n. 3.

284 Schürer (Vermes), *History*, 2:574 n. 76.

285 So Dupont-Sommer, *Essene Writings*, 94 n. 3; Leaney, *Rule of Qumran*, 227–8.

286 For a list of the copies of prophetical writings found at Qumran, as well as citations of such writings in other Qumran literature, see Fitzmyer, *Dead Sea Scrolls: Major Publications*, 163–70.

287 Dupont-Sommer, *Essene Writings*, 255. See also Horgan, *Pesharim*, 229.

288 Horgan, *Pesharim*, 229.

289 See further G. Vermes, "Interpretation (History of) at Qumran and in the Targums," *IDBSup* (1976), 440–1.

290 Other Qumran texts also mention the "mysteries" or "hidden things" of God's will: 1QS 4:6; 9:13, 18–19; 11:3–9; CD 3:13–14.

291 Thus Vermes, *Discovery*, 57 n. 176; cf. Michel and Bauernfeind, *De bello judaico*.

292 Dupont-Sommer, *Essene Writings*, 35 n. 3.

293 So Pelletier, *Guerre des Juifs*, 2:210. Admittedly, this still leaves τριετίᾳ unexplained. Assuming that the text is correct, why would three years be necessary for such a test of fertility? Perhaps Josephus is using τριετίᾳ loosely, to indicate "three cycles."

294 H. R. Moehring, "Josephus on the Marriage Customs of the Essenes," *Early Christian Origins*, ed. A. Wikgren (Chicago: Quadrangle Books, 1961), 124 n. 22; so also Leaney, *Rule of Qumran*, 206.

295 Using the Loeb edition, in *J. W.* 2 §119–61 230 lines are devoted to the Essenes, with eleven each for the Pharisees and Sadducees. In *Ant.* 18 §11–22, twenty-six lines are spent on the Essenes, twenty-seven on the Pharisees, and ten on the Sadducees.

296 Thackeray et al., *Josephus*, 7:311; R. Shutt, "The Concept of God in the Works of Flavius Josephus," *JJS* 31 (1980), 183–6; Rengstorf, *Concordance*, 2:26; E. Merrill, *Qumran and Predestination: A Theological Study of the Thanksgiving Hymns*, STDJ 8 (Leiden: Brill, 1975), 8, 13; M. Mansoor, *The Thanksgiving Hymns*, STDJ 3 (Leiden: Brill, 1961), 98n.; cf. G.F. Moore, "Fate and Free Will in the Jewish Philosophies according to Josephus," *HTR* 22 (1929), 371–89.

297 Merrill, *Qumran and Predestination*, 8.

298 Ibid., 12–13.

299 See further J.P. Hyatt, "The View of Man in the Qumran *Hodayot*," *NTS* 2 (1955–6), 276–85; J. Licht, "The Doctrines of the Thanksgiving Scroll," *IEJ* 6 (1956), 1–13; Mansoor, *Thanksgiving Hymns*, 55–8; H. Ringgren, *The Faith of Qumran: Theology of the Dead Sea Scrolls* (Philadelphia: Fortress, 1963), 52–63, 110–12; and Merrill, *Qumran and Predestination*, 12–58, esp. 16–23.

300 W. Whiston, *Josephus: Complete Works* (Grand Rapids: Kregel, 1963 [orig. edn, 1737]), 377; Dupont-Sommer, *Essene Writings*, 36.

301 Strugnell, "Josephus and the Essenes," 108–9; Thackeray et al., *Josephus*, 9:15–16n.

302 This determination is based largely on the slightly superior external evidence in favor of omitting οὐκ. The case for or against οὐκ based on internal evidence can be made strongly either way: see, for example, J. Thomas, *Le mouvement baptiste*, 12–19, who argues for οὐκ, and J. Strugnell, "Josephus and the Essenes," 113–15, who argues against it. Other scholars who believe οὐκ is genuine include E. Schürer, *Geschichte des jüdischen Volkes*, 2:663 n. 50; J. Lightfoot, *Colossians*, 371 (both prior to the discovery of the Dead Sea Scrolls); M. Delcor, "Le Midrash d'Habacuc," *RB* 58 (1951), 544–5; D. Wallace, "The Essenes and Temple Sacrifice," *TZ* 13 (1957), 335–8; A. Dupont-Sommer, *Essene Writings*, 36 n. 3; and J. Nolland, "A Misleading Statement of the Essene Attitude to the Temple," *RQ* 9 (1977–8), 558. Others who omit the οὐκ include B. Niese, *Flavii Josephi opera*, 4:143; W. Bauer, "Essener," 398; M.J. Lagrange, *Le Judaïsme avant Jésus-Christ* (Paris: J. Gabalda, 1931), 316 (all three prior to the Dead Sea Scrolls); R. Marcus, "Pharisees, Essenes, and Gnostics," *JBL* 73 (1954), 158; M. Black, *Scrolls*, 39–42; and L. Feldman, *Josephus*, 9:16–17.

303 As R. Marcus ("Pharisees," 158) and others have noted, εἰργόμενοι is always passive, not middle, in Josephus, and thus should be translated "they are excluded," not "they removed themselves."

304 For example, Brownlee, *Manual of Discipline*, 34; Dupont-Sommer, *Essene Writings*, 93; Vermes, *Dead Sea Scrolls in English*, 87; and Leaney, *Rule of Qumran*, 210.

305 Milik, "Manuale disciplinae," 151; J. Carmignac, "L'utilité ou l'inutilité des sacrifices sanglants dans la 'Règle de la Communauté' de Qumrân," *RB* 63 (1956), 524–32; Wernberg-Møller, *Manual of Discipline*, 35, 133 n. 9.

306 Carmignac, "L'utilité ou l'inutilité des sacrifices sanglants," 525–6. He argues that the author of the *War Scroll* had 1QS 9:3–5 in mind when he wrote.
307 Ibid., 532.
308 This was the original position of J. M. Baumgarten, "Sacrifice and Worship," 41–2.
309 This is J. M. Baumgarten's more recent view of the passage ("The Essenes and the Temple: A Reappraisal," *Studies in Qumran Law*, 70–1).
310 Baumgarten, "Sacrifice and Worship," 44; Baumgarten, "Essenes and the Temple," 70; S. H. Steckoll, "The Qumran Sect in Relation to the Temple of Leontopolis," *RQ* 6 (1967–9), 64; Charles, *Apocrypha and Pseudepigrapha*, 2:828.
311 Charles, *Apocrypha and Pseudepigrapha*, 2:790.
312 Delcor, "Midrash d'Habacuc," 543. So also Driver, *Judaean Scrolls*, 119.
313 Marcus, "Pharisees," 158; Baumgarten, "Sacrifice and Worship," 67; Yadin, *Scroll of the War*, 201.
314 Baumgarten, "Sacrifice and Worship," 52–4.
315 Kuhn, "Lord's Supper," 260 n. 15; so also Vermes, *Discovery*, 56; Wallace, "Temple Sacrifice," 338; B. Gärtner, *The Temple and the Community in Qumran and the New Testament*, SNTSMS 1 (Cambridge: Cambridge University Press, 1965), 11–13.
316 Cross, *Ancient Library*, 102 n. 120; Thackeray et al., *Josephus*, 9:17; Strugnell, "Josephus and the Essenes," 113–14 n. 33. Baumgarten himself recognized the force of this argument in a later article, and changed his position ("Essenes and the Temple," 58).
317 Cross, *Ancient Library*, 102; Steckoll, "Qumran Sect," 55–69; Strugnell, "Josephus and the Essenes," 113.
318 De Vaux, *Archaeology*, 14.
319 Steckoll, "Qumran Sect," 57.
320 Baumgarten, "Essenes and the Temple," 59. See further the discussion above, pp. 63–4 (*J. W.* 2 §132–3).
321 R. Beckwith, "The Qumran Calendar and the Sacrifices of the Essenes," *RQ* 7 (9971), 589.
322 So Milik, *Ten Years*, 105 n. 2: "There is no trace of an altar at Qumran."
323 Black, *Scrolls*, 40.
324 Baumgarten, "Essenes and the Temple," 62–7. M. J. Lagrange reached a similar conclusion almost fifty years ago (*Le Judaïsme avant Jésus-Christ*, 316–17 n. 5).
325 So Buchanan, "Role of Purity," 405–6.
326 See further above, pp. 9, 135–6 n. 35.
327 Whiston, however, translates the passage as follows: "They also appoint certain stewards to receive the incomes of their revenues, and of the fruits of the ground; such as are good men and priests, who are to get their corn and their food ready for them" (*Josephus*, 377). See further Strugnell, "Josephus and the Essenes," 110–11.

328  A. Dupont-Sommer, "On a Passage of Josephus Relating to the Essenes (*Antiq.* 18 §22)," *JSS* 1 (1956), 361–6.
329  So J. Carmignac, "Conjecture sur un passage de Flavius Josèphe relatif aux Esséniens," *VT* 7 (1957), 318; Thackeray et al., *Josephus*, 9:21. See also S. Isser, "The Conservative Essenes: A New Emendation of *Antiquities* 18 §22," *JSJ* 7 (1976), 177–8.
330  Carmignac, "Conjecture," 317–18. See also Burrows, *More Light*, 361.
331  Isser, "Conservative Essenes," 179–80.
332  Thackeray et al., *Josephus*, 9:20; LSJ, 1434.
333  Thackeray et al., *Josephus*, 9:20.

**Appendix**

1  Yadin, *Temple Scroll*, 1:301–4; Yadin, "Gate of the Essenes," 90–1. So also Cornfeld, *Josephus*, 336; Caquot, "Le rouleau du Temple de Qoumrân," 447; Milgrom, "Temple Scroll," 117. J. Charlesworth ("Origin and Subsequent History of the Authors of the Dead Sea Scrolls," 227) notes that J. Fleming has excavated the southwest corner of the first wall, and has exposed what he believes is the Essene Gate.
2  C. T. Fritsch's evaluation of Josephus' account is entirely negative: according to Fritsch, the account "must be taken with a large grain of salt" ("Herod the Great," 181 n. 26).
3  E. Zeller, *Die Philosophie der Griechen*, 5th edn (3 vols., Hildesheim: Georg Olms Verlagsbuchhandlung, 1923), 3:365–77; Schürer, *Geschichte des jüdischen Volkes*, 2:573–84; I. Lévy, *La légende de Pythagore de Grèce en Palestine* (Paris: Champion, 1927), 264–93; Lagrange, *Judaïsme avant Jésus-Christ*, 325–8; Dupont-Sommer, "Le problème des influences étrangères," 75–92.
4  In addition to the references given above (n. 3), see Dupont-Sommer, *Jewish Sect*, 104–5, 112–17, 123 n. 12, 128, 132, 135, 161–2.
5  Milik, "Review," 415.
6  See M. Hengel, *Judaism and Hellenism* (2 vols., London: SCM, 1974), 1:107–8.
7  Vermes, *Discovery*, 60. See also R. Marcus' discussion in Thackeray et al., *Josephus*, 8:179; Hengel, *Judaism and Hellenism*, 1:243–7.

# BIBLIOGRAPHY

## A. Primary sources for Dead Sea Scrolls

### 1. Manual of Discipline

The principal edition of 1QS is found in M. Burrows et al., eds., *The Dead Sea Scrolls of St. Mark's Monastery*, vol. 2, fasc. 2 (New Haven: American Schools of Oriental Research, 1951), cols. I–XI; see also F. M. Cross et al., eds., *Scrolls from Qumrân Cave I: The Great Isaiah Scroll, the Order of the Community, the Pesher to Habakkuk* (Jerusalem: Albright Institute of Archaeological Research and the Shrine of the Book, 1972), pp. 125–47 (with black-and-white and color photographs of columns). Main variants from Cave 4 texts are listed by Milik, "Review of Wernberg-Møller" (see n. 25 above), 412–16. Both 1QSa and 1QSb are found in D. Barthélemy and J. T. Milik, *Qumrân Cave I*, DJD 1 (Oxford: Clarendon Press, 1955), 108–30 and pls. XXIII–XXIX.

### 2. Damascus Document

The best available edition of the *Damascus Document* is that of C. Rabin, *The Zadokite Documents: I. The Admonition; II. The Laws*, 2nd edn (Oxford: Clarendon Press, 1958), but it is not perfect. Much of the Qumran material remains unpublished. 4QD^a (= 4Q266) may be found in J. T. Milik, "Fragment d'une source du Psautier (4Q Ps 89)," *RB* 73 (1966), 103–6 and "Numérotation des feuilles des rouleaux dans le scriptorium de Qumrân," *Sem* 27 (1977), 79; while readings from 4QD^a and 4QD^e (= 4Q270) are given in Milik, "Milkî-sedeq et Milkî-resa'," *JJS* 23 (1972), 135–6. 5QD (= 5Q12) and 6QD (= 6Q15) are both published in M. Baillet, J. T. Milik, and R. de Vaux, *Les "Petites Grottes" de Qumrân*, DJD 3 (2 vols.: part 1: Textes, part 2: Planches, Oxford: Clarendon Press, 1962), 128–30 and pl. XXVI (= 6QD), 181 and pl. XXXVII (= 5QD).

### 3. War Scroll

The principal edition of 1QM is found in E. L. Sukenik, *The Dead Sea Scrolls of the Hebrew University* (2 parts: Plates and Transcriptions; Jerusalem: Hebrew University and Magnes Press, 1955), pls. 16–34, 47. 4QM^a–f have now been published in M. Baillet, *Qumrân Grotte 4: III (4Q482–4Q520)*, DJD 7 (Oxford: Clarendon Press, 1982), 12–68 and pls. V–VIII, X, XII, XIV, XVI, XVIII, and XXIV. A text previously identified in a preliminary report as 4QM^g by M. Baillet ("Les manuscrits de la Règle de la guerre de la grotte 4 de Qumrân," *RB* 79 [1972], 217–26) is now listed separately in DJD 7 (pp. 69–72 and pl. XXVI) as a text similar to the *War Scroll*, but not a seventh copy of it.

### 4. *Hodayot*

The principal edition of 1QH is, like the *War Scroll*, found in Sukenik's *Dead Sea Scrolls of the Hebrew University*, pls. 35–58.


### 5. *Pesharim*

The principal editions of the *Pesharim* are contained in three different publications. 1QpHab may be found in M. Burrows et al., eds., *The Dead Sea Scrolls of St. Mark's Monastery*, vol. 1 (1950), pls. LV–LXI (see also Cross, *Scrolls from Qumrân Cave I*, pp. 149–63). The remainder of the Cave 1 *Pesharim* (1QpMic, 1QpZeph, and 1QpPs) are found in Barthélemy and Milik, *Qumrân Cave I*, 77–82 and pl. XV. The *Pesharim* of Cave 4 (4QpIsa[a-e], 4QpHos[a,b], 4QpNah, 4QpMic [?], 4QpZeph, 4QpPs[a,b]) are contained in J. M. Allegro, *Qumrân Cave 4: I (4Q158–4Q186)*, DJD 5 (Oxford: Clarendon Press, 1968), 11–53 and pls. IV–XVIII. See J. Strugnell, "Notes en marge du volume V des 'Discoveries in the Judaean Desert of Jordan,'" *RQ* 7 (1969–71), 183–220 for helpful clarifications of and corrections to Allegro's work on the Cave 4 *Pesharim*. A helpful volume that contains text, translation, and notes on all the *Pesharim* listed above is M. P. Horgan, *Pesharim: Qumran Interpretation of Biblical Books*, CBQMS 8 (Washington, D.C.: The Catholic Biblical Association of America, 1979).


### 6. *Temple Scroll*

The principal edition of the *Temple Scroll* is the three-volume publication by Y. Yadin, *The Temple Scroll* (3 vols., Jerusalem: Israel Exploration Society, The Institute of Archaeology of the Hebrew University of Jerusalem, The Shrine of the Book, 1983 [Hebrew edn, 1977]). For an English translation (other than Yadin's), see J. Maier, *The Temple Scroll: An Introduction, Translation and Commentary*; for a German translation, see J. Maier, *Die Tempelrolle vom Toten Meer* (Munich: E. Reinhardt, 1978); for a French translation, see Caquot, "Le Rouleau du Temple de Qoumrân," 451–500; and for a Spanish translation, see F. Garcia, "El rollo de Templo," *EstBib* 37 (1978), 247–92.


### 7. *Other Qumran literature*

Five fragments from Cave 4 (4QOrd[a], 4QFlor, 4QTestim, 4QAgesCreat, and 4QWiles) have been published in Allegro, *Qumrân Cave 4: I (4Q158–4Q186)*. Three other fragments (4QPBless, 4QPrNab, and 4QŠirŠabb) are available in provisional form in journal articles: 4QPBless, J. M. Allegro, "Further Messianic References in Qumran Literature," *JBL* 75 (1956), 174–6; 4QPrNab, J. T. Milik, "'Prière de Nabonide' et autres écrits d'un cycle de Daniel," *RB* 63 (1956), 407–11; 4QŠirŠabb, J. Strugnell, "The Angelic Liturgy at Qumrân – 4Q Serek Šîrôt 'Ôlat Haššabbāt," *Congress Volume, Oxford, 1959*, VTSup 7 (Leiden: Brill, 1960), 318–45.

The published Qumran texts of *Enoch* may be found in J. T. Milik, *The Books of Enoch: Aramaic Fragments of Qumrân Cave 4* (Oxford: Clarendon,

1976). Not all the Enoch literature from Qumran has been published. See further J. A. Fitzmyer, "Implications of the New Enoch Literature from Qumran," *TS* 38 (1977), 341–2.

## B. General bibliography

Abbott, E. A. *Notes on New Testament Criticism*, London: A. &C. Black, 1907

Adam, A. *Antike Berichte über die Essener*, Kleine Texte für Vorlesungen und Übungen 182, 2nd edn, Berlin: de Gruyter, 1972

Albright, W. F. *From the Stone Age to Christianity*, 2nd edn, Baltimore: Johns Hopkins University Press, 1957

Allegro, J. M. "Further Messianic References in Qumran Literature," *JBL* 75 (1956), 174–87

*The Mystery of the Dead Sea Scrolls Revealed*, New York: Gramercy, 1981

*Qumrân Cave 4: I (4Q158–4Q186)*, DJD 5, Oxford: Clarendon Press, 1968

"The Wiles of the Wicked Woman: A Sapiential Work from Qumran's Fourth Cave," *PEQ* 96 (1964), 53–5

Amoussine, J. D. "Observatiunculae Qumraneae," *RQ* 7 (1969–71), 533–52

Attridge, H. W. *The Interpretation of Biblical History in the Antiquitates Judaicae of Flavius Josephus*, HDR 7, Missoula, MT: Scholars, 1976

Audet, J.-P. "Qumrân et la notice de Pline sur les Esséniens," *RB* 68 (1961), 346–87

Avigad, N. "The Palaeography of the Dead Sea Scrolls and Related Documents," *Aspects of the Dead Sea Scrolls*, Scripta Hierosolymitana 4, Jerusalem: Magnes, 1957, 56–87

Baillet, M. "Fragments du Document de Damas. Qumrân, Grotte 6," *RB* 63 (1956), 513–23

"Les manuscrits de la Règle de la guerre de la grotte 4 de Qumrân," *RB* 79 (1972), 217–26

*Qumrân Grotte 4: III (4Q482–4Q520)*, DJD 7, Oxford: Clarendon Press, 1982

Baillet, M., J. T. Milik, and R. de Vaux. *Les 'Petites Grottes' de Qumrân: Exploration de la falaise, les grottes 2Q, 3Q, 5Q, 6Q, 7Q à 10Q, le rouleau de cuivre*, DJD 3, 2 vols. (part 1: Textes, part 2: Planches), Oxford: Clarendon Press, 1962

Baillet, M., et al. "Le travail d'édition des fragments manuscrits de Qumrân," *RB* 63 (1956), 49–67

Bardtke, H., ed. *Qumran-Probleme: Vorträge des Leipziger Symposions über Qumran-Probleme vom 9. bis 14. Oktober 1961*, Berlin: Akademie-Verlag, 1963

Barthélemy, D. "Notes en marge de publications récentes sur les manuscrits de Qumrân," *RB* 59 (1952), 187–218

Barthélemy, D., and J. T. Milik. *Qumran Cave I*, DJD 1, Oxford: Clarendon Press, 1955

Bauer, W. "Essener," *PWSup* 4 (1924), 386–430

Baumgarten, J.M. "The Beginning of the Day in the Calendar of Jubilees,"
    Studies in Qumran Law, SJLA 24, Leiden: Brill, 1977, 124–30
    "The Essene Avoidance of Oil and the Laws of Purity," RQ 6 (1967–9),
    183–92
    "The Essenes and the Temple: A Reappraisal," Studies in Qumran Law,
    SJLA 24, Leiden: Brill, 1977, 57–74
    "Qumran Studies," Studies in Qumran Law, SJLA 24, Leiden: Brill,
    1977, 3–12
    Review of Y. Yadin, Megillat ha-Miqdaš, The Temple Scroll, JBL 97
    (1978), 584–9
    "Sacrifice and Worship among the Jewish Sectarians of the Dead Sea
    (Qumran) Scrolls," Studies in Qumran Law, SJLA 24, Leiden: Brill,
    1977, 39–56
Beckwith, R. "The Qumran Calendar and the Sacrifices of the Essenes,"
    RQ 7 (1971), 587–91
    "The Significance of the Calendar for Interpreting Essene Chronology
    and Eschatology," RQ 10 (1980), 167–202
Benoit, R.P., and R.B. Boismard. "Un ancien sanctuaire chrétien à
    Béthanie," RB 58 (1951), 200–51
Benoit, P., J.T. Milik, et R. de Vaux. Les Grottes de Murabba'at, DJD 2,
    2 vols.: part 1: Texte, part 2: Planches, Oxford: Clarendon Press, 1961
Betz, O. "Essenes," IDBSup (1976), 277–9
Birnbaum, S.A. The Hebrew Scripts. Part One: The Text, Leiden: Brill,
    1971; Part Two: The Plates, London: Palaeographia, 1954–7
    The Qumrân (Dead Sea) Scrolls and Paleography, BASOR Supplemen-
    tary Studies, 13–14, New Haven: American Schools of Oriental
    Research, 1952
Black, M. "The Account of the Essenes in Hippolytus and Josephus," The
    Background of the New Testament and Its Eschatology, ed. W.D.
    Davies and D. Daube, Cambridge: Cambridge University Press, 1956,
    172–5
    The Essene Problem, London: Heffer & Sons, 1961
    The Scrolls and Christian Origins: Studies in the Jewish Background of
    the New Testament, London: Thomas Nelson & Sons, 1961
    ed. The Scrolls and Christianity: Historical and Theological Significance,
    London: SPCK, 1969
Bornkamm, G. "πρέσβυς," TDNT 6 (1968), 651–83
Bowman, J. "Did the Qumran Sect Burn the Red Heifer?," RQ 1 (1958–9),
    73–84
Brock, S.P. "Some Syriac Accounts of the Jewish Sects," A Tribute to Arthur
    Vööbus: Studies in Early Christian Literature and Its Environment,
    Primarily in the Syrian East, ed. R.H. Fischer, Chicago: Lutheran
    School of Theology, 1977, 265–76
Brown, R.E. "The Messianism of Qumran," CBQ 19 (1957), 53–82
Brownlee, W.H. "A Comparison of the Covenanters of the Dead Sea Scrolls
    with Pre-Christian Jewish Sects," BA 13 (1950), 49–72
    The Dead Sea Manual of Discipline: Translation and Notes, BASOR
    Supplementary Studies, 10–12, New Haven: American Schools of
    Oriental Research, 1951

"Light on the Manual of Discipline (DSD) from the Book of Jubilees,"
*BASOR* 123 (1951), 30–2

*The Midrash Pesher of Habakkuk*, SBLMS 24, Missoula, MT: Scholars,
1979

Bruce, F. F. *Second Thoughts on the Dead Sea Scrolls*, 2nd edn, Grand
Rapids: Eerdmans, 1961

Buchanan, G. W. "The Role of Purity in the Structure of the Essene Sect,"
*RQ* 4 (1963–4), 397–406

Burchard, C. "Die Essener bei Hippolyt," *JSJ* 8 (1977), 1–41

"Pline et les Esséniens. A propos d'un article récent," *RB* 69 (1962),
533–69

Review of A. Adam, *Antike Berichte über die Essener*, *RQ* 5 (1964–6),
131–5

Burkert, W. *Lore and Science in Ancient Pythagoreanism*, Cambridge, Mass.:
Harvard University Press, 1972

Burnet, J. *Early Greek Philosophy*, 4th edn, London: A. & C. Black, 1930

Burrows, M. *The Dead Sea Scrolls*, New York: Viking, 1955

"The Discipline Manual of the Judaean Covenanters," *OTS* 8 (1950),
156–92

*More Light on the Dead Sea Scrolls*, New York: Viking, 1958

Burrows, M., et al., eds. *The Dead Sea Scrolls of St. Mark's Monastery*,
2 vols., New Haven: American Schools of Oriental Research, 1 (1950),
2 (1951)

Burton, D., J. B. Poole, and R. Reed. "A New Approach to the Dating of
the Dead Sea Scrolls," *Nature* 184 (1959), 533–4

Caquot, A. "Le rouleau du Temple de Qoumrân," *ETR* 53 (1978), 443–500

Carcopino, J. *Le mystère d'un symbole chrétien: L'ascia*, Paris: Arthème
Fayard, 1955

Carmignac, J. "Conjecture sur un passage de Flavius Josèphe relatif aux
Esséniens," *VT* 7 (1957), 318–19

"Les éléments historiques des 'Hymnes' de Qumrân," *RQ* 2 (1960),
205–22

"Localisation des fragments 15, 18 et 22 des Hymnes," *RQ* 1 (1958–9),
425–30

"Poème allégorique sur la secte rivale," *RQ* 5 (1964–6), 361–74

"Qui était le Docteur de Justice?," *RQ* 10 (1980), 235–46

"The Qumran Problem," *Introduction to the New Testament*, ed. A.
Robert and A. Feuillet, New York: Desclée, 1965, 73–7

"Remarques sur le texte des Hymnes de Qumrân," *Biblica* 39 (1958),
139–55

Review of S. Schechter, *Documents of Jewish Sectaries*, *RQ* 7 (1969–71),
607–8

"L'utilité ou l'inutilité des sacrifices sanglants dans la 'Règle de la
communauté' de Qumrân," *RB* 63 (1956), 524–32

Carmignac, J., P. Guilbert, E. Cothenet, and H. Lignée. *Les textes de
Qumran traduits et annotés*, 2 vols., Paris: Letouzey et Ané, 1961,
1963

Cerfaux, L. "Le baptême des Esséniens," *Recueil Lucien Cerfaux*, BETL
6–7, Gembloux: Duculot, 1954, 321–36

Charles, R. H., ed. *The Apocrypha and Pseudepigrapha of the Old Testament*, 2 vols.: vol. 1: Apocrypha; vol. 2: Pseudepigrapha, Oxford: Clarendon Press, 1913

*The Book of Jubilees*, London: Adam and Charles Black, 1902

Charlesworth, J. H. "A Critical Comparison of the Dualism in 1QS 3:13–4:26 and the 'Dualism' contained in the Fourth Gospel," *NTS* 15 (1969), 389–418

"The Origin and Subsequent History of the Authors of the Dead Sea Scrolls: Four Transitional Phases Among the Qumran Essenes," *RQ* 10 (1979–81), 213–33

ed. *The Old Testament Pseudepigrapha*. Vol. 1: *Apocalyptic Literature and Testaments*, Garden City, NY: Doubleday, 1983

Cleve, F. *The Giants of Pre-Sophistic Greek Philosophy*, 2 vols., The Hague: Martinus Nijhoff, 1973

Colson, F. H., and G. H. Whitaker, trans., *Philo*, LCL, 10 vols., Cambridge, Mass.: Harvard University Press, 1929–62

Coppens, J. "Le célibat essénien," *Qumrân: Sa piété, sa théologie et son milieu*, ed. M. Delcor, BETL 46, Leuven: Leuven University Press, 1978, 295–303

Cornfeld, G. *Josephus: The Jewish War*, Grand Rapids: Zondervan, 1982

Cross, F. M. *The Ancient Library of Qumran and Modern Biblical Studies*, rev. edn, Grand Rapids: Baker, 1980

"The Development of the Jewish Script," *The Bible and the Ancient Near East: Essays in Honor of William Foxwell Albright*, ed. G. E. Wright, New York: Doubleday, 1961, 133–202

"The Early History of the Qumran Community," *New Directions in Biblical Archaeology*, ed. D. N. Freedman and J. C. Greenfield, Garden City: Doubleday, 1969, 63–79

"The Oldest Manuscript from Qumran," *JBL* 74 (1955), 147–72

Cross, F. M., et al., eds. *Scrolls from Qumrân Cave I: The Great Isaiah Scroll, the Order of the Community, the Pesher to Habakkuk*, Jerusalem: Albright Institute of Archaeological Research and the Shrine of the Book, 1972

Cullmann, O. "Die neuentdeckten Qumrantexte und das Judenchristentum der Pseudoklementinen," *BZNW* 21 (1954), 35–51

Dahl, N. A. "The Origin of Baptism," *Interpretationes ad Vetus Testamentum pertinentes Sigmundo Mowinckel septuagenario missae*, Oslo: Fabritius & Sonner, 1955, 36–52

Daniel, C. "Esséniens et Eunuques (Matt. 19:10–12)," *RQ* 6 (1967–9), 353–90

"'Faux Prophètes': surnom des Esséniens dans le Sermon sur la Montagne," *RQ* 7 (1969–71), 45–78

"Les 'Hérodiens' du Nouveau Testament sont-ils des Esséniens?," *RQ* 6 (1967–9), 31–53

Daniélou, J. "La communauté de Qumran et l'organisation de l'église ancienne," *RHPR* 35 (1955), 104–15

*The Dead Sea Scrolls and Primitive Christianity*, Baltimore: Helicon, 1958

Davies, P. R. *The Damascus Covenant*, JSOT Supplement Series 25,
    Sheffield: University of Sheffield, 1982
  "Eschatology at Qumran," *JBL* 104 (1985), 39–55
  *1QM, the War Scroll from Qumran: Its Structure and History*, BibOr 32,
    Rome: Biblical Institute, 1977
Delcor, M. "Contribution à l'étude de la législation," *RB* 61 (1954), 533–53
  *Les Hymnes de Qumran (Hodayot)*, Paris: Letouzey et Ané, 1962
  "L'immortalité de l'âme dans le Livre de la Sagesse et les documents de
    Qumrân," *NRT* 77 (1955), 614–30
  "Le Midrash d'Habacuc," *RB* 58 (1951), 521–48
  "Repas cultuels esséniens et thérapeutes, Thiases et Haburoth," *RQ* 6
    (1967–9), 401–25
  ed. *Qumrân: Sa piété, sa théologie et son milieu*, BETL 46, Leuven:
    Leuven University Press, 1978
Del Medico, H. E. *The Riddle of the Scrolls*, New York: Robert M. McBride,
    1959
Denis, A.-M. *Les thèmes de connaissance dans le Document de Damas*, Studia
    Hellenistica 15, Louvain: Publications Universitaires, 1967
Driver, G. R. *The Judaean Scrolls: The Problem and a Solution*, Oxford:
    Blackwell, 1965
Dupont-Sommer, A. "Contribution à l'exégèse du Manuel de discipline x
    1–8," *VT* 2 (1952), 229–43
  "Culpabilité et rites de purification dans la secte juive de Qoumrân,"
    *Sem* 15 (1965), 61–70
  *The Dead Sea Scrolls: A Preliminary Survey*, Oxford: Basil Blackwell,
    1952
  *The Essene Writings from Qumran*, Gloucester, Mass.: Peter Smith, 1973
    (orig. French edn, 1961)
  *The Jewish Sect of Qumran and the Essenes*, 2nd edn, London: Valentine,
    Mitchell & Co., 1954
  "Le Livre des Hymnes découvert près de la mer Morte (1QH)," *Sem* 7
    (1957), 5–120
  "On a Passage of Josephus Relating to the Essenes (*Antiq.* 18 §22),"
    *JSS* 1 (1956), 361–6
  "Le problème des influences étrangères sur la secte juive de Qoumrân,"
    *RHPR* 35 (1955), 75–94
  "Le Psaume CLI dans 11QPs[a] et le problème de son origine essénienne,"
    *Sem* 14 (1964), 25–62
Eck, W. "Die Eroberung von Masada und eine neue Inschrift des L. Flavius
    Silva Nonius Bassus," *ZNW* 60 (1969), 282–9
Ewing, W. "Linen," *A Dictionary of the Bible*, ed. J. Hastings, 4 vols., New
    York: Scribners, 1901, 3:124–5
Farmer, W. R. "The Economic Basis of the Qumran Community," *TZ* 11
    (1955), 295–308
  "Essenes," *IDB* 2 (1962), 143–4
Feldman, L. H. *Josephus and Modern Scholarship (1937–1980)*, Berlin:
    W. de Gruyter, 1984
  *Scholarship on Philo and Josephus (1937–1962)*, Studies in Judaica 1,
    New York: Yeshiva University, n.d.

Ferguson, E. "Qumran and Codex 'D,'" *RQ* 8 (1972–5), 75–80

Fitzmyer, J.A. "The Aramaic Language and the Study of the New Testament," *JBL* 99 (1980), 5–21

"A Bibliographical Aid to the Study of the Qumran Cave IV Texts 158–186," *CBQ* 31 (1969), 59–71

"The Date of the Qumran Scrolls," *America* 104 (1961), 780–1

*The Dead Sea Scrolls: Major Publications and Tools for Study*, SBLSBS 8, Missoula, MT: Scholars, 1977

*The Genesis Apocryphon of Qumran Cave 1: A Commentary*, 2nd rev. edn, BibOr 18a, Rome: Biblical Institute, 1971

"Glory Reflected on the Face of Christ (2 Cor 3:7–4:6) and a Palestinian Jewish Motif," *TS* 42 (1981), 630–44

"Implications of the New Enoch Literature from Qumran," *TS* 38 (1977), 332–45

"Jewish Christianity in Acts in the Light of the Qumran Scrolls," *Essays on the Semitic Background of the New Testament*, London: Geoffrey Chapman, 1971, 271–303

"The Matthean Divorce Texts and Some New Palestinian Evidence," *TS* 37 (1976), 197–226

"The Qumran Scrolls, the Ebionites and their Literature," *Essays on the Semitic Background of the New Testament*, London: Geoffrey Chapman, 1971, 435–80

"The Story of the Dishonest Manager (Lk 16:1–13)," *Essays on the Semitic Background of the New Testament*, London: Geoffrey Chapman, 1971, 161–84

Freedman, D.N., and J.C. Greenfield, eds. *New Directions in Biblical Archaeology*, Garden City: Doubleday, 1969

Fritsch, C.T. "Herod the Great and the Qumran Community," *JBL* 74 (1955), 173–81

"The So-called 'Priestly Messiah' of the Essenes," *JEOL* 6 (1959–66), 242–8

Garcia, F. "El rollo de Templo," *EstBib* 37 (1978), 247–92

Gärtner, B. *The Temple and the Community in Qumran and the New Testament*, SNTSMS 1, Cambridge: Cambridge University Press, 1965

Gaster, T. *The Dead Sea Scriptures*, 3rd edn, Garden City: Doubleday, 1976

Gerhardsson, B. *Memory and Manuscript*, ASNU 22, Uppsala: Gleerup, 1961

Ginsburg, C.D. *The Essenes: Their History and Doctrines*, London: Longman, Green, Longman, Roberts, and Green, 1864

Ginzberg, L. *An Unknown Jewish Sect*, New York: Jewish Theological Seminary of America, 1976

Gnilka, J. "Das Gemeinschaftsmahl der Essener," *BZ* 5 (1961), 39–55

Goranson, S. "'Essenes': Etymology from '*šh*," *RQ* 11 (1982–4), 483–98

"On the Hypothesis that Essenes lived on Mt. Carmel," *RQ* 9 (1977–8), 563–7

Gottstein, M.H. "Anti-Essene Traits in the Dead Sea Scrolls," *VT* 4 (1954), 141–7

Grelot, P. "L'eschatologie des Esséniens et le livre d'Hénoch," *RQ* 1 (1958–9), 113–31

Grintz, Y.M. "Die Männer des Yaḥad-Essener. Zusammenfassungen,
    Erläuterungen und Bemerkungen zu den Rollen vom Toten Meer,"
    *Zur Josephus-Forschung*, ed. Abraham Schalit, Darmstadt: Wissen-
    schaftliche Buchgesellschaft, 1973, 294–336
Gross, E. "Noch einmal: Der Essenereid bei Josephus," *TLZ* 82 (1957),
    73–4
Guthrie, W. *A History of Greek Philosophy*. Vol. 1: *The Earlier Presocratics
    and the Pythagoreans*, Cambridge: Cambridge University Press, 1962,
    146–340
Hengel, M. *Judaism and Hellenism*, 2 vols., London: SCM, 1974
Hennecke, E. *New Testament Apocrypha*, 2 vols., Philadelphia: Westminster,
    1963–5
Higgins, A.J.B. "The Priestly Messiah," *NTS* 13 (1966–7), 211–39
Hippolytus, *Philosophumena or the Refutation of All Heresies*, trans. F.
    Legge, 2 vols., New York: Macmillan, 1921
Hoenig, S. "Qumran Fantasies," *JQR* 63 (1973), 247–67, 292–316
Holm-Nielsen, S. *Hodayot: Psalms from Qumran*, Acta Theologica Danica
    2, Aarhus: Universitetsforlaget, 1960
Hooke, S.H. "Symbolism in the Dead Sea Scrolls," *SE* (1959), 600–12
Horgan, M.P. *Pesharim: Qumran Interpretations of Biblical Books*, CBQMS
    8, Washington, D.C.: The Catholic Biblical Association of America,
    1979
Humble, B.J. "The *Mebaqqer* in the Dead Sea Scrolls," *Restoration
    Quarterly* 7 (1963), 33–8
Hunzinger, C.-H. "Beobachtungen zur Entwicklung der Disziplinarordnung
    der Gemeinde von Qumrân," *Qumran-Probleme*, ed. H. Bardtke,
    Berlin: Akademie-Verlag, 1963, 231–47
    "Fragmente einer älteren Fassung des Buches Milhamā aus Höhle 4 von
    Qumrân," *ZAW* 69 (1957), 131–51
Hurvitz, A. "The Usage of *Šeš* and *bûs* in the Bible and Its Implication for
    the Date of P," *HTR* 60 (1967), 117–21
Hyatt, J.P. "The View of Man in the Qumran *Hodayot*," *NTS* 2 (1955–6),
    276–85
Isser, S. "The Conservative Essenes: A New Emendation of Antiquities
    XVIII.22," *JSJ* 7 (1976), 177–80
Iwry, S. "Was There a Migration to Damascus? The Problem of *šby yśr'l*,"
    *W.F. Albright Volume* (*Eretz-Israel* 9 [1969]), 80–8
Jastrow, M. *A Dictionary of the Targumim, the Talmud Babli and
    Yerushalmi, and the Midrashic Literature*, 2 vols., New York: Putnams,
    1903
Jaubert, A. "Le calendrier des Jubilés et de la secte de Qumrân: Ses origines
    bibliques," *VT* 3 (1953), 250–64
    "Le pays de Damas," *RB* 65 (1958), 214–48
Jones, H.L. *The Geography of Strabo*, LCL, 8 vols., Cambridge, Mass.:
    Harvard University Press, 1917–32
Jongeling, B. *Le Rouleau de la guerre des manuscrits de Qumrân*, Studia
    semitica neerlandica 4, Assen: Van Gorcum, 1962
Keck, L. "The Poor among the Saints in Jewish Christianity and Qumran,"
    *ZNW* 57 (1966), 54–78

Kittel, B. *The Hymns of Qumran: Translation and Commentary*, SBLDS 50, Chico, CA: Scholars, 1981

Knibb, M. A. *The Ethiopic Book of Enoch: A New Edition in the Light of the Aramaic Dead Sea Fragments*, 2 vols., Oxford: Clarendon Press, 1978

"Keeping up with Recent Studies: III. The Dead Sea Scrolls: Reflections on Some Recent Publications," *ExpTim* 90 (1979), 294–300

Kohler, K. "Essenes," *The Jewish Encyclopedia* 5 (1903), 224–32

Kuhn, K. G. *Konkordanz zu den Qumrantexten*, Göttingen: Vandenhoeck & Ruprecht, 1960

"The Lord's Supper and the Communal Meal at Qumrân," *The Scrolls and the New Testament*, ed. K. Stendahl, New York: Harper, 1957, 65–93

"The Two Messiahs of Aaron and Israel," *The Scrolls and the New Testament*, ed. K. Stendahl, New York: Harper, 1957, 54–64

Kutsch, E. "Der Eid der Essener. Ein Beitrag zum Problem des Textes von Josephus Bell. jud. 2,8,7 (§142)," *TLZ* 81 (1956), 495–8

Lagrange, M. J. *Le Judaïsme avant Jésus-Christ*, Paris: J. Gabalda, 1931

Laperrousaz, E.-M. "'Infra hos Engadda.' Notes à propos d'un article récent," *RB* 69 (1962), 369–80

*Qoumrân: L'établissement essénien des bords de la Mer Morte. Histoire et archéologie du site*, Paris: A. & J. Picard, 1976

Lapp, P. W. *Palestinian Ceramic Chronology 200 B.C. – A.D. 70*, New Haven: American Schools of Oriental Research, 1961, 137–220

Laurin, R. B. "The Question of Immortality in the Qumran *Hodayot*," *JSS* 3 (1958), 344–55

Leaney, A. R. C. *The Rule of Qumran and Its Meaning: Introduction, Translation and Commentary*, Philadelphia: Westminster, 1966

Lévy, I. *La légende de Pythagore de Grèce en Palestine*, Paris: Champion, 1927

*Recherches esséniennes et pythagoriciennes*, Genève: Librairie Droz, 1965

Licht, J. "An Analysis of the Treatise of the Two Spirits in DSD," *Aspects of the Dead Sea Scrolls*, Scripta Hierosolymitana 4, Jerusalem: Magnes, 1957, 88–100

"The Doctrines of the Thanksgiving Scroll," *IEJ* 6 (1956), 1–13

Lieberman, S. "The Discipline in the So-Called Dead Sea Manual of Discipline," *JBL* 71 (1952), 199–206

Lightfoot, J. B. *Saint Paul's Epistles to the Colossians and to Philemon*, rev. edn, London: Macmillan, 1879

Lipsius, R. A., and M. Bonnet. *Acta apostolorum apocrypha post Constantinum Tischendorf*, 2 vols., Lipsiae: Mendelssohn, 1891–8

Macalister, R. A. S. *The Excavation of Gezer*, 3 vols., London: John Murray, 1912, 1:274–6; 3: pl. 54

Maier, J. *Die Tempelrolle vom Toten Meer*, Munich: E. Reinhardt, 1978

Mansoor, M. *The Thanksgiving Hymns*, STDJ 3, Leiden: Brill, 1961

Marcus, R. "Pharisees, Essenes, and Gnostics," *JBL* 73 (1954), 157–61

"Philo, Josephus and the Dead Sea *Yaḥad*," *JBL* 71 (1952), 207–9

"The Qumrân Scrolls and Early Judaism," *Biblical Research* 1 (1956), 9–47

"Textual Notes on the Dead Sea Manual of Discipline," *JNES* 11 (1952), 205–11

Marx, A. "Les racines du célibat essénien," *RQ* 7 (1969–71), 323–42

Masterman, E. W. G. " 'Ain el-Feshkhah, el-Ḥajar el-Aṣbaḥ, and Khurbet Ḳumrân," *PEFQS* (1902), 160–7

"Observations on the Dead Sea Level," *PEFQS* (1904), 83–95

McCready, W. O. "The Sectarian Status of Qumran: The Temple Scroll," *RQ* 11 (1982–4), 183–91

Merrill, E. *Qumran and Predestination: A Theological Study of the Thanksgiving Hymns*, STDJ 8, Leiden: Brill, 1975

Michel, O. "Der Schwur der Essener," *TLZ* 81 (1956), 189–90

Michel, O., and O. Bauernfeind, eds. *De bello judaico: Der jüdische Krieg*, Darmstadt: Wissenschaftliche Buchgesellschaft, Munich: Kösel, 1960–9

Milgrom, J. "Further Studies in the Temple Scroll," *JQR* 71 (1980), 1–17, 89–106

"The Temple Scroll," *BA* 41 (1978), 105–20

Milik, J. T. *The Books of Enoch: Aramaic Fragments of Qumrân Cave 4*, Oxford: Clarendon Press, 1976

"Ecrits préésséniens de Qumrân: d'Hénoch à Amram," *Qumrân: Sa piété, sa théologie et son milieu*, ed. M. Delcor, BETL 46, Leuven: Leuven University Press, 1978, 91–106

"Fragment d'une source du Psautier (4QPs 89)," *RB* 73 (1966), 94–106

"Hénoch au pays des aromates (ch. 27–32). Fragments araméens de la grotte 4 de Qumran," *RB* 65 (1958), 70–7

"Manuale disciplinae," *Verbum domini* 29 (1951), 129–58

"Milkî-ṣedeq et Milkî-reša'," *JJS* 23 (1972), 95–144

"Numérotation des feuilles des rouleaux dans le scriptorium de Qumrân," *Sem* 27 (1977), 75–81

"La patrie de Tobie," *RB* 73 (1966), 522–30

" 'Prière de Nabonide' et autres écrits d'un cycle de Daniel," *RB* 63 (1956), 407–15

Review of P. Wernberg-Møller, *The Manual of Discipline Translated and Annotated*, *RB* 67 (1960), 410–16

*Ten Years of Discovery in the Wilderness of Judaea*, SBT 26, London: SCM, 1959

"Le Testament de Lévi en araméen: Fragment de la grotte 4 de Qumrân," *RB* 62 (1955), 398–406

"Le travail d'édition des manuscrits du Désert de Juda," *Volume du Congrès, Strasbourg, 1956*, VTSup 4, Leiden, Brill, 1957, 17–26

Moehring, H. R. "Josephus on the Marriage Customs of the Essenes," *Early Christian Origins*, ed. A. Wikgren, Chicago: Quadrangle Books, 120–7

Montgomery, M. W., and M. Seligsohn. "Solomon," *The Jewish Encyclopedia* 6 (1905), 436–48

Moore, G. F. "Fate and Free Will in the Jewish Philosophies according to Josephus," *HTR* 22 (1929), 371–89

Mueller, J. "The Temple Scroll and the Gospel Divorce Texts," *RQ* 10 (1980), 247–56

Murphy-O'Connor, J. "The Critique of the Princes of Judah (CD VIII, 3–19)," *RB* 79 (1972), 200–16
"An Essene Missionary Document? CD II,14 – VI,1," *RB* 77 (1970), 201–9
"The Essenes and Their History," *RB* 81 (1974), 215–44
"The Essenes in Palestine," *BA* 40 (1977), 100–24
"La genèse littéraire de la règle de la communauté," *RB* 76 (1969), 528–49
"A Literary Analysis of Damascus Document VI,2 – VIII,3," *RB* 78 (1971), 210–32
"A Literary Analysis of Damascus Document XIX,33 – XX,34," *RB* 79 (1972), 544–64
*Paul and Qumran*, London: Chapman, 1968
"Remarques sur l'exposé du Professeur Y. Yadin," *RB* 79 (1972), 99–100
"The Translation of Damascus Document VI,11–14," *RQ* 7 (1971), 553–6
Negoïtsa, A. "Did the Essenes Survive the 66–71 War?," *RQ* 6 (1967), 517–30
Nickelsburg, G. W. E. "Future Life in Intertestamental Literature," *IDBSup* (1976), 348–51
*Resurrection, Immortality, and Eternal Life in Intertestamental Judaism*, HTS 26, Cambridge, Mass.: Harvard University Press, 1972
Niese, B. *Flavii Josephi opera*, 2nd edn, 7 vols., Berlin: Weidmann, 1955 (orig. pub. 1887–95)
Nolland, J. "A Misleading Statement of the Essene Attitude to the Temple," *RQ* 9 (1977–8), 555–62
North, R. "The Damascus of Qumran Geography," *PEQ* 87 (1955), 33–48
Pelletier, A. *Flavius Josèphe: Autobiographie*, Collection des Universités de France, Paris: Belles Lettres, 1959
*Josèphe: Guerre des Juifs*, Collection des Universités de France, Paris: Belles Lettres, 1975 (vol. 1), 1980 (vol. 2)
Perles, F. "The Hebrew Names of the Essenes and Therapeutae," *JQR* 17 (1926–7), 405–6
Perrot, C. Review of A. Schalit, *Zur Josephus-Forschung*, *RQ* 9 (1977–8), 275–6
Pfeiffer, R. H. *History of New Testament Times*, New York: Harper & Row, 1949
Philip, J. *Pythagoras and Early Pythagoreanism*, Toronto: University of Toronto Press, 1966
Pinner, B. *An Essene Quarter on Mount Zion?*, Jerusalem: Franciscan Printing, 1976
Ploeg, J. van der. "The Belief in Immortality in the Writings of Qumrân," *BO* 18 (1961), 118–24
"Le 'Manuel de Discipline' des rouleaux de la Mer Morte," *BO* 8 (1951), 113–26
"The Meals of the Essenes," *JSS* 2 (1957), 163–75
Ploeg, J. van der, et al. *La secte de Qumrân et les origines du christianisme*, Bruges: Desclée de Brouwer, 1959
Pouilly, J. *La règle de la communauté de Qumrân: son évolution littéraire*, Cahiers de la Revue Biblique 17, Paris: J. Gabalda, 1976

Priest, J.F. "Mebaqqer, Paqid, and the Messiah," *JBL* 81 (1962), 55–61
"The Messiah and the Meal in 1QSa," *JBL* 82 (1963), 95–100
Pryke, E.J. "The Identity of the Qumran Sect: A Reconsideration," *NovT* 10 (1968), 43–61
Rabin, C. "On a Puzzling Passage in the Damascus Fragments," *JJS* 6 (1955), 53–4
*Qumran Studies*, London: Oxford University Press, 1957
*The Zadokite Documents: I. The Admonition; II. The Laws*, 2nd edn, Oxford: Clarendon Press, 1958
Rabinovitz, I. "A Reconsideration of 'Damascus' and '390 Years' in the 'Damascus' ('Zadokite') Fragments," *JBL* 73 (1954), 11–35
Rajak, T. *Josephus: The Historian and His Society*, Philadelphia: Fortress, 1983.
Reike, B. "The Constitution of the Primitive Church in the Light of Jewish Documents," *The Scrolls and the New Testament*, ed. K. Stendahl, New York: Harper & Bros., 1957, 143–56
Rengstorf, K.H. *A Complete Concordance to Flavius Josephus*, 4 vols., Leiden: Brill, 1973–83
Ringgren, H. *The Faith of Qumran: Theology of the Dead Sea Scrolls*, Philadelphia: Fortress, 1963
Roberts, B.J. "The Qumrân Scrolls and the Essenes," *NTS* 3 (1956–7), 58–65
Rokéah, D. "The Temple Scroll, Philo, Josephus, and the Talmud," *JTS* 34 (1983), 515–26
Rost, L. *Die Damaskusschrift*, Berlin: De Gruyter, 1933
"Zur Struktur der Gemeinde des neuen Bundes im Lande Damaskus," *VT* 9 (1959), 393–8
Roth, C. "Were the Qumran Sectaries Essenes? A Re-examination of Some Evidences," *JTS* 10 (1959), 87–93
"Why the Qumran Sect Cannot Have Been Essenes," *RQ* 1 (1958–9), 417–22
"The Zealots and Qumran: The Basic Issue," *RQ* 2 (1959–60), 81–4
Rowley, H.H. *From Moses to Qumran: Studies in the Old Testament*, New York: Association, 1963
"The Qumran Sectaries and the Zealots: An Examination of a Recent Theory," *VT* 9 (1959), 379–92
*The Zadokite Fragments and the Dead Sea Scrolls*, Oxford: Blackwell, 1956
Rubinstein, A. "The Essenes According to the Slavonic Version of Josephus' Wars," *VT* 6 (1956), 307–8
Sanders, J.A. "The Dead Sea Scrolls – A Quarter Century of Study," *BA* 36 (1973), 109–48
*The Psalms Scroll of Qumrân Cave 11*, DJD 4, Oxford: Clarendon, 1965
Schalit, A. *Namenwörterbuch zu Flavius Josephus*, Supplement 1 to *A Complete Concordance to Flavius Josephus*, ed. K.H. Rengstorf, Leiden: Brill, 1968
*Zur Josephus-Forschung*, Darmstadt: Wissenschaftliche Buchgesellschaft, 1973
Schechter, S. *Documents of Jewish Sectaries*, with prolegomenon by J.A. Fitzmyer, 2 vols. in one, New York: KTAV, 1970

Schiffman, L. H. "Communal Meals at Qumran," *RQ* 10 (1979–81), 45–56
    *The Halakhah at Qumran*, SJLA 16, Leiden: Brill, 1975
Schneider, J. "Σχῆμα, μετασχηματίζω," *TDNT* 7 (1971), 954–8
Schubert, K. *The Dead Sea Community: Its Origin and Teachings*, New York:
    Harper, 1959
Schürer, E. *Geschichte des jüdischen Volkes im Zeitalter Jesu Christi*, 4th edn,
    4 vols., Leipzig, J. C. Hinrichs'sche Buchhandlung, 1907, 2:651–80
    *The History of the Jewish People in the Age of Jesus Christ (175 B.C.–
    A.D. 135)*, rev. English edn, ed. G. Vermes, F. Millar, and M. Black,
    Edinburgh: T. & T. Clark (vol. 1) 1973, (vol. 2) 1979
Segal, M. H. "The Habakkuk 'Commentary' and the Damascus Fragments,"
    *JBL* 70 (1951), 131–47
Seitz, O. J. F. "Two Spirits in Man: An Essay in Biblical Exegesis." *NTS*
    6 (1959–60), 82–94
Shutt, R. "The Concept of God in the Words of Flavius Josephus," *JJS* 31
    (1980), 171–89
    *Studies in Josephus*, London: SPCK, 1961
Silberman, L. H. "Manus Velatae: The Significance of 1QS 7:13–14, 15,"
    *JANESCU* 5 (1973), 383–8
Smith, M. "The Dead Sea Sect in Relation to Ancient Judaism," *NTS* 7
    (1960–1), 347–60
    "The Description of the Essenes in Josephus and the Philosophumena,"
    *HUCA* 29 (1958), 273–313
    "'God's Begetting the Messiah' in 1QSa," *NTS* 5 (1958–9), 218–24
Steckoll, S. H. "Preliminary Excavation Report in the Qumran Cemetery,"
    *RQ* 6 (1967–9), 323–36
    "The Qumran Sect in Relation to the Temple of Leontopolis," *RQ* 6
    (1967–9), 55–69
Stendahl, K., ed. *The Scrolls and the New Testament*, New York: Harper &
    Row, 1957
Strugnell, J. "The Angelic Liturgy at Qumrân – 4Q Serek Šîrôt 'Ôlat
    Haššabbāt," *Congress Volume, Oxford, 1959*, VTSup 7, Leiden: Brill,
    1960, 318–45
    "Flavius Josephus and the Essenes: *Antiquities* XVIII.18–22," *JBL* 77
    (1958), 106–15
    "Notes en marge du volume V des 'Discoveries in the Judaean Desert of
    Jordan,'" *RQ* 7 (1969–71), 163–276
Stukenrath, R. "On the Care and Feeding of Radiocarbon Dates," *Archae-
    ology* 18 (1965), 277–81
Sukenik, E. L., ed. *The Dead Sea Scrolls of the Hebrew University*, 2 parts:
    Plates and Transcriptions, Jerusalem: Hebrew University and Magnes
    Press, 1955
Sutcliffe, E. F. "Baptism and Baptismal Rites at Qumran?," *HeyJ* 1 (1960),
    179–88
    *The Monks of Qumran*, Westminster, MD: Newman, 1960
    "Sacred Meals at Qumran?," *HeyJ* 1 (1960), 48–65
Talmon, S. "The Calendar Reckoning of the Sect from the Judaean Desert,"
    *Aspects of the Dead Sea Scrolls*, Scripta Hierosolymitana 4, Jerusalem:
    Magnes, 1957, 162–99

"A Further Link between the Judean Covenanters and the Essenes," *HTR* 56 (1963), 313–19

"The 'Manual of Benedictions' of the Sect of the Judaean Desert," *RQ* 2 (1959–60), 475–500

Teicher, J. L. "Puzzling Passages in the Damascus Fragments," *JJS* 5 (1954), 139–43

Thackeray, H. St. J. *Josephus: The Man and the Historian*, New York: KTAV, 1967

Thackeray, H. St. J., R. Marcus, A. Wikgren, and L. H. Feldman, *Josephus*, LCL, 9 vols., Cambridge, Mass.: Harvard University Press, 1926–65

Thesleff, H. "Pythagoreanism," *Encyclopaedia Britannica*, 15th edn, 30 vols., Chicago: Encyclopaedia Britannica, 1978, 15:322–6

Thomas, J. *Le mouvement baptiste en Palestine et Syrie (150 v. J.-C.–300 apr. J.-C.)*, Gembloux: Duculot, 1935

Tosato, A. "The Law of Leviticus 18:18: A Re-examination," *CBQ* 46 (1984), 199–214

Tricot, A. "The Essenes, According to Philo and Josephus," *Introduction to the New Testament*, ed. A. Robert and A. Feuillet, New York: Desclée, 1965, 70–3

Vaux, R. de. *Archaeology and the Dead Sea Scrolls*, London: Oxford University Press, 1973

"Fouilles de Khirbet Qumran," *RB* 63 (1956), 533–77

"Une hachette essénienne?," *VT* 9 (1959), 399–407

"Les manuscrits de Qumrân et l'archéologie," *RB* 66 (1959), 87–110

Vermes, G. *The Dead Sea Scrolls in English*, 2nd edn, Harmondsworth, Middlesex: Penguin Books, 1975

*The Dead Sea Scrolls: Qumran in Perspective*, Cleveland: Collins & World, 1978

*Discovery in the Judean Desert*, New York: Desclée, 1956

"Essenes and Therapeutai," *RQ* 3 (1961–2), 495–504

"The Etymology of 'Essenes,'" *RQ* 2 (1959–60), 427–43

"Interpretation (History of) at Qumran and in the Targums," *IDBSup* (1976), 438–43

*Jesus the Jew*, New York: Macmillan, 1974

*Post-Biblical Jewish Studies*, SJLA 8, Leiden: Brill, 1975

*Scripture and Tradition in Judaism*, SPB 4, 2nd edn, Leiden: Brill, 1973

"Sectarian Matrimonial Halakhah in the Damascus Rule," *JJS* 25 (1974), 197–202

Vogel, C. de. *Pythagoras and Early Pythagoreanism*, Assen: Van Gorcum, 1966

Wacholder, B. Z. *The Dawn of Qumran: The Sectarian Torah and the Teacher of Righteousness*, Cincinnati: Hebrew Union College, 1983

Wallace, D. "The Essenes and Temple Sacrifice," *TZ* 13 (1957), 335–8

Weinert, F. D. "4Q159: Legislation for an Essene Community Outside Qumran?," *JSJ* 5 (1974), 179–207

Wernberg-Møller, P. *The Manual of Discipline Translated and Annotated*, STDJ 1, Leiden: Brill, 1957

"A Reconsideration of the Two Spirits in the Rule of the Community," *RQ* 3 (1961–2), 413–41

Whiston, W. *Josephus: Complete Works*, Grand Rapids: Kregel, 1963 (orig. edn, 1737

Williamson, G. A., trans. *Josephus: The Jewish War*, Baltimore: Penguin Books, 1959

*The World of Josephus*, Boston: Little, Brown, 1964

Yadin, Y. "L'attitude essénienne envers la polygamie et le divorce," *RB* 79 (1972), 98–9

"The Gate of the Essenes and the Temple Scroll," *Jerusalem Revealed: Archaeology in the Holy City 1968–1974*, ed. Y. Yadin, New Haven: Yale University Press, 1976, 90–1

*The Scroll of the War of the Sons of Light Against the Sons of Darkness*, Oxford: Oxford University Press, 1962

*The Temple Scroll*, 3 vols., Jerusalem: Israel Exploration Society, The Institute of Archaeology of the Hebrew University of Jerusalem, The Shrine of the Book, 1983 (Hebrew edn, 1977)

"The Temple Scroll," *BA* 30 (1967), 135–9

Zeitlin, S. "Josephus and the Zealots: A Rejoinder," *JSS* 5 (1960), 388

*The Zadokite Fragments. Facsimile of the manuscripts in the Cairo Genizah Collection in the possession of the University Library, Cambridge, England: with an Introduction*, JQRMS 1, Philadelphia: The Dropsie College for Hebrew and Cognate Learning, 1952

Zeller, E. *Outlines of the History of Greek Philosophy*, 13th edn, New York: Harcourt, Brace & Co., 1931

*Die Philosophie der Griechen*, 5th edn, 3 vols., Hildesheim: Georg Olms Verlagsbuchhandlung, 1923

# INDEX OF PASSAGES

**B New Testament**

**C Apocrypha**

**D Pseudepigrapha**

## G Greek and Latin writers

# INDEX OF AUTHORS

# SUBJECT INDEX

*198*